Memorial and Gift Fund

The Davee Foundation

Winnetka-Northfield
Public Library District

BERTRAM GOODHUE

*What is Life? An illusion, a shadow, a story. And the greatest good
is little enough: for all life is a dream, and dreams themselves are only dreams . . .
but whether it be dream or truth, to do well is what matters.*

     —PEDRO CALDERÓN DE LA BARCA, *Life Is a Dream*, ACT II, Scene 1

BERTRAM GOODHUE

His Life and Residential Architecture

ROMY WYLLIE

W. W. NORTON & COMPANY

New York • London

For information about permission to reproduce selections from
this book, write to Permissions, W. W. Norton & Company, Inc.,
500 Fifth Avenue, New York NY 10110

Manufacturing by Chroma Graphics/KHL Printing
Book design by Abigail Sturges
Production manager: Leeann Graham

Library of Congress Cataloging-in-Publication Data

Wyllie, Romy.
   Bertram Goodhue : his life and residential architecture / Romy Wyllie.
       p. cm.
   Includes bibliographical references and index.
   ISBN-13: 978-0-393-73219-1 (hardcover)
   ISBN-10: 0-393-73219-3 (hardcover)
   1. Goodhue, Bertram Grosvenor, 1869-1924. 2. Architects--United
States--Biography. 3. Architecture, Domestic--United States. I.
Title.

   NA737.G6W95 2007
   720.92--dc22
   [B]
                                        2006018342
ISBN 13: 978-0-393-73219-1
ISBN 10: 0-393-73219-3

W. W. Norton & Company, Inc.,
500 Fifth Avenue, New York NY 10110
www.wwnorton.com

W. W. Norton & Company Ltd., Castle House,
75/76 Wells Street, London W1T 3QT

0 9 8 7 6 5 4 3 2 1

To the family of Bertram Grosvenor Goodhue,
especially Nicholas,
for keeping alive an extraordinary architectural legacy

Goodhue's pen-and-ink wash of a proposed townhouse in Boston, Massachusetts, c. 1900.

Contents

FOREWORD

ROBERT C. RIPLEY AIA, Capitol Administrator, Nebraska State Capitol

Bertram Goodhue was one of the most gifted and complex architects in America during the early years of the twentieth century. By examining Goodhue's smaller-scale architectural achievements, Romy Wyllie's book delves into a relatively unexplored realm of his work, adding much new information about his illustrious career. Moreover, the book provides unprecedented insight into the personality of a brilliant man, whose skillful synthesis of contemporary and traditional forms, respect for craftsmanship, and exploration of new building techniques remain relevant to current directions in architectural thought.

An architect's work lives on through his buildings, but awareness of the man behind the work fades quickly. In addition to correspondence and other documents available in libraries, the author was also granted access to Goodhue's personal and professional papers still in the possession of his descendants. This has added a remarkable perspective on his family background, as well as a better understanding of his dynamic character, which played such an important role in the making of his career. Excerpts from Goodhue's correspondence provide the reader with insights into the architect's opinions and ideas; quotations from his published writings demonstrate Goodhue's belief in the importance of using indigenous materials and architectural forms to help create an architecture applicable to its region and environmental setting.

Although his career was not founded on residential commissions, their value to his evolving development as an architect in an era of strict architectural dogma is undeniable. Always refining and reinventing his work, Goodhue displays in his residential projects a track of experimentation parallel to that evolving in his larger and more prominent work. In recent years, perhaps more than at any time since his death in 1924, the example of Goodhue's work and of his insistent refusal to conform to any rigid architectural doctrine finds a sympathetic reception among contemporary architects, who strive to recapture his confident handling of mass, his masterful skill at detail realized through craft, and his belief in the past being the foundation on which to enrich the present.

This volume makes a significant contribution to a broader understanding of the impressive body of work created by Bertram Grosvenor Goodhue, and of his place in early-twentieth-century American architecture.

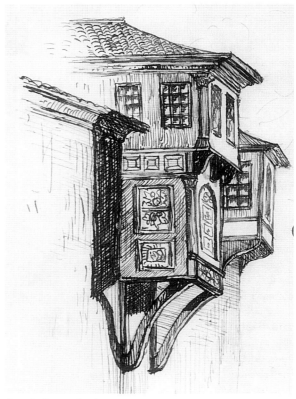

Scene in Constantinople

PREFACE

Bertram Grosvenor Goodhue (1869–1924) was an architect of exceptional vision, with an unusually fertile imagination and a fascination with the past. Making everything beautiful became his goal in life. A rare gift for drawing, a gift that had been carefully nurtured by his mother, contributed to this quest. In 1914 a selection of Goodhue's drawings and designs was published as *A Book of Architectural and Decorative Drawings*,[1] and during his lifetime his architectural work, sketches, book designs, and writings appeared frequently in professional magazines. Richard Oliver, the author of the 1983 monograph Bertram Grosvenor Goodhue,[2] wrote: "Goodhue's drawings were and are, of course, breathtakingly beautiful, and are among the most awesome architectural drawings of this century."[3]

However, one of the greatest American architects of the early twentieth century has been sadly neglected in contemporary literature. Except for the publication in 1925 by the American Institute of Architects of a magnificent memorial volume, *Bertram Grosvenor Goodhue: Architect and Master of Many Arts*, edited by Charles Harris Whitaker,[4] there is a dearth of books that recognize Goodhue's contribution to the world of architecture. There have been a few publications on specific buildings, but Goodhue was overlooked for the most part until Oliver returned his name to the architectural arena in 1983.

The purpose of my book is twofold: to examine Goodhue's residential designs within the framework of his ecclesiastical and secular projects and to take a closer look at the architect as a person, with the hope that my study will stimulate a renewed interest in this remarkable man. The word "secular" is used in this book for all nonresidential and nonecclesiastical projects whether they are civic, institutional, or educational.

I have spent the last twenty years immersed in the architecture that Goodhue created for the campus of the California Institute of Technology. My involvement has included lecturing about Goodhue's master plan to hundreds of alumni, taking many visitors on tours of the campus, and writing a book on the history of the campus architecture.[5] I became especially intrigued to learn more about Goodhue's personality after meeting his son, Hugh, and developing a close relationship with his grandchildren.

In order to broaden our understanding of Goodhue's designs, I decided to focus on a less-known part of his portfolio. Oliver's excellent monograph deals primarily with his ecclesiastical and secular work, and mentions only five completed and five proposed residences. My book discusses twenty built and six unbuilt houses that provide new insights into the evolution of Goodhue's architecture during the thirty-three-year period of his remarkable career.[6] Although they made up only a relatively small portion of his total work, these projects are rich in architectural expression. Goodhue's residential clients provided him with the opportunity to experiment with various interpretations of historical styles, to realize some of his romantic dreams, to put into practice the goals of the Arts and Crafts Movement, and to advance his search for stylistic freedom. By examining Goodhue's domestic work we see that many of his experiments found fuller expression in his secular commissions. For instance, Waldron Gillespie's California estate was the proving ground for a Persian landscaping scheme that became Goodhue's signature in several civic and educational projects. Goodhue's residential portfolio also provides a unique glimpse of life in the early twentieth century, the era of the great industrialists and their grand estates.

The book concludes with a discussion of Goodhue's place in the history of architecture, with particular attention to how his role in the modern movement has been evaluated with renewed interest and fresh eyes in the postmodern period.

Bertram Grosvenor Goodhue as a young man.

In order to follow Goodhue's career and clarify the interplay between his ecclesiastical, secular, and residential work, the book includes brief mentions of those non-residential commissions that played a significant role in making him one of the leading architects of his time. Initially, Goodhue's greatest impact came through his ecclesiastical designs, such as the Cadet Chapel of the U.S. Military Academy at West Point and churches in New York City—in particular, the Chapel of the Intercession, St. Thomas, St. Vincent Ferrer, and St. Bartholomew's. Although church commissions might encompass parish houses and manses, I have not included them because they are an integral part of the ecclesiastical work. Beginning in 1915 with the Panama-California Exposition in San Diego, Goodhue executed several outstanding educational and civic projects, including the National Academy of Sciences in Washington, D.C., the Nebraska State Capitol, and the Los Angeles Public Library. Goodhue garnered praise for the broad diversity of his architectural work, which ranged from Classical, Gothic, Tudor, and Spanish to a new style free of historical references. His unusual versatility gave him an advantage in an era of eclectic architecture.

Goodhue's education was as unconventional as was his work. His lack of a formal education strengthened his belief that "the architect, like the poet, is born, not made."[7] He spent much of his childhood developing his exceptional drawing skills; his only architectural training was a six-year apprenticeship, supplemented by extensive reading and travels to foreign lands. Trips to Mexico and Persia early in his career along with his love of England, especially its medieval and Gothic Revival architecture, strongly influenced the direction of his future work.

Goodhue became famous in his lifetime for his leadership in the world of architecture, for training and teaching young architects, for the pen-and-ink renderings that brought buildings to life, and for his contribu-

tions to the renewal of the arts of printing and illumination. I have attempted to discover the man behind the drawing board by reading his letters and studying previously unknown family archives. I have learned about his personality, his warmth and charm, his mood changes and health concerns, and above all his caring relationship and deep compassion for family, friends, and colleagues. His longtime partner, Ralph Adams Cram, described Goodhue's personality as "baffling."[8] Goodhue was a complex man. An outward shyness masked a dynamic character; he was a person who knew his own mind, often displaying a strong determination to have his way whether in an intellectual discussion or in the execution of an architectural design. At times he could be unnecessarily outspoken and high-handed. On other occasions he could beguile his companions with an infectious vivacity through song, stories, or discussion. Even in the last minutes of his life Goodhue impressed the attending doctor, who reported that he had "never met a more entertaining man in his life."[9]

Sir Giles Gilbert Scott, one of his closest friends and most respected colleagues, remarked: "I knew Goodhue intimately. I knew him as a man and as an artist. . . . He was a man of extraordinarily captivating personality, whom one could not help but like the moment one met him. He was of a very nervous temperament, such as one would expect to find in an artist of his ability, and very retiring—not at all the typical caricature type of an American."[10]

ACKNOWLEDGMENTS

Architectural historian Dr. Robert Winter's question "Why don't you write something more about Goodhue?" triggered the thought process that evolved into this book. Aided by the ease of electronic mail, I have been overwhelmed by the cooperation and kindness of the many people who have contributed information and material for my research.

I owe a large debt of gratitude to the current owners of the residences who have welcomed me into their homes and shared histories and photographs. My thanks go to Roberta Arena, Scarborough; R. O. Blechman, guardian for nearly thirty years of the Goodhue studio in New York City; Riz Chand and Laura Colhouer, Pittsburgh; Gary and Norma Cowles, Pasadena; Gail Jansen and Kellam de Forest of the Austin Val Verde Foundation, Montecito; Father Januario of St. Josaphat's Monastery, Long Island; Daniel and Fiona McKee, Duluth; Robert and Concetta Mitro, Pittsburgh; Bruce and Paula Rice, Lloyd Harbor; Bruce Richards and Kim Kanatami, Dobbs Ferry; Leonard Ross, Montecito; and Robert and Janey Wetzel, Pasadena. The Rices introduced me to Marjorie Lloyd-Smith's granddaughter, Jenny Lawrence, who provided photographs and a detailed history of her family. Elizabeth Hartley Carden loaned me photographs taken by her father, a professional photographer and son of Cavour Hartley, of the Hartley residence in Duluth. Gary Cowles shared not only his house and all the materials that he had collected on Goodhue, but searched libraries for some of the historical articles on Goodhue.

Archivists and librarians have helped me discover innumerable sources of valuable information. I am especially grateful to Janet Parks of the Avery Architectural and Fine Arts Library, Columbia University; Janice Chadbourne, Curator of Fine Arts, Boston Public Library; Charlotte Erwin, Associate Archivist, California Institute of Technology; Janice Goldblum, Archivist,

National Academy of Sciences; Karen Wagner, Archivist, Nebraska State Capitol; and George Bain, Head, Archives and Special Collections, Ohio University. The many other dedicated librarians, researchers, and photographers who have contributed materials have been acknowledged in the Notes and Illustration Credits.

Every manuscript needs readers to criticize and generally prod and stimulate an author. Pamela Kingsbury, Robert Ripley, Albert Tannler, and Robert Winter graciously gave of their time and expertise. Albert Tannler also became a valuable mentor, sharing his own research on Bertram Goodhue's brother and nephew, as well as his discovery of previously unrecorded residential designs.

I am especially appreciative of the enthusiastic cooperation of Goodhue's descendants and relatives: Jane Hamilton provided much of the information on General Grosvenor's house in Ohio; Sylvia Danenhower produced a trove of treasures found in the Grosvenor house in Pomfret, Connecticut; great-grandson John Rivers lent me his thesis on Goodhue and negatives of Goodhue's drawings; grandchildren Yates Satterlee and Fay Engle shared original drawings and memorabilia, and read the text; Jill Goodhue Hoeksma and Nicholas Goodhue gave me access to files, photographs, and books that their parents Hugh and Fanny Goodhue had saved. Most of all, I want to thank Nicholas Goodhue for providing valuable research assistance.

It has been a pleasure and a privilege to work with editor Nancy Green, copy editor Fred Wiemer, designer Abigail Sturges, and the excellent staff at W. W. Norton. Last but by no means least, my heartfelt thanks to my husband, Peter Wyllie, for keeping me company on my research travels and for his patience and encouragement throughout this project.

Chapter 1

An Architect Is Born

1869–1891

I was born of poor but honest parents in Pomfret, Connecticut.

—Bertram Grosvenor Goodhue[1]

A silver-trimmed, dove-gray sombrero cast a shadow over the handsome features of the young man as he sat sketching the cityscape spread across the distant horizon. With an occasional puff on a fragrant cigar and with a pencil balanced between his delicate fingers, he recorded quickly the forms and heights, light and shade, of the domes and towers of Guadalupe, Mexico. The year was 1891 (fig. 1-1).

Who was this precocious young artist who had just completed an architectural apprenticeship in New York City and at the age of twenty-two won a competition for the design of the Cathedral of St. Matthew in Dallas, Texas? He was Bertram Grosvenor Goodhue, but during a sojourn in Mexico he favored "Beltran," the Spanish version of his name, which a beautiful dark-eyed señorita had bestowed upon him.[2] By taking a close look at Bertram's upbringing, we can observe many of the factors that contributed to his creative brilliance and distinction as an architect.

Bertram Goodhue's artistic ability and innate romanticism were nurtured in his formative years. He was born in Pomfret, Connecticut, on April 28, 1869. Pomfret, in the County of Windham, is a small, sleepy town nestled in a densely wooded area set among the rolling hills of northeast Connecticut. The center of the hamlet has changed little since Goodhue's childhood. Many of the original white clapboard houses remain, sitting well back from the road, surrounded by tall trees and separat-

ed from their neighbors by broad green spaces. Streams meander through the surrounding forests with occasional ponds, small lakes, or farms breaking the timbered landscape.

Bertram came from a thoroughly British background, having forebears on both sides of his family who had sailed over on the *Mayflower* in 1620. On his father's side he was descended from William Goodhue of Kent, a weaver who settled in Ipswich, Massachusetts, in 1635. On his mother's side, John Grosvenor came from Bridgnorth, Salop (Shropshire), England, around 1670 and settled in Roxbury, Massachusetts, where he had a tanning business and held the office of Town Constable. He became "one of the six original purchasers from Maj. James Fitch, 1 May 1686, of the Mashamoquet grant of 15,100 acres, which included the territory of the present towns of Pomfret, Brooklyn, and Putnam, and the parish of Abington, Conn."[3] Pomfret was incorporated as a town in 1713. Unfortunately, complications over the title and divisions prevented John from settling on his land before his death in 1691 at the age of forty-nine. But by 1700 his wife, Esther, and their seven children were able to conclude the settlement. Esther built at least two houses in Pomfret before constructing Grosvenor Place in 1725 (or in 1710, according to some accounts). This fine, framed house has always been owned by members of the Grosvenor and Goodhue families and is still standing (fig. 1-2).[4] Esther's great-grand-

FIG. 1-1. *Goodhue's sketch of Guadalupe in* Mexican Memories.

son, Colonel Thomas Grosvenor, became the most renowned individual of the family. As a member of the revolutionary forces, he fought at Bunker Hill, Trenton, Princeton, and Monmouth. He is immortalized in John Trumbull's famous 1786 painting *The Battle of Bunker's Hill* (fig. 1-3).

Around 1790, Colonel Grosvenor built a house for himself in Pomfret, and this became Bertram's childhood home. Bertram's parents were Charles Wells Goodhue and Helen Grosvenor Eldredge, a cousin of Charles's first wife, who had died prematurely (figs. 1-4 and 1-5). Charles Wells Goodhue grew up in Brattleboro, Vermont, where his father was president of the First National Bank. After their marriage Charles and Helen moved to Pomfret to live in the house built by Helen's grandfather, Colonel Thomas Grosvenor. The house was originally known as the Homestead but in a later photograph was identified as the Meadows (fig. 1-6). Though Charles Goodhue changed the original form of the house by enlarging it and adding piazzas, it was considered to be "a fine example of that sound craftsmanship and sense of proportion and refinement which distinguished the architecture of the period."[5]

Charles Goodhue's occupation was listed as "Country Gentleman."[6] Evidently, he started out as a manufacturer of sacking and other materials, and then turned to farming.[7] Family lore records that he spent much of his time racing horses, which he trained around the large

FIG. 1-2. *Grosvenor Place, Pomfret, built by Esther Grosvenor c. 1725.*

FIG. 1-3. *Col. Grosvenor and his servant from John Trumbull's painting* The Battle of Bunker's Hill.

FIG. 1-4. *Charles Wells Goodhue.*

FIG. 1-5. *Helen Grosvenor Eldredge.*

FIG. 1-6. *The Meadows, Bertram's childhood home (originally named the Homestead). "Its raising was accompanied by great mirth and festivity, a young Indian delighting the crowd by dancing upon its ridgepole."* Ellen D. Larned, History of Windham County, Connecticut (*Worcester, Mass.: published by the author, 1874–1880*)

Fig. 1-7. *Bertram in the arms of his mother.*

Fig. 1-8. *Bertram as a young child.*

pond at the back of his property.[8] There were five boys in the family: Wells, by the father's first wife; Bertram Grosvenor (1869–1924) (figs. 1-7 and 1-8); Harry Eldredge (1873–1918);[9] Edward Eldredge (Ned) (1875–1943); and Donald Mumford (1876), who died at four months. Bertram and Harry were the artists of the family, Harry becoming a well-known stained-glass designer and fabricator who passed on his gift and skills to his son, Wright. Ned, the youngest, became a career officer in the U.S. Navy and never married.[10]

Growing up in a small rural community did not mean that the boys were deprived of education or culture. Their father appreciated music and was especially fond of opera. Many evenings were spent around the piano with the mother playing and the father leading his children in song.[11] In adult life Bertram enjoyed playing the guitar and singing. He always had a piano in his home and, with his wife, attended the opera regularly. His son, Hugh, remembered him whistling the whole of "Di Provenza il mar, il suol," from *La Traviata*, which he had learned from his father. Harry played the violin, and he and his pianist wife participated in recitals.

Helen Goodhue was a skilled horsewoman (cousin Constance remembered "how well she rode horseback, and how supremely beautiful she was—on horseback or off").[12] She was also a highly educated woman who had

attended the Troy Female Seminary in Troy, New York, founded by Emma Willard, a pioneer in creating educational opportunities for women.[13] Helen received a well-rounded education, which led to an interest in history, literature, and the arts. Throughout her life she took great pride in maintaining an autograph book, which she had inherited from her mother (the daughter of Colonel Thomas Grosvenor). The book contains the signatures of authors, artists, historians, senators, and United States presidents. Its pages were filled with such illustrious names as Charles Dickens, Henry Longfellow, George Bancroft, Jack Barrymore, Charles Eliot Norton, Brigham Young, Henry Irving, and Presidents James Buchanan, James Monroe, John Quincy Adams, and Ulysses Grant.[14] Familiarity with such names as well as his mother's connections with famous people must have prepared the way for Bertram to feel at ease with the men and women of importance that he encountered as he became established in his chosen profession.

Helen spent many hours with her children and, instead of sending them to the local school, made use of her own excellent education and training to teach them at home, a circumstance that strongly influenced their future lives, especially that of Bertram. The boys' education also benefited from the influence of their Aunt Hattie (Frances Harriet Eldredge, Helen's spinster sister), who lived with

FIG. 1-9. *A drawing by Helen Goodhue given to her son, Bertram, on the occasion of his tenth birthday, April 28, 1879.*

the family, and relatives Mary Ann and Edward Eldredge, who had been brought up in Bahia, Brazil.[15]

Helen herself was a proficient artist and soon recognized her eldest son's drawing ability (fig. 1-9). She became an important influence on his development, encouraging his learning through conversation and reading, and filling his fertile mind with the stories of St. Augustine and St. Francis of Assisi. She made space in her attic studio, which the burgeoning artist fashioned into a special retreat where visitors could only come by invitation. The words ART PRE-EXISTS IN NATURE, AND NATURE IS REPRODUCED IN ART, which were lettered on the wood paneling above the dormer, became a motto for his future work.[16] In his adult life he rebuilt a townhouse in New York and created an attic retreat where he could read and think uninterrupted as he had done in his childhood. When he wanted to take a break from drawing, young Bertram would immerse himself in the legends of King Arthur and other medieval heroes. He loved to explore the family's library, where books full of adventure and mystery opened up a world of knowledge and enchantment that nourished the young man's imagination. In his twenties this early preparation found fulfillment in compelling compositions about imaginary places. Writing to cousin Constance in 1919, he said:

> I am not "cocky" when I say that I'd have gotten nowhere at all if it hadn't been for the habit of sitting on the floor in the library in Pomfret and reading everything I could get my hands on from Harvey's *Meditations Among the Tombs* and Burton's *Anatomy of Melancholy* down, or up, to Roderick Ramdon or the Farmers' Almanac.[17]

Bertram's childhood was by no means confined to drawing and reading. He loved the outdoors and with his brothers and friends spent many hours exploring the woods and streams around Pomfret, discovering the excitement of hunting rabbits or catching fish. A love of hunting and fishing stayed with him for the rest of his life and became an important release from hard work. In a letter explaining his qualifications as a sportsman, he wrote:

> From my earliest youth, I have been devoted to tobacco and the chase. Finding bent pins and angle worms indifferent as a lure for the trout that inhabited the little streams of my native valley, I later graduated into the use of artificial flies and a 4½ oz. Lanman rod, though I cannot yet claim to be able to keep a floating fly floating over thirty seconds. When I first began to use a shot gun, I cannot remember, the date being lost in the mist of antiquity, but I couldn't have been over nine or ten years old. At first, I rather confined my attentions to woodchuck and grey squirrels, game birds of all kinds having an awkward habit of not flying straight . . . and finally broke my first gun—a very beautiful French one of my father's—trying to dig a woodchuck out of the wall with it.[18]

Even his ancestry qualified him as a hunter:

> On my mother's side, I am descended from the Grosvenors, the first of which family was Master of the Hounds to William the Conqueror; in fact the word, "Grosvenor," which is my middle name, means just this, though anyone who is charitably disposed might be willing to translate it roughly as "Great hunter." Anyhow, a taste for the woods is in the blood of us all.[19]

When he became established in his career, he was able to expand his hunting horizons with annual expeditions to join a group of friends, who formed a hunting club and leased two large tracts of land amounting to about 105 square miles near Lake St. John in Canada. The main purpose was to fish and to hunt moose, though the area also had small game. Such expeditions became an essential relaxation from a professional life that became increasingly stressful with each success.

> Certainly there is nothing in the world to compare with the woods as a restorative. . . . My membership in the Meno Keosawin Club is one of the things that I am proudest of and now that I have gotten a really fine head with which to adorn the reception room here at my office I am prouder than ever.[20]

With his brother Harry he also hunted deer in Maine, and whenever he could find the time, he went trout fishing in Connecticut, the Catskills, California, or Canada.[21]

In addition to sports and exploration, the outdoors provided young Bertram with an endless canvas, which he filled with a multitude of pen and pencil drawings. The tall trees of the woods may have given him his first sense of the vertical, which became such a vital element of his ecclesiastical architecture and in his revolutionary design for Nebraska's Capitol building.[22]

Theatrical activities also played an important role in Bertram's childhood. The Goodhue brothers, with their cousins and friends, put on annual plays in Pomfret Hall, which had been built as an entertainment venue in 1877. Bertram created the playbills and sometimes designed the costumes. In 1883 a local newspaper, reporting on a performance of *Loan of a Lover*, wrote that the "young people not only remembered what was to be said, but they knew how to say it."[23] Amateur theatricals became a lifelong passion for Goodhue. During their years in Boston both Bertram and Harry were involved with the annual theatrical festivals of the Boston Art Students' Association, and an annual pageant at Christmas became part of office life, both in partnership with Cram and Ferguson and later at his own firm in New York City.

Bertram had stated clearly at the young age of nine that he was going to become an architect, but his parents decided that before becoming a teenager he should attend Russell's Collegiate and Commercial Institute in New Haven, founded in 1834. In an article on the headmaster, William Huntington Russell (1809–1885),[24] bookseller and author Reverdy Whitlock described the curriculum: "Although it offered . . . a strong dosage of the classics, it was primarily a military school and reflected the Spartan disciplines of the master."[25] The students wore hot, uncomfortable uniforms, and discipline pervaded every aspect of the school experience.[26]

Presumably, the intent of Goodhue's parents was to obtain a sound education for their eldest son rather than point him toward a military career. There is no clear record of the exact age at which Bertram entered Russell's or of the number of years that he spent there, but correspondence with former school friends indicates approximately two years. Many years later a schoolmate wrote:

> My rather vivid recollection of him at school is of a rather chubby, jolly, little chap, with a round head covered with light brown or rather yellow, curly hair, who spent most of this time, when in the school room, drawing caricatures of his school mates, and fancy pictures. It was all good-natured. His devotion to his drawing was far greater than that to his studies, and I do not recall that he entered prominently into the sports or the drills. . . . After I left, in June, 1883, I lost sight of Goodhue, though we had always been good friends and [I] had taken a fancy to him—he was a general favorite.[27]

Though he failed to shine academically in this short period, he formed worthwhile friendships and left lasting impressions on his classmates. In 1906, Goodhue renewed contact with his school friend Jorge Bird y Arias of Puerto Rico. The two men corresponded intermittently for several years. Bird y Arias expressed his approval that Goodhue had "taken up a profession which certainly is in line with your natural inclination." He observed: "The nice flowers, birds, and landscapes, which you so frequently painted to decorate our writing papers, is something that I have never forgotten and has helped to keep your memory fresh in mine, so that I had to make no effort to know who was Goodhue. It is very pleasant indeed to hear from our school friends, as with their memories, we go back to the happiest period of life when everything is bright and our minds and hearts are free from selfishness, and all is noble and true."[28]

Following publication of some of his professional successes, Goodhue heard from other schoolmates. In 1913, David Small wrote to inquire "whether or not you are the 'Bertram Goodhue' of Russell's C.C.I. of 1881–3?"[29] In reply to Goodhue's response Small's next letter is addressed to "'is 'ighness, Bertram Goodhue." He writes, "Your acknowledgment of your identity is before me; it gives me hearty good pleasure to learn of the great success of the 'Artist' of the old C.C.I."[30] After hearing from Harry Crosby in 1916, Goodhue wrote, "I am indeed the very same Goodhue that used to be the victim of your spit balls and the like at Russell's."[31] Goodhue had made a sketch in Crosby's autograph book of a moonlit tropical scene. It was signed and dated January 26, 1883.[32]

Later in 1883, presumably at the end of the school year, Goodhue returned to Pomfret, where he was given private tutoring by the Reverend Frederick Burgess, who went on to become the Bishop of Long Island. The reason for his leaving Russell's is not known, though it is possible that the high fees—Whitlock wrote that only the wealthiest families could afford to send their sons to C.C.I.[33]—had become a strain on the Goodhues' limited resources, especially if their son did not seem to be making the most of the educational opportunity. According to architect and author Charles Harris Whitaker, Goodhue's "impressionable mind had no need of what is called education in the school sense, and it is very likely true that his genius took seed and blossomed and bore a fruit that might have been less to the taste had that genius been interfered with by pedantry or academicism."[34] Whitaker remarked further that "Bertram Goodhue was an avid absorber. . . . He sought and studied, read and remembered, and there is no piece of his work, in any field, that is not imbued with as much knowledge as skill."[35]

Bertram's education may have been unconventional, but it was broad and varied, providing a freedom not usually afforded to children in a regular school setting. The combination of his mother's instruction, his own exploration of books, and his natural gift of creativity laid the seeds for his development as an architect renowned for his creativity and independent thinking. His upbringing gave him an inner freedom as well as a chance to develop his individuality unhampered by the structure of formal educational establishments.

At the age of fifteen, young Bertram sold his horse and bird dog and went to the big city to earn his livelihood[36] (fig. 1-10). In September 1884, Charles Goodhue signed an agreement with the firm of Renwick, Aspinwall & Russell in New York City for his son to become an architectural apprentice, a common form of professional training at that time.

> I hereby agree that my son shall obey all the rules of the office, shall be as regular as possible in attendance at the office, being there from 9:30 A.M. until 5 P.M. each day (Sundays, Public Holidays, and one month vacation each summer, after this summer, being excepted) until September 1st 1886, unless prevented by illness; and that he may leave between now and September 1st 1886 and have his obligation cancelled only by the payment of three hundred dollars by me to RENWICK, ASPINWALL and RUSSELL, and further should he be prevented from attendance for more than two weeks during the time above described, such time shall be added to his term of service.[37]

It is not known why the Goodhues chose Renwick, Aspinwall & Russell for their son's apprenticeship. With her interest in high-quality education, Helen Goodhue would certainly have looked for the best architects to educate her gifted son. The firm, which was renowned for its ecclesiastical and Gothic Revival work, may well have appealed to young Bertram's interest in history. His unusual drawing ability, which developed rapidly during his apprenticeship as illustrated by some intricate pen-and-ink drawings of Howard Hoppin's Gothic Revival houses in Pomfret (fig. 1-11), would have appealed to James Renwick, Jr. (1818–1895). Renwick was best known for his Gothic Revival designs of Grace Church, New York (1843–1846), the Smithsonian Institution, Washington, D.C. (1847–1855), and St. Patrick's Cathedral, New York (1858–1879). Though the senior partner was nearing retirement during Goodhue's tenure at his firm, he must have strongly influenced the young apprentice to follow the same path. At Renwick's death Goodhue recalled "his lovable qualities and unfailing kindliness as a man and teacher. . . . Over and over again he has taken the pencil from my hands, and motioning me to one side, with his own trembling fingers traced a correction on the incomplete drawing."[38]

About seven months into his apprenticeship, the firm decided to pay Goodhue $5 a month, as stated in a letter written by William Hamilton Russell—the Russell of Renwick, Aspinwall & Russell—to someone who evidently had expressed concern about Goodhue's straitened circumstances:

> I received your note about Goodhue, and, talking the matter over with Aspinwall we decided to give him $5.00 a month. He is a very nice boy and does very well for one who has been so short a time in an office; but we do not want to pay him more salary as the other boys would think we had not treated them well.—It is not our custom to pay anything to pupils, and in many offices it is the custom to charge them.
>
> I am very sorry to hear that he has had such hard lines, and if you consider him really in want I will be glad to help him personally.[39]

Goodhue was an office boy for two years; in 1886 he graduated to draftsman for another five and half years. As an office boy, his responsibilities would have included tracking and filing drawings, which would have helped him become familiar with the firm's style and techniques. As a draftsman, he would have spent much of his time tracing the drawings of the more senior men. In the late 1800s there were no blueprinting machines to do this important work. Goodhue would also have been permitted to design small items for churches, such as ornament or chancel furniture. Because of his special skill in delineation, he occasionally drew perspectives of proposed buildings.[40]

For some aspiring architects a college career was followed by attendance at the École des Beaux-Arts in Paris, where training in the classical language of architecture was augmented by travel in Europe.[41] As a prac-

with architecture for the next fifteen years. He also joined the Sketch Club, where he made friends easily and quickly became popular. Though "shy and modest, to a fault,"[44] he didn't hesitate to participate in a discussion, often choosing to take an opposing viewpoint and demonstrating that even at this young age he was quickly forming his own, unique ideas on architecture. A description of him quoted in Whitaker's biographical account gives us a vivid picture of this handsome young man:

> He lived in a hall bedroom on Madison Avenue [no. 112] where, with a small drawing board, he used to experiment with spatterdash work done with a toothbrush, and other mechanical methods of getting ink on paper expeditiously and effectively.
>
> He was recognized among the younger men as an independent thinker and worker who would not accept the trail left by the fellow ahead. His motto seemed to be not "whatever is, is right"—but "whatever is, is wrong." He was always very determined and tenacious, this amounting to obstinacy at times. . . .
>
> . . . He was always very slight and boyish looking, having very blond hair, vivid blue eyes and very red cheeks. He seemed to have discovered the fountain of perpetual youth.[45]

FIG. 1-10. *Goodhue as a teenager. This was probably taken around the time that he left home to become an architectural apprentice in New York City.*

Even at this stage in his life Goodhue recognized the importance of getting his work published. Membership in the Sketch Club provided such an outlet, giving Goodhue the chance to enter architectural competitions sponsored by the Sketch Club in New York and the T-Square Club in Philadelphia. With his natural ability and apprenticeship experience, Goodhue was able to produce a competent drawing for a "House & Lodge Designed for Erection on the Sea-coast of Oregon." This Richardsonian-inspired design with a double-gabled roof, arched entry, and stone facade, along with a floor plan, was published in *Building* magazine in 1887.[46] He was awarded "First Mention" for a drawing of "A Toll-gate and Lodge for a Country Road" (fig. 1-12).

In 1889, at the age of twenty, Goodhue had the temerity to enter a competition for the Cathedral of St. John the Divine in New York City. A young Boston firm, Cram & Wentworth, also submitted a design. Neither one was chosen, but it was the publication of these sketches that brought together two exceptional young men.

In 1890, Goodhue turned twenty-one, and in 1891 his success in winning the competition for the Episcopal cathedral in Dallas marked a turning point and a clear indication that it was time to leave the nest of apprenticeship and begin his career as a full-fledged architect.

Goodhue realized that winning a competition was only a small beginning and that converting his design

ticing architect, Goodhue's fundamental belief in a person's natural gift of creativity made him critical of architectural schools with their rules and regulations. He held strongly to his creed that "the architect, like the poet, is born, not made."[42] Ambivalent about his own education, he sometimes expressed pride, at other times regret, that he had never been "a college man." Perhaps he had once harbored dreams of following in the footsteps of his renowned ancestor, Colonel Thomas Grosvenor, who as a Connecticut man attended Yale. Certainly his mother and the Grosvenor family, more than the Goodhues, stressed the importance of education.[43] But regardless of the monetary burden, his parents may have felt that an apprenticeship in the offices of a well-known architect where he would have the advantage of a hands-on education was the most suitable course for a young man of Goodhue's gifts and personality. Harry, also artistically inclined, went to an art school in Boston instead of college. Only Ned, the youngest son, went to college, attending Harvard after graduating from the Cambridge Latin School.

While learning the architectural profession in New York, Goodhue made full use of his spare time to read voraciously and explore different avenues of art. He started experimenting with the art of typography, an avocation that competed for his attention on equal terms

FIG. 1-11. *Goodhue's pen-and-ink sketches, dated 1886–1887, of houses designed by Howard Hoppin in Pomfret. The Rectory still stands on the main street.*

Oberthal.
Dr. F.W. Chapin's Cottage
H. Hobbin, Archt

The 'Lodge' ~ 'Rathlin'
The Estate of
Geo. L. Bradley Esq'.
Van Brunt & Howe
Arch'ts

S·C·N·Y·Monthly·Competition.
A·Toll-gate·and
Lodge·for·a·Country·road

First·mention·awarded·to·
Bertram·Grosvenor·Goodhue·

Design·svbmitted·by·"The·Kings·Highway·"

FIG. 1-12. *Goodhue's drawing for "A Toll-gate and Lodge for a Country Road," for which he was awarded "First Mention."*

into reality would require connection with an established architectural office. After seeing Cram's competition design for St. John the Divine and learning that the partners were young and had been in business in Boston for only a few years, Goodhue contacted them in May 1891 but didn't join them until the fall of the same year.[47] Thus began one of the most important chapters in the lives of Ralph Adams Cram and Bertram Grosvenor Goodhue, both of whom became more important leaders in their profession because of the influence they exerted on each other. Their partnership will be examined in detail in later chapters.

Before settling down to the serious work of architecture, Goodhue took the train to Dallas to speak with the bishop about the cathedral project. This gave him an opportunity to follow his romantic inclinations and discover the rough country south of the border, where the lifestyle was so different from the formal life of New York City. He spent the next several months exploring Mexico by train and horseback, falling in love with the architecture and the people, especially the beautiful señoritas. This first contact with Spanish Colonial architecture stirred the soul of an impressionable young man and remained a dominant influence in his career. In 1892 he published *Mexican Memories*,[48] a book about his experiences. As the train approached Mexico City, Goodhue described his first impressions: ". . . rapidly growing larger and larger . . . was the City itself, whose thousand domes and white walls glistened in the first

rays of sunlight like a dream city. Dominating all appeared the towers of the cathedral itself. . . . Tremendous as it is, however, it was now reduced to pigmy size by the blue bases and dazzling white snow caps of the two volcanos, which, rising through the perfect clarity of the atmosphere, seemed terribly near, indeed, almost overhanging the whole scene."[49]

Though traveling was difficult and sometimes dangerous (Goodhue and his Mexican companion carried guns when journeying by horseback), the author appreciated the warm hospitality of the people, the relaxed atmosphere, and the simplicity of the peasants' way of life. Having designed costumes for his childhood theatrical activities, Goodhue was fascinated by the Mexican's "tight breeches, with silver spangles down the seams (or golden if you are rich)—short velvet jacket likewise ornamented, bright colored sash and gorgeous sombrero." He indulged in the purchase of a sombrero, but it was "quietly respectable . . . being dove-gray with heavy silver 'trimmins.'"[50] Goodhue could wear it in Mexico but knew that he would shock New Yorkers if he ever wore it on Broadway. It eventually hung on the wall in his attic studio. He attended a bullfight and shouted his support as loudly as the natives; he enjoyed a night in a country hacienda, especially the evening song and guitar music provided by Señorita Inez with her dancing black eyes; he purchased an especially valuable painting by Sebastián de Arteaga of "San Antonio gazing caressingly at the infant Saviour, whom he holds in his arms."[51]

This eventually took pride of place over the mantel in Goodhue's New York townhouse. But most of all he became fascinated by the cathedrals with their Churrigueresque designs, "masses of ornament, pilasters above pilasters, masques and garlands without end." This florid ornament presented a marked contrast to the "heavy, almost sombre, work of the cathedral."[52] "Churrigueresque"—a luxuriantly decorated style of the Baroque period—is named after three architect brothers, the eldest being José Benito de Churriguera (1665–1725). The brothers were members of a Barcelona family of sculptors known for their elaborately carved decorations of altar backdrops.[53]

Before his vacation came to an end, Goodhue stopped in a village called Santa Ana, which he describes as situated in a peaceful valley in northeastern Mexico,[54] to see a particularly interesting confessional in the church. Staying at an inn nearby, he met a young señorita named Dolores. Her novio (fiancé) was away tending his herds, and while her father was busy looking after his patrons, she joined Goodhue on the roof, where he retired to smoke his cigars (fig. 1-13). A lack of fluency in Spanish didn't prevent a certain respectable intimacy from developing between them. But it was short-lived. Goodhue received a letter from home telling him his furlough was at an end. On his departure he bade Dolores a tender goodbye: "During the moment's silence which followed something happened, I don't remember what very clearly, and then holding both her hands in mine I bade her farewell." She watched him mount his horse and, almost whispering, said, "Adiós, Beltran; vaya usted con Dios."[55]

This was the first of many foreign journeys undertaken by Goodhue. Such experiences added an important element to his architectural development. Observing and absorbing the culture, history, and architecture of other countries broadened his horizons, nurtured his romanticism, and gave him a wealth of material for his own designs. Although Goodhue initially became known for his Gothic Revival architecture, he never forgot this first visit to Mexico and his early fascination with Spanish Colonial architecture, which was strengthened later by a second tour of Mexico and visits to Spain, where he could observe the original Renaissance designs. These experiences helped Goodhue develop a style that influenced the future architecture of California and Hawaii for decades to come. He also used his "Spanish" inspirations to develop a simpler architectural language devoid of decoration. Now, in the fall of 1892, with his explorations of Mexico at an end, he was ready to embark on the first stage of what would become an increasingly successful career.

On·the·Roof·of·the·Fonda
(with Dolores)
Looking westward

FIG. 1-13. *Goodhue's sketch in* Mexican Memories *of the view from the roof of the inn where he enjoyed a romantic interlude with Señorita Dolores.*

Chapter 2

THE BOSTON YEARS

1891–1903

From a professional point of view he was my alter ego *and I like to think that I was his.*

—RALPH ADAMS CRAM[1]

On his return from Mexico in the fall of 1891, Goodhue joined the firm of Cram & Wentworth. Around the same time, his brother Harry also moved to Boston. Both men qualified for membership in the Boston Art Students' Association (BASA). A few years later Harry began designing glass for his brother's firm at the Boston studio of Phipps, Slocum & Company.[2] Harry (1873–1918) soon became an important player in his brother's life and work, making a significant contribution to Bertram's Arts and Crafts agenda. As Albert M. Tannler notes, Harry Goodhue, Otto Heinigke (1850–1915), and William Willet (c. 1867–1921) were "the first American stained glass craftsmen to revive the art and craft of medieval glazing"[3]—an important feature of Cram's and Goodhue's Modern Gothic churches. Though he was a brilliant artist and was recommended for commissions by his architect brother, Harry had a poor sense of business and struggled financially.

On March 7, 1891, the brothers' father, Charles Goodhue, died. Two years later Helen Goodhue gave up the Pomfret home[4] and joined her sons in Boston. At first, the family took lodgings at 40 Russell Street, moving later to 7 Buckingham Place, where Mrs. Goodhue stayed until her death from apoplexy in 1906.[5] Cousin Constance recalled a scene in this house when she thanked Bertram for sending *A Book of Architectural and Decorative Drawings*: "You know how proud I always am of your work and of you, so it is an especial joy to possess so much of it for my very own. So many of these, too, I saw grow under your pen, in the living room of 7 Buckingham Place and I have only to shut my eyes to see the dear group, you at the desk and the blessed aunts and the rest of us gathered about."[6]

One might think that Bertram and Harry would have found it a burden to live with their mother while they were exploring a social life that revolved around gatherings at the Tavern Club, the Association of Pewter Mugs, and the Visionists.[7] On the contrary, Helen Goodhue and her sister, Hattie, received callers, had their own social circle, and participated in the amateur theatricals that gave Bertram and Harry, cousin Constance, and Bertram's new business associate, Ralph Cram, an opportunity to continue an activity that they had all enjoyed as children. A photograph in Con's scrapbook of a group of debonair young adults had a note: "Bertram belonged to our little 'Cambridge Comedy Club'" (fig. 2-1).[8] Evidently, they performed plays in aid of a "Fund for Children's Country Week" at a studio in Cambridge. But their most ambitious activities were for the BASA annual ball. A Boston newspaper reported on *The Pageant of Life*, an allegory of the seven ages of man (fig. 2-2):

In a series of tableaux, brief plays and illuminated poems the arts students, with the assistance of some of the most

FIG. 2-1. *The "Cambridge Comedy Club." Back row from left #1 Harry, #4 Cousin Constance. Front row from right #3 Bertram.*

cultivated ladies of Boston, gave a presentation of the same idea, unique in its conception, artistic in its arrangement and historically real.

Mr. Bertram Grosvenor Goodhue was Prologue, and in the gorgeous costume of a herald repeated the appropriate lines to a large audience of the city's most appreciative people, "All the world's a stage . . . his acts being seven ages."[9]

In 1893, the theme of the student festival was "Renaissance." Goodhue was Renée of Provence with his queen and a retinue of followers; Cram was Pope Leo with a court of his own. Another year "Bertram was Cimabue, Harry was Ancassin, Aunt Helen (Mrs. Goodhue) was Empress Maud, and I (Constance) was Desdemona." Cousin Con's description included a note about "Trumpets and Crusaders (the Tavern Club marched in together in marvelous ringing armor, with clanking mailed feet and swords, shouting St. George and Merry England)." In addition to playing roles, Goodhue often helped to design the scenery and costumes.[10] What great times these must have been for the artists, architects, writers, poets, and musicians of Boston. It was a Bohemian lifestyle, a time of free expression, exploration, and camaraderie. Moreover, participation in amateur theatricals nurtured Goodhue's artistic imagination and gave him an opportunity to recreate the beauty that he found in the past.[11]

There was also work to do. Goodhue's new employer, Ralph Adams Cram (1863–1942), was five years older

FIG. 2-2. *Bertram Goodhue as Prologue in* The Pageant of Life *performed by BASA for their 1892 ball.*

than he and the son of a Unitarian minister in Hampton Falls, New Hampshire. Like Goodhue, he never went to college but began his architectural career as an apprentice, in his case with the firm of Rotch & Tilden in Boston. At the end of five years, having failed to win any competitions, young Cram left the conservative firm feeling disillusioned with architecture. After a brief interlude he obtained a job as an architectural critic and reporter for the *Transcript*, a Boston newspaper. Travels in Europe introduced him to Anglo-Catholicism and renewed his interest in architecture. After winning second prize for the design of an extension to the Massachusetts State House, Cram found a solid business partner in Charles Wentworth and started his own office in 1889. Cram is described as having "sandy hair, firm chin, and boyish good looks."[12] He was thought of as a dandy who liked to dress in colorful clothes, and "though not, perhaps, charming, [he] had increasingly the reputation of being both earnest and brilliant, as well as precocious,"[13] attributes that were similar to those of his new employee (fig. 2-3).

Oliver felt that there was some uncertainty as to whether Goodhue initially joined the firm as its head draftsman or as an equal partner.[14] Goodhue's first contact with Cram and Wentworth was in May 1891, when he traveled to Boston to meet them. At that time the three men appear to have discussed a partnership arrangement, but in a letter of June 24, 1891, Cram wrote to Goodhue apologizing for having to postpone the proposal because certain projects had failed to materialize. He suggested an interim plan: "You shall have as much room in our three rooms as you want. You shall use our men as much as you like and in return shall give us as much of your time at the rate of $25 per week as will pay for the time our men give you at the rates we pay them. Room rent we will throw in. Of course, you would have your name on the door of the third room, and would realize all your commissions on whatever you did." Cram went on to explain that they did not want to lose Goodhue under any circumstances.[15] However, before he mailed his letter, Cram received a note from Goodhue, to which he responded as follows: "Your letter of the 23rd has arrived. Our letter answers it we think. . . . You need not hurry back on our account."[16] Cram was referring to Goodhue's decision to take some time off to visit Dallas and travel on to Mexico before joining the Boston firm.

When listing his qualifications in 1916, Goodhue wrote: "Went to Boston in 1891 as head draughtsman for the firm of Cram & Wentworth. The following year became a member of the firm, the name being changed to Cram, Wentworth & Goodhue."[17] This is confirmed by an announcement in cousin Con's scrapbook: "Messrs. Cram & Wentworth, Exchange Building, 53 State

Street, Boston, have the pleasure of announcing that Mr. B. G. Goodhue has become a member of the firm, and that on and after January 1, 1892, the firm name will be Cram, Wentworth & Goodhue."[18] Business was still slow and no doubt it was economically more feasible to give Goodhue a share of the profits than to pay him a salary.

Wentworth was the business partner and anchor of the firm. He took on the responsibility of trying to balance a precarious budget, and borrowed money from his family when desperate. In addition to financial worries, Wentworth found Goodhue's personality irksome and at one time advised Cram to let him go because he felt Goodhue was spending too much time on projects that never materialized. The Dallas cathedral job proved to be especially frustrating. Cram & Wentworth had also submitted a design for the competition, so it should have been a workable project for the new team. However, the bishop was dissatisfied with the initial drawings, complained about the cost, and failed to raise the money or make a single payment toward the promised $150,000. Finally, Cram, as the principal architect of the firm, decided that they couldn't continue to produce drawings without compensation and withdrew.[19] Goodhue had also been working on a memorial arch for Chickamauga, Georgia, which his cousin General Charles Grosvenor had brought to the firm. Goodhue had done at least two sketches, one a "very formal and classical design," the other a "castellated structure with a certain military effect," but a congressional bill asking for an appropriation to cover the cost of the design and construction was unsuccessful.[20] It probably didn't help that Wentworth was suffering the effects of tuberculosis. He retired from the firm in 1895 and died in California in 1897 at the age of thirty-six.[21] Cram then hired Frank William Ferguson (1860–1926) as engineer, business manager, and general controller of construction. The firm was Cram, Goodhue & Ferguson through December 1913 when they split and Goodhue formed his own office in New York City.

Cram and Goodhue became firm friends and developed a comfortable professional rapport. Many years later Cram wrote a vivid description of his partner and friend:

> A genius takes his place in no recognized category, and Bertram was this, to a degree I have seldom met with during an over-long life. As a master of decorative detail of every sort he had no rival then nor had had for some centuries before; his pen-and-ink renderings were the wonder and the admiration of the whole profession, while he had a creative imagination, exquisite in the beauty of its manifestations, sometimes elflike in its fantasy, that actually left one breathless.
>
> His personality was as baffling to any powers of description as was his artistic facility. Exuberantly enthusiastic, with an abounding and fantastic sense of humour, he flung gaiety and abandon widely around whenever he was in the temper to do so. On the other hand, he could be moody and dispirited on occasion, though this mood lasted only for brief moments, vanishing as quickly as it came. I remember him best in two aspects: sitting hunched up over a drawing-board, his lips writhing nervously around innumerable drooping cigarettes, shifting his pen from one hand to another (he was ambidextrous) as he wrought out some inimitable study in dazzling black and white; or perched crosslegged on the edge of a table, a stein of beer beside him while he sang riotous or sentimental songs to improvised accompaniment on the Spanish guitar. He could be playboy or philosopher, visionary or fierce protagonist of outrageous and impossible theories—most of which he did not believe, but defended stoutly. He was an almost universal genius. He was Bertram Grosvenor Goodhue, and in saying that you have said all.[22]

As indicated by the above description and by comments of other colleagues, Goodhue, like many creative people, was emotional and prone to excessive moods. He himself admitted that he suffered from neurasthenia, a psychic disorder that can cause fatigue, depression, headaches, indigestion, and circulatory problems. In 1912 he wrote to his English friend Cecil Brewer, referring to his health problems: "I suppose I suffer somewhat (perhaps it is a part of the damned neurasthenic fiddlesticks) from what Milton calls, 'the last infirmity of a noble mind'; in other words, the desire for fame."[23] In addition to the nervous disorder Goodhue had a heart murmur, which required a special risk proviso in a hard-to-obtain life insurance policy.[24] Although he suffered from various ailments throughout his too short life, Goodhue worked extremely hard. But conscious of his weaknesses, he tried to take regular breaks either to go hunting or fishing or to travel overseas.[25]

Although the firm, with its newly formed partnership, was hoping for ecclesiastical and public projects, much of their early work was devoted to residential designs. Cram wrote: "For a year or two all we did was in the field of domestic architecture, and in all sorts of places around Boston, most of it along the lines of the English half-timber work (imitation) then coming into vogue."[26] Cram had already executed several residential projects as a result of articles that he had published in *Architectural Review, Decorator and Furnisher,* and *Ladies' Home Journal.*[27] Cram was a capable draftsman, but now he was able to make use of his new partner's exceptional rendering skills to create lifelike illustrations of his proposed designs (fig. 2-4). In 1899, Cram wrote to a client, "Unfortunately Mr. Goodhue, who makes all our show drawings, is in Mexico, so I must apologize for the badness of this particular sketch for which I alone am to be held responsible."[28] Early house designs were generally two- or three-story half-timbered structures over a ground elevation of brick. Groups of leaded casement windows were placed under a range of gabled slate roofs combined with dormers and elegant brick chimneys—all created in a traditional Tudor Revival milieu to appeal to New England inhabitants still steeped in their British heritage.

During this period Cram, as the principal architect, was responsible for the planning. At first, Goodhue's involvement may have been limited to illustrating Cram's plans, but the very act of drawing a three-dimensional view of the building must have had some bearing on the ultimate design. Moreover, in view of Goodhue's creative intensity, we can presume that he would not have been shy about expressing his ideas. From the firm's early correspondence it is clear that Cram was the principal contact and designer for some projects, and Goodhue for others.[29] In fact, Cram soon came to rely on Goodhue's special skills not only in rendering but also in creating the details. Cram described their working relationship:

> What ability I had stopped short at one very definite point. I could see any architectural problem in its mass, proportion, composition, and articulation, and visualize it in three dimensions even before I set pencil to paper. I had

FIG. 2-4. *Pen-and-ink perspective of a house for publication in the* Ladies' Home Journal.

FIG. 2-5. *Pen-and-ink perspective for the proposed* Walter Dodge *house in Simsbury, Connecticut, 1893.*

PERSPECTIVE VIEW OF
A PROPOSED HOUSE FOR
JOSEPH MERRILL ESQ.
LITTLE BOAR'S HEAD
N.H.

FIG. 2-6. *Sketch for the proposed Joseph Merrill house at Little Boar's Head, New Hampshire, 1895.*

FIG. 2-7. *Joseph Merrill house, Little Boar's Head, New Hampshire—alternate Colonial Revival design.*

also the faculty of planning, and I generally blocked out all our designs at quarter-scale. There my ability ceased. I had neither the power nor the patience to work out any sort of decorative detail. At this point Bertram entered the equation, to go on without a break to the completion of the work. And this detail was marvelous, no less. . . . Little by little we began to learn something from each other.[30]

In 1893, Cram, Wentworth & Goodhue entered a design competition for a residence for Walter Phelps Dodge in Simsbury, Connecticut. The Phelps and Dodge families, who were descended from early Massachusetts Bay settlers, had intermarried and become successful overseas traders. They used their profits to invest in a variety of enterprises that included railroads, banking, and copper mining.[31] Walter Dodge, a less illustrious member of the family, decided to build a country house on family-owned land in Simsbury where Walter's father and uncle owned houses, called Beaverbrook and Four Corners, on Bushy Hill.[32]

Cram, Wentworth & Goodhue's design for the proposed Walter Dodge house followed closely the designs that they had published in the *Ladies' Home Journal*. If anything, the scheme was more authentically Tudor, with a half-timbered second floor and carefully detailed wood cornice overhanging the brick base. The first-floor plan was organized around a large hall or great room with reception and dining rooms on one side, and

library, office, conservatory, and octagonal warming room on the other side (fig. 2-5). According to the firm's records, their scheme for Walter's house was not the winning design.

The firm's early domestic work reflects some of the forms and details found in the architecture of Edwin Landseer Lutyens (1869–1944), whose success lay in his ability to bring a fresh approach to English vernacular architecture. In 1894, Cram, perhaps influenced by Edward S. Morse's magic-lantern lectures on Japanese architecture[33] and by Japanese forms found in the work of H. H. Richardson (1838–1886),[34] designed a Japanese-style house with Western amenities for the Reverend Arthur May Knapp, pastor of the Unitarian Society in Fall River, Massachusetts. The exotic design caused quite a stir in its traditional New England neighborhood. In 1898 the Reverend Knapp, who worked for many years as a Unitarian missionary in Japan, suggested that the firm propose a design for the imperial Japanese parliament buildings in Tokyo. Armed with drawings and a stunning perspective by Goodhue, Cram traveled to Japan to present their scheme. The design was well received and an order was placed for further drawings; but the government that supported the project was ousted, and the job was canceled.[35]

Goodhue continued to create beautiful renderings for residential designs. In 1895 he drew two designs for a house for Joseph Merrill in Little Boar's Head, New Hampshire. One perspective view showed a gabled

FIG. 2-9. *Richmond Court, Brookline, Massachusetts, 1899. This was one of the first open-court plans in the United States.*

house with casement windows and a wide porch supported by a fieldstone base wrapping around one corner. It appeared to be a more rustic version of the Walter Dodge house. In place of the half-timbering the upper level was finished in clapboard (fig. 2-6). The same client was also shown a rendering of a much more formal two-story Colonial Revival mansion with tall first-floor windows framed by shutters and topped with scrolled pediments. A Palladian window emphasized the center of the symmetrical façade (fig. 2-7). Neither of these designs was built, but they demonstrate that the firm was experimenting in several architectural styles and was versed in the classical orders. Throughout his career Goodhue was critical of the Beaux-Arts training. However, neither he nor Cram was against the principles of classical architecture; they just questioned rigid adherence to the rules with no opportunity for innovative expression.

Cram, feeling unsatisfied with individual residences, turned to designing apartment houses. This would produce more challenging planning and give the firm some welcome publicity for tackling a relatively new form of living accommodation. In 1898, Cram created the plan and Goodhue drew a perspective for the Hammond House block, on Johnson Avenue, Charlestown, Massachusetts (fig. 2-8). The six-story building was broken into segments with separate entrances. The general impression here was of a restrained elegance that might be found in London or Paris. To judge from the number of letters and payments, this apartment house was actually built.

In the same year, Goodhue had initiated discussions with Horace Slingluff about a proposed apartment house in Baltimore, and in December of 1898, Cram sent Slingluff some floor plans which he had drawn on the basis of Goodhue's notes. In his letter accompanying the drawings Cram added, "Mr. Goodhue wished me to say that he had made inquiries in Baltimore after seeing you,

and found that it would be perfectly possible to raise 60% of the valuation of the building and land."[36] However, nothing more came of this project.

The partners' 1899 design for Richmond Court (named after Richmond Palace, England) in Brookline, Massachusetts, was one of the first open-court plans in the United States (fig. 2-9). The design was simpler, crisper, and more modern than that of the Hammond House.[37] The building was divided into entries or halls, each one named after one of Cram's friends. Cram wrote that it was "the first attempt to camouflage an apartment house through the counterfeit presentment of a great Tudor mansion."[38]

In December 1898, Goodhue caught pneumonia and was dangerously ill for several weeks. A month later Goodhue wrote, "I am on the eve of sailing for Mexico. . . . I have been forced through illness to take this trip."[39] No doubt the doctor had recommended recuperation in a warmer climate. This time he traveled with Sylvester Baxter and Henry Greenwood Peabody to gather information and photographs for a book, eventually published as *Spanish-Colonial Architecture in Mexico.*[40] Peabody was the photographer and Baxter the primary author. Goodhue was responsible for the drawings and contributed to the text, which helped to establish him as an authority on Spanish Colonial architecture. He published an article on his experiences in *The Churchman.*[41] In order to finance his trip Goodhue borrowed money from the firm. Ferguson explained that "our resources were taxed severely by the sickness of Mr. Goodhue, who was obliged to draw heavily in order that he might go to Mexico for his health. This has left us sailing pretty closely into the wind."[42] Goodhue was away for four months, returning in May 1899.

Soon after his return Goodhue began work on a residence in Athens, Ohio, for his cousin, General Charles Henry Grosvenor (1833–1917).[43] General Grosvenor,

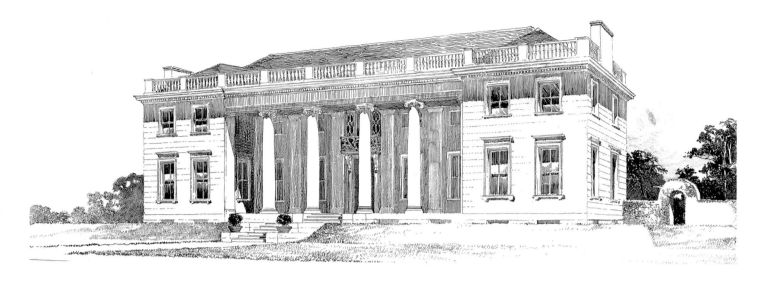

FIG. 2-10. *Pen-and-ink rendering of the first design for General Charles Grosvenor, Athens, Ohio, 1899.*

FIG. 2-11. *General Grosvenor house—Scheme 1: first-floor plan.*

FIG. 2-12. *General Grosvenor house—Scheme 1: second-floor plan.*

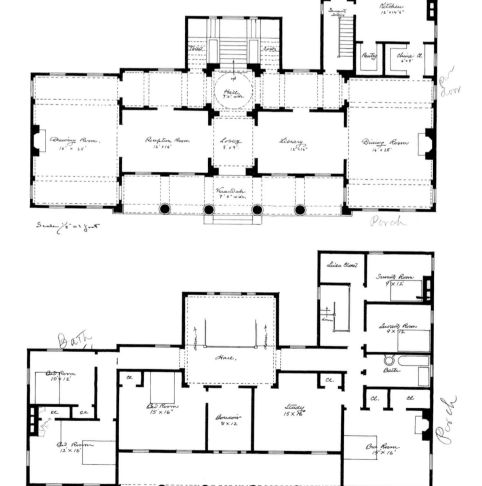

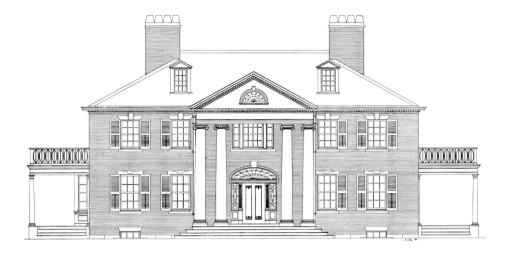

FIG. 2-13. *General Grosvenor house—Scheme 2, 1899: front elevation.*

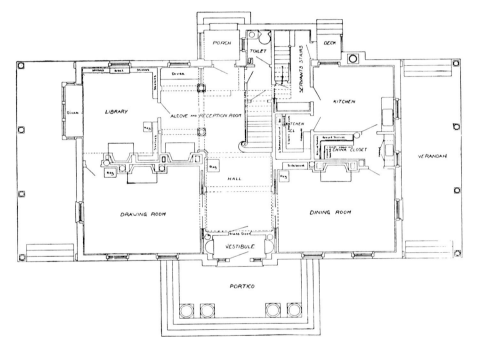

FIG. 2-14. *General Grosvenor house—Scheme 2: first-floor plan. In the final construction, the first floor was flipped over so that the dining room and kitchen were on the left side as you entered.*

who is described as having a "magnificent head of snow-white hair and snowy whiskers reaching clear down to his waist,"[44] trained as a lawyer before joining the army and serving with honor in the Civil War. Soon after resuming his law practice in Athens, he was elected to the Ohio House of Representatives, and then to Congress. On retirement from politics he resumed his law practice,[45] and in 1899 he hired Bertram Goodhue to design a grand home for himself and his second wife on land that he owned in Athens.

Two schemes were developed. The first one was a gracious Colonial Revival mansion that would use two lots (fig. 2-10). The main feature of the house was a long inset veranda with four Ionic columns set within a perfectly balanced façade featuring paired windows. As with most of the firm's residential floor plans, a central lobby divided the first floor, with reception and drawing rooms on one side, and a library and a dining room on the other (fig. 2-11). The upstairs consisted of four bedrooms, a boudoir, a study, and servants' rooms (fig. 2-12). The design, which was symmetrical and beautifully proportioned, demonstrated a fresh interpretation of a classical theme.

Although General Grosvenor had expected to build his house on the two lots that he owned, the family who rented a house on the second lot begged him not to demolish their home.[46] In acceding to their wishes, General Grosvenor asked his cousin to modify the design in order to make it fit on one lot. As a result, the final design became a more conventional Georgian Revival mansion. According to Jane Hamilton, it is quite possible that her grandmother, Constance Stewart Grosvenor (General Grosvenor's daughter), who owned a house on the same street, had some say in the changes.[47] The recessed veranda of the first scheme became a more cumbersome pedimented porch attached to the front of the house (figs. 2-13 and 2-14). The interior, now revised and smaller, featured fluted columns and pilasters, gracious Adams-style fireplaces, paneled wainscots, and built-in cabinets.[48] A small building at the back housed the carriages, with rooms for a manservant.

Before the drawings were completed and the house constructed, Goodhue went on another extended tour, this time to the Mediterranean, Persia, and India with his friend and new client James Waldron Gillespie. Trying to catch up with business on his return, he wrote to his cousin in October 1901:

> With regard to the windows, we all feel that it would be better to make both upper and lower sash single sheets of glass, if Mrs. Grosvenor objects to the small panes. The small panes are much more Colonial in effect.
>
> We are rather at sea regarding the condition of your building. Mr. Cram tells me that during my seven months absence no details have been called for.[49]

A month later Goodhue wrote about compensation for the "labour involved in reversing the house." The office was now busy drafting full-size details, but

> we must point out, however, that there is every reason to believe that your contractor has deviated largely from our plans and specifications and, therefore, the full size drawings may not be absolutely correct for the building as constructed. . . . Trusting that everything will now proceed smoothly and harmoniously. . . .[50]

The comment about "reversing the house" referred to reversing the first-floor plan from one side to the other (see caption for fig. 2-14).

General Grosvenor died in 1917, but the house remained in the family for approximately fifty years before his granddaughter Constance Lette, an Ohio University professor emerita of French, donated it to the Episcopal Church of the Good Shepherd, which leased it back to the university. The building became the Konneker Alumni Center in 1981 (fig. C-1).[51]

In 1899, at the same time Goodhue began work on his cousin's house, Cram became involved in the design of a house in Greensburg, Pennsylvania, for William Augustus Huff (1856–1928), who was president of the

Safe Deposit & Trust Company.[52] Cram was initially hired to design the interior of the house, but he couldn't resist making suggestions for improvements to the architecture even though he wrote, "We want him [Huff's architect] to distinctly understand that we are making no attempt to supplant him."[53] Cram felt that the house would be more authentically "Colonial" if Huff made certain changes: "First, if it can possibly be done, the frontage of the house be extended and its depth diminished. . . . The round bay windows I should certainly try to get rid of as they are never used in Colonial work. . . . In the second place may I recommend common red brick laid up in Flemish bond in white mortar in place of the cream color brick you suggest. . . . I send you by mail a plan and elevation of a similar house though considerably smaller, which we are building for Congressman Grosvenor in Ohio."[54]

A week later Cram sent modifications for the plan and a rough sketch of his exterior suggestions: "I need not remind you that the essence of Colonial architecture is its formality, stateliness, regularity and simplicity. . . . In the sketch that I send you I have tried to obtain regular rooms arranged formally and with doors so located that you can get long straight vistas."[55] At some point during these discussions the Huff family visited the Boston office of Cram, Goodhue & Ferguson: "We went to Boston to see the architect. . . . We met Mr. Cram but spent most of our time with Mr. Goodhue."[56]

Though larger in size, the final result was a house strikingly similar to General Grosvenor's house in Athens, Ohio. Both houses fall into the category of "Colonial Revival" using classical vocabulary. The Athens house, which might be described as "Colonial Georgian," appears to be more gracious, with symmetrical shuttered windows giving a lighter feel to the front elevation, and chimneys placed behind the dormers, making them less obvious. Even if the final result was more rustic, Cram had succeeded in persuading the client's architect to make the Huff house more authentically classical through the use of elements from the late Colonial Georgian and post-Colonial Federalist years. The building has survived and is now the YWCA of Westmoreland County (fig. C-2).[57]

For both Cram and Goodhue, the Boston years were filled with a variety of endeavors. Their church designs had begun with All Saints' Church in Ashmont, outside Boston, and each year brought more ecclesiastical commissions (mostly in the Gothic style) in Massachusetts and as far away as Detroit, Michigan. To further this area of their practice Cram published a series of eight articles on ecclesiastical design in *The Churchman* (September 2, 1899, through August 18, 1900). A year later the articles were revised, augmented with illustrations by Goodhue, and published as a book called *Church*

Building.[58] This was the first of several books on church architecture by Cram, who wrote many articles on the subject. Cram had also become an ardent Anglican, with most of the firm's church commissions being Episcopal.

It was also a time of learning and experimentation. Cram's tendency toward starkness and simplicity was soon softened by Goodhue's more decorative contributions. Cram described their working relationship: "So intimately and simultaneously did we work that it sometimes seemed to me that we were less two individuals than the two lobes of one brain. It was from Bertram Goodhue, however, that the inspiration seemed to flow. His personality was so dynamic that it seemed to stream out into and infect everyone within the office walls."[59]

Cram admitted that he was more archaeological in his approach to historic architecture, tending to "reproduce rather than to recreate."[60] Goodhue, on the other hand, was a designer, not a historian. He had a special gift for reworking period designs and bringing them into a modern context, using contemporary methods and materials. "He [Goodhue] demonstrated very clearly that Gothic was not a dead style, but, at least at his hands, could be recovered, revitalized, and continued into new times and new fields with added glory."[61] His aim was to select those elements of Gothic, whether medieval or Revival, that were appropriate to his designs. The fact that Gothic architecture, unlike classical, was not bound by strict rules and codes enabled Goodhue to reinterpret this earlier style as he chose.

Both partners found inspiration in the work of Augustus Welby Northmore Pugin (1812–1852), "one of the most brilliant and picturesque figures of the Gothic Revival"[62] in England, and the writings of John Ruskin (1819–1900), the great Victorian critic of art and society who glorified the Middle Ages and condemned the ugliness resulting from the Industrial Revolution. Goodhue was also a great admirer of William R. Lethaby (1857–1931), a well-known English architect, theorist, and Arts and Crafts practitioner who exerted more influence on the architectural community through his writings than through his designs. Lethaby's first book, *Architecture, Mysticism and Myth*, published in 1891, expressed the theory "that architecture and symbolism are inextricably related."[63] This became Goodhue's area of expertise.

Cram and Goodhue were strong advocates of the Arts and Crafts Movement, which originated in England to counteract the lack of creativity in machine-made products and revive the art of handcrafted materials. In 1897 the partners became founding members of the Boston Society of Arts and Crafts, whose activities included manual training, model housing for the poor, bookmaking, education, and exhibits to encourage the revival of handicrafts. The firm excelled at finding the best arti-

sans for wood carving, stained glass, metal or stone sculpture, tile work, paintings, and even embroidery in the churches. For All Saints' Church in Ashmont, Goodhue produced exquisite drawings for the altar decorations, a jeweled cross, and eight candlesticks, and also designed several altar textiles. In 1898, Cram discovered twenty-year-old Lee Lawrie (1877–1963) and commissioned him to do the first of many sculptures for the office. Lawrie maintained a close working relationship with Goodhue and brought to fruition all of the latter's major sculptural decorations.

As publisher Ingalls Kimball observed, "Bertram Grosvenor Goodhue . . . was recognized by Architects, the world over, as a master in his chosen profession; to those who love books he was a master of the Craft of Printing."[64] During the Boston years he gave equal time and effort to book design (figs. 2-15 to 2-19). This was another pursuit in which Cram and Goodhue were two lobes of the same brain. Cram wrote both prose and poetry with zest and imagination, and Goodhue created the decorations, whether they were covers, elaborate borders, full pages, frontispieces, beautifully executed initials and colophons, tailpieces, endpapers, printer's marks and seals, or bookplates.[65]

Now "through that singular quality that drew all sorts of interesting and provocative people within the sphere of his dynamic personality,"[66] Goodhue joined forces with publisher-photographer F. Holland Day and

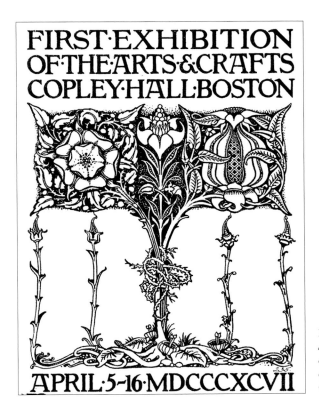

FIG. 2-15. *Goodhue's design for the brochure of the First Exhibition of the Arts and Crafts, Boston.*

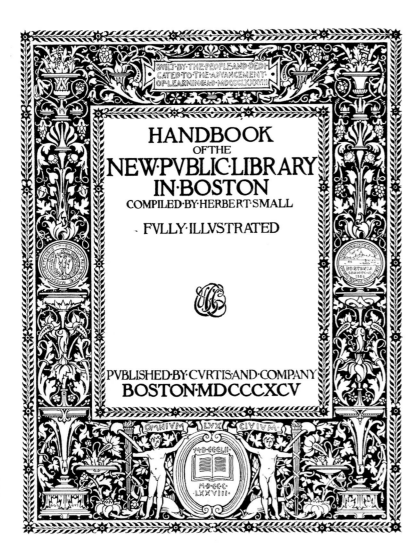

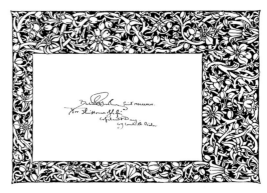

FIG. 2-16. *Goodhue's design for a handbook of the New Public Library in Boston.*

FIGS. 2-17 TO 2-19 *Miscellaneous book-cover designs by Goodhue.*

his partner Herbert Copeland, with publishers D. B. Updike, Stone & Kimball, and Small, Maynard & Company, and with the poet Bliss Carman and other writers to follow the lead of their English counterpart, William Morris (1834–1896), in reviving the art of bookmaking. Morris epitomized the Arts and Crafts Movement through his combination of art, ideals, and production. He founded the Art Workers Guild and the Society for the Protection of Ancient Buildings and became one of the leaders of the British Arts and Crafts Movement. Though he focused his efforts on the decorative arts, Morris founded the Kelmscott Press in 1890 for the production of fine books. Goodhue was inspired by Morris's work. He had studied medieval book decoration and was especially skilled in Gothic ornament. Cram wrote that "he would design a font of type or a sumptuous set of initials as quickly as he would clothe an architectural form with the splendid vesture of intricate Gothic ornament."[67]

Goodhue designed the cover, the borders, the initials, and the Merrymount type font for the *Altar Book of the Episcopal Church*, an outstanding work of art. He also created the Cheltenham type, which is still in use today. Cram edited the contributions, and Goodhue designed the cover, frontispiece, and initials, for *The Knight Errant*, a magazine closely related to Morris's *Hobby Horse*, and which aimed at being "as Medieval as possible" (fig. 2-20).[68] The magazine included articles by Cram and Goodhue themselves as well as essays and poems contributed by friends Bliss Carman, Richard Hovey, and Louise Guiney. Of the two articles written by Goodhue, the second, entitled "The Final Flowering of Age-End Art" (January 1893), championed an objective that pervaded his whole career: "a return to greater simplicity— subtler simplicity is a better term—and directness of method."[69] According to Oliver, this theme "implied the use of materials in a way that revealed their inherent qualities and beauty; it ruled out extraneous ornament; it

railed against pretension; it endorsed a clarity of structural system in the creation of architectural space and form; and it implied a preference for hand-crafted elements and finishes in a building."[70] Goodhue reiterated this theme when he wrote for other publications, but *The Knight Errant* had a short life. After its first publication in 1892 only three more issues were produced.

In the office Goodhue's typographical skills helped to create beautiful booklets used to solicit funds for their ecclesiastical projects. The hand-printed booklets combined up-to-date printing techniques with the spirit of a medieval production. The text and illustrations represented a church that respected the past but was in tune with contemporary conditions.[71]

When successes in the field of architecture became the dominant factor in Goodhue's life, he found it necessary to put aside typography. However, as a member of the Council of the Grolier Club, a New York club named after Jean Grolier de Servières (1479–1565), a French bibliophile and patron of writers and printers,[72] Goodhue continued to make contributions to an art that had played a significant role in his early career.

The Boston years (1891–1903) were exciting times in the lives of two exceptional men embarking on their architectural careers. Within a few years both men would be married,[73] and the dynamics of the firm would change. The award of a major project would require the opening of a second office in New York City, leading to a greater separation of work and responsibilities. Cram summed up their development:

> Little by little we began to learn something from each other: he [Goodhue] came to see problems more in the large, as consistent and unified conceptions, where detail was *only* a detail; while I slowly sloughed off some of my archaeological predispositions and realized the inherent value in his originality and modernism. While this process . . . helped vastly in the work we did at the time, it was in the end . . . the cause of our separation . . .[74]

FIG. 2-20. *Goodhue's design for the cover of* The Knight Errant, *a quarterly magazine.*

Chapter 3

FROM PERSIA TO MONTECITO

1901–1906

*But the poetry is here, and the mystery, and, above all else, the art—an art and craft of garden-making
no less perfect than that of Italy, but set in the midst of surroundings as different as east is from west.*

—BERTRAM GROSVENOR GOODHUE[1]

In 1896, during the Boston years, Goodhue, in one of his most romantic phases, wrote a series of travel essays illustrated with exquisite drawings of towns he had visited and buildings he had studied. Guided by the author's rich text and realistic illustrations, readers were transported to these faraway places. They were enchanted with Traumburg (which means Dream City), a medieval German town in Bohemia where the author had measured and drawn in detail St. Kavin's Church and its accompanying monastery. They were taken to Monteventoso and its lovely Church of Santa Caterina in northern Italy (fig. 3-1), and to a remote island in the Adriatic where they toured the dilapidated Villa Fosca (fig. 3-2) and met its guardian, Signor Orgogliese.

The writings and illustrations were so vivid in their detail that the reader had no doubt about the authenticity of the locations or the fact that the writer had spent many months exploring them. And yet, it turned out that these were pseudo travel articles. They were created in the young writer's imagination. Goodhue, who was only twenty-seven, had visited Mexico but had yet to travel to Europe. One New England editor rejected the articles because the names were not on any of his maps, but they were published in 1896 and 1897 in several issues of *Architectural Review* and the *Brickbuilder*, and much later in *A Book of Architectural and Decorative Drawings.*[2]

In a letter to his close friend, the journalist and screenwriter Ruth Ann Baldwin, Goodhue explained "that no

one else has ever tried to picture and write up an entire imaginary place in this fashion. Every now and then a novelist does it . . . but this isn't quite the same thing."[3] The essays and drawings demonstrated the author's knowledge of history and architecture, and more importantly, they revealed Goodhue's intense romanticism and his architectural dreams. The shapes and forms in the illustrations would appear many times in his future work. Was the elegant tower of St. Kavin's Church the forerunner of the Spanish Colonial tower of the Panama-California Exposition project in San Diego or the domed tower of the Nebraska State Capitol? It seems very likely that the Villa Fosca formed the basis of Goodhue's next residential project, a Roman villa in California.

In 1898, Cram traveled for several months in Japan. Three years later, in 1901, it was Goodhue's turn to take an extended leave from the Boston firm to go on his first real journey of exploration through Europe, the Mediterranean, Persia, and India in the company of his friend and new client, James Waldron Gillespie. Gillespie had purchased some 30 acres of land in Montecito, California, a suburb of Santa Barbara, where he had begun to plant exotic tropical trees, eventually acquiring 125 varieties of palms. He also wanted to build a grand villa with elaborate gardens. Because of the desert climate of California he needed to devise a method of using water, both functionally and aesthetically. So Gillespie invited his young architect to travel

MONTEVENTOSO

FIG. 3-1. *Pen-and-ink drawing of Monteventoso, an imaginary city.*

with him to explore the use of water in different climates, in particular in Persia, where the arid landscape was similar to that of California.

According to correspondence with his cousin General Charles Grosvenor,[4] Goodhue and Gillespie spent seven months traveling the world. Their adventures included an 800-mile horseback ride from the Caspian Sea to the Persian Gulf.[5] Some years later Goodhue wrote on the front endpaper of his copy of Benjamin Burges Moore's *From Moscow to the Persian Gulf*: "Ex Libris Beltrami G. Goodhue, who, in 1901 with his friend Waldron Gillespie, rode the length of Persia from Ehzeli (Resht) on the Caspian through Kasvin, Teheran, Ispahan & Shiraz to Bushire."[6] Goodhue recorded their experiences in an essay (this time based on reality) and a wonderful collection of pen-and-ink sketches (fig. 3-3).[7]

Before reaching Persia, Gillespie and Goodhue visited Italy, where they saw many famous gardens, enabling them to compare the horticultural art of the Renaissance with the Islamic gardens of Persia. Goodhue was especially conscious of the contrast in the use of water. In Italy water was almost too abundant: "At Tivoli and Frascati, the Anio, tumbling and rushing through its rocky gorges, fills every fountain with sparkle and makes musical every leafy alley." Everywhere there were fountains spewing forth volumes of water with rushing streams flowing into vast lakes that were "deep, dark, and full of mysterious movement."[8]

FIG. 3-2. *Pen-and-ink drawing of the Villa Fosca, an imaginary villa on an island in the Adriatic.*

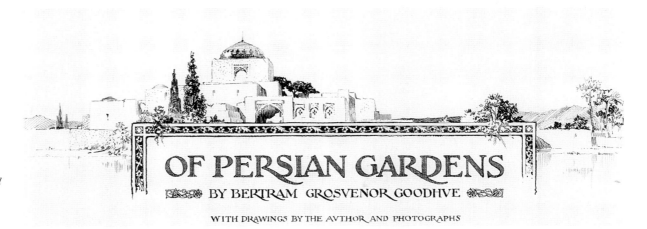

OF PERSIAN GARDENS
BY BERTRAM GROSVENOR GOODHVE
WITH DRAWINGS BY THE AVTHOR AND PHOTOGRAPHS

FIG. 3-3. *Illustrated title for Goodhue's essay "Of Persian Gardens."*

In Persia water was "a rare and precious thing to be carefully cherished and used . . . over and over again." Persian pools were "shallow, lucent and motionless," and lined with blue-green tiles, giving the appearance of reflecting a cloudless sky. The pools were generally eighteen inches deep or less and were fed by small three-layered fountains with the bottom layer in the shape of a square, the second one an octagon, and the top one circular, "resembling nothing so much as a squat rifle bullet." The published text continued: "Simple as it is, this is a not ungraceful form." But Goodhue's original typed version read: "a not ungraceful form and probably phallic in origin,"[9] which was censored before publication but provided a clearer image, especially when linked to the following: "At the apex a microscopic orifice emits a gurgling thread of water, which breaks immediately upon reaching outer air, only to fall noiselessly in a thin, glistening surface over the stone to the pool below causing not even the tiniest ripple in its progress."

The water was usually transported from one place to another in narrow, shallow channels sunk into the surface alongside or down the center of a pathway. Goodhue felt that the prevailing rectilinear shapes of the pools, walks, and terraces in Persia provided a more restful atmosphere than the "tortuous sinuosities of late Italian work."[10]

Except where cities were able to use water from the melting snows of the mountains or had their own underground springs, water in general was very scarce. In the 1600s the Persians had built subterranean canals, called kanats, which were marked by long lines of earth mounds, to bring water from the mountain gorges over many miles to towns and villages in the plains. After a day's ride through the pitiless glare of the desert, the two travelers would arrive at a walled city or traveler's inn and be startled and refreshed by the beauty of the gardens and courtyards within.

Goodhue described the different types of gardens. Invariably, city houses had small and rigidly formal gardens set inside courtyards (fig. 3-4). A second type of garden, most typical of Persia, was more ambitious. It needed a level site to accommodate the axial layout of tree-lined avenues. Watering was provided by shallow canals, which could be closed or opened as needed. Garden houses built as simple domed structures in square or cruciform shapes formed covers for pools at the intersection of the allées (fig. 3-5). In contrast, expensive gardens had more complicated sites, often on several levels. Terraces were used to create cooling water gardens. At Bagh-i Takht (Garden of the Throne) overlooking Shiraz, a small watercourse ran through the midst of the crumbling palace before breaking "in a sort of rigidly confined and box-like cascade over the highest terrace, appearing and reappearing in various fashions on most of the seven terraces that lead to the great lake-like pool at the base of the eminence" (fig. 3-6). The terraces differed in shape and size, and beyond the cypress-bordered pool a double avenue led to the gatehouse. But "the focus of the whole design, the crowning perfection of all, was not this gatehouse but the greenish-golden dome of the principal mosque far away in the heart of the city."[11]

Gillespie, who had some knowledge of horticulture, observed that there was not much variety in trees and flowers but that the cypress trees, which were native to Persia, were especially tall and stately. In addition, chenars (Oriental plane trees), which were thin and poplarlike, were used to great effect (fig. 3-7).

This and other journeys exposed Goodhue to a vast resource of architectural styles, which gave him ample material to draw on for future projects. Above all, he became entranced by the exoticism and mystery of Islamic architecture, whose influence could be found in Spanish Renaissance and Byzantine buildings. Tiled domes, towers decorated like minarets, plain adobe wall surfaces contrasting with concentrations of ornament around doors and windows, mashrabiyyas (decorative stone grilles covering window openings), water foun-

FIG. 3-4. *"Court of the Telegrapher's House, Shiraz."*

FIG. 3-5. *"Central Avenue, Dul-go-Sha, Shiraz"* with a shallow canal down the center.

tains set in colorfully tiled alcoves, and shallow reflecting pools came to form the basis of an architectural style that pervaded much of his secular and domestic work.

On their return Goodhue started work on the design of Gillespie's estate in Montecito. Waldron Gillespie (1866–1954) was the only child of William Mitchell Gillespie and Harriet Emily Bates. The Gillespies, who were of Scottish origin, had come to New York by way of Canada. Waldron's grandfather had invested successfully in real estate in upstate New York. His father was a civil engineer and educator who became the first professor of civil engineering at Union College, Schenectady, New York. He published an important treatise on roadbuilding and land surveying, and developed engineering formulas for constructing railroad tracks around curves.[12] The latter work proved to be especially valuable in the new age of railroads, and he wisely took his consultation compensation in the form of stock in the fast-growing companies. When he died of tuberculosis in 1868, his two-year-old son had a large fortune waiting for him.[13]

Young Waldron grew up in New York, attended the North Granville Military Academy northeast of Albany, and became enamored of the natural beauty of the countryside. He used his inheritance to build an elaborate house on a recently purchased farm in Middle Granville. He called the place Merevale after a nearby mere, which had been enlarged by a dam. Though he had a house in New York City and soon acquired two other homes, the Middle Granville house became his principal residence[14] and one that Bertram Goodhue and his family visited frequently. Gillespie was a restless man who became an inveterate traveler and never married. He bought property in Mariel, a suburb of Havana, Cuba, and beginning in 1890 gradually acquired several parcels of land in Montecito.

With the ocean on one side and mountains on the other, Santa Barbara is blessed with an ideal climate. Don Sebastián Vizcaíno, the Spaniard who discovered the area in 1602, sent the following description to King Philip III of Spain: "This land has a genial climate, its waters are good, and its soil fertile. . . . It is thickly settled with people, whom I found to be of gentle disposition, peaceable and docile."[15] It would be another hundred years before the Spaniards colonized Alta California, and it would become a Mexican dependency before being occupied by Americans. Owing to its relative inaccessibility, Santa Barbara escaped the concentrated development that established Los Angeles as a large metropolis in the late 1800s.

FIG. 3-6. "The Seven Terraces of the Bagh-i-Takht, Shiraz."

OPPOSITE
FIG. 3-7. "Central Avenue of Cypress and Chenars, Afiabad, Shiraz."

CENTRAL AVENVE OF CYPRESS
AND CHENARS 'AFIABAD' SHIRAZ

B.G.Goodhue

"El Fureidis"
Estate of
J.W. Gillespie, Esq
at Montecito, California

General Plan showing
House, Gardens, Terraces, etc.

CRAM, GOODHUE & FERGUSON
ARCHITECTS

KEY TO THE GENERAL PLAN

A House	G Pavilion	M Tennis Court	S Greenhouses	Y Olive Orchard
B Patio	H Steps	N Jungle	T Ancient Causeway	Z Pasture
C Pools	I Bridges	O Shrine	U Gardener's House	
D Stable	J Pergola	P Rose Garden	V Lattice House	
E Paddock	K Exedra (Chapel)	Q Lemon Orchard	W Flower Garden	
F Fountain	L Javanese Hut	R Reservoir	X Terminal Stairway	

FIG. 3-8. General plan of the Gillespie estate, Montecito, California, 1902–1906.

"Montecito" means "little forest" (not "little mountain," as sometimes stated).[16] The rolling hills, situated between the ocean and the mountains, were covered in oak trees, and there were therapeutic hot springs nearby. The open landscape and dry climate were ideal for the establishment of large and moderate-sized estates. At first, easterners and midwesterners came to winter in Santa Barbara and Montecito, but they soon returned to build permanent homes. These early inhabitants built their new retreats in revival styles with which they were familiar, Queen Anne, Shingle, or Colonial. The City of Santa Barbara, conscious of its heritage, introduced a Spanish Mission Revival style, but many of the new inhabitants were looking for a more sophisticated architecture.[17]

Fresh from the worlds of Persia and the Mediterranean, Gillespie asked Goodhue to design a Roman villa set amid gardens combining Persian and Italian elements. The style of the house and gardens initiated a new trend for the community. A long driveway bordered by tall, elegant date palms formed the approach to the estate from Parra Grande Lane. From here a winding road led up to the house sited at the top of a steep slope (fig. 3-8). The tree-bordered drive is no longer part of the property, but the original setting of the house and gardens is relatively intact. There are no formal flower beds or manicured lawns, just a simple white Roman villa set on a hill with a deep cerulean sky above the tinted peaks of the Santa Ynez Mountains that form a dramatic backdrop (fig. C-3). In front of the house an uncluttered formation of red-brick walkways outlines a quadrant of reflecting pools and delicate fountains. Beyond a wall, a long flight of steps, bordered by cypress and palm trees, descends to three long, narrow pools that terminate in a colonnaded pavilion (fig. C-4). The original pavilion, sometimes referred to as the casino, was modeled on the gatehouse of the Bagh-i Takht Palace in Shiraz (fig. 3-9). It was washed away in the disastrous flood of 1914 and was replaced with a simpler version. Here a visitor can sit and meditate or enjoy the view of the house and mountains (fig. 3-10). From the house the scene is a dense forest of trees pierced by the concrete steps and pools falling away toward a winding creek.

The pools, steps, and walkways, which formed the main axis of the gardens, were built first. Construction on the house itself did not begin until 1905 and was completed a year later.[18] Goodhue was responsible for the design, with his firm executing the drawings. Myron Hunt, an established architect who had come recently to California, was the on-site construction supervisor. For Gillespie's villa Goodhue took his inspiration from the visionary design he had devised for his essay on the Villa

Fosca "set on a forgotten islet in the Adriatic." The imaginary villa was "irregularly regular in plan, set about three sides of a court. A five-arched loggia adorns one of these sides, the columns of which are perhaps those originally used in the *peristylium* of the Roman house which once occupied the site."[19]

Gillespie's villa of approximately 10,000 square feet had four sides forming an interior courtyard. The main entry from the driveway approach was on one end of the north two-story wing (fig. 3-11). The other three wings were one story high. In place of the Villa Fosca's five-arched loggia, the garden façade featured symmetrical paired windows linked by a shallow, implied loggia supported by eight columns with Ionic capitals. The design of this section was a simplified version of the original 1899 scheme that Goodhue created for General Grosvenor's house in Athens, Ohio (fig. 2-10). For Gillespie's residence the classical features were stripped down. The central portion was only slightly recessed, the columns were no longer freestanding but engaged in the façade, and the banded cornice was undecorated except for simple pediments over the windows. Decoration was confined to nine bas-reliefs of the Arthurian legends,

FIG. 3-9. *Goodhue's pen-and-ink drawing of the original pavilion at the end of the allée of pools. This pavilion was destroyed in a flood in 1914 and replaced with a simpler version.*

FIG. 3-10. *View of the Gillespie estate from the pavilion.*

highly decorative Corinthian capitals supported a silk canopy whose other end was attached to a beam running along the top of a group of four columns, these with Ionic capitals (fig. 3-12). If Goodhue had to accede to his client's wish for a classical theme, it is likely that he would have wanted to keep his columns simple and retain a sense of continuity in the style of the capitals, but the twisted marble columns were among the treasures that Gillespie had collected on his travels through Italy (fig. C-8).

The house was built with double-thick reinforced walls of sandstone quarried on the site. The walls provided excellent insulation and were coated in whitewashed stucco, which glistened in the California sun and formed a perfect backdrop to the wrought-iron window grilles, the bands of colored tiles around doors and pools, the terracotta planters, and the dark red brick of the terrace and paths.

For a description of the interior written in the period in which it was built, nothing can compete with the words of author and movie art director Una Nixson Hopkins:

> The formal entrance to the villa is through a carved door of remarkable workmanship which once graced the entrance to a palace; this admits you into a hall, charming in its simplicity. The delicately wrought-iron balustrade is in striking contrast to the white walls; aside from a carved chest and a few antique chairs, the room has no furniture other than hanging lamps of old brass and potted palms. But supplementing the hall is the court or atrium, open to the sky, shaded by orange trees, bananas and palms, with a floor of white marble, and in the center a pool bordered with blue tile. The court is a charming bit of The Little Paradise, encompassed within four white walls.[23]

Here the host and his guests dined alfresco unless inclement weather forced them indoors (fig. 3-13).

Hopkins was also enraptured by the formal dining room (figs. 3-14 and C-6):

> The vaulted ceiling of the long room, at one end of which is a musicians' gallery hung with elaborate old embroideries, has a painted frieze on panels of gold leaf, interrupted by bands of delicate tracery, all inscribed with great decorative charm. . . . The side walls are copper stippled, and the doors at each end of the room are copper covered and fire proof, while the French doors opening onto the court, are hung with fine old velvet very like the wall in tone.[24]

The room was furnished with a long oak table, which had a heavily carved edge, and antique chairs upholstered in tooled leather with intricate designs. The chairs had once belonged to a Spanish nobleman. On his many travels in Italy, Spain, Portugal, Cuba, Persia, and Mexico,

sculpted by Lee Lawrie, forming a band between the tops of the columns (fig. C-5). Though the tales of King Arthur might seem inappropriate on a classical façade, for Gillespie they symbolized the defense of classical civilization against the Teutonic barbarians.[20] Goodhue did not know it at the time, but this exercise in restrained classical architecture would contribute to his solution for blending the National Academy of Sciences building with the Roman environment of Washington, D.C.

Goodhue described his friend Waldron Gillespie as "a curious type; but as far from being a fool as almost anyone I know."[21] He was certainly eccentric, with strong ideas of what he wanted. He had gone to a great deal of trouble and expense to take his architect on a journey to many foreign countries to study styles of buildings and gardens, but he wasn't ready to follow all of his design ideas. According to John Rivers, Goodhue's great-grandson and also an architect, Gillespie designed much of the house himself. In a letter to Cecil Brewer, Goodhue wrote: "The three pictures of my friend Gillespie's place you may have seen before. Please don't credit me with the twisted columns or even the concrete benches."[22] At one side of the house a pair of pink, twisted columns with

Gillespie collected antiques, artwork, and tapestries to furnish and decorate his California retreat. Antique Italian chairs, tables, and a grand piano filled the rooms (fig. 3-15). The floors were covered in Oriental rugs, the walls were hung with tapestries and heavy velvet draperies, and a painting by Caravaggio in an ornate Baroque frame hung above a heavily carved fireplace constructed from a Spanish altarpiece (fig. 3-16).

The pièce de résistance of the house was a sunken conversation room (figs. 3-17 and C-7):

> Beyond the living room is the conversation room, with floor of white marble, and a central tiled pool—out of which rises a delicate pedestal, supporting a bronze figure. Lined against the four walls are low marble seats cushioned in bronze velvet, the tone of the lower part of the wall, while above, there is an elaborate surface decoration, worked out in bronze and blue and gold changing in character according to the architectural requirements of the room until finally it reaches the top of the domed ceiling. Here a great suspended globe of amber glass sheds a subtle light of gold—a place wrought by Aladdin, and the light from his wonderful lamp![25]

Henry Saylor, who published an article about the house at the same time as Hopkins, complained that "it has too many pools in the floors, hazards for the unwary guest."[26] In addition to the rooms described by Hopkins, there were two guest suites on the ground floor and five bedrooms and baths on the second floor. Bathing facilities were augmented by a large Roman pool, a sauna, and steam rooms.

Gillespie chose to call his new estate El Fureidis. *Fureidis* is an Arabic term meaning "little paradise."[27] Gillespie interpreted the name to mean "pleasance," or piece of land laid out for the purposes of pleasure.[28] When in residence, the master entertained lavishly. His home, known as "the Gillespie Place," became an important center for Santa Barbara's social life and was used for weddings, masked balls, and other grand occasions. In his absence Gillespie sometimes rented the house to winter visitors. On several occasions Goodhue and his family stayed there, and Gillespie's cousin, Henry Dater, and his wife Molly used the place until their house, also designed by Goodhue, was built on an adjacent acreage.

After World War I, Gillespie spent more time at his estate in Cuba. Following the Depression, the cost of maintaining El Fureidis was taking its toll. Gillespie still visited Montecito, but he had less interest in entertaining and spent more time reading and taking long walks, either to bathe in the hot springs or to lunch at the Santa Barbara Club on Chapala Street, a five-mile walk. Historian and cartographer David Myrick provided a colorful description of the man: "With a cloak, tennis shoes and a jauntily-worn Panama hat, he cut quite a figure."[29] Yates Satterlee, a grandson of Bertram Goodhue, remembers visiting Gillespie in his old age. He had sold his estates in Cuba and California and retreated with one servant to his

FIG. 3-11. *Goodhue's pen-and-ink drawing of the main entrance and two-story wing of the Gillespie house.*

FIG. 3-12. *Gillespie's twisted marble columns, which he had collected on his travels.*

FIG. 3-13. *Goodhue's pen-and-ink drawing of the original central atrium. The rectangular pool represents a Roman impluvium for collecting rainwater from the surrounding roofs.*

FIG. 3-14. *El Fureidis—the formal dining room with its original furnishings.*

FIG. 3-15. *Gillespie's living room with its original furnishings.*

OPPOSITE
FIG. 3-17.

FIG. 3-16. *Gillespie's original Baroque fireplace, constructed from a Spanish altarpiece. The antiques dealer who bought the house from Gillespie sold the fireplace surround and the Caravaggio painting.*

OPPOSITE
FIG. 3-17. *Conversation room with its original furnishings.*

integrity of the original building form. Thus architectural history has been well served by the restraint of succeeding owners.

In 1915, *Country Life in America* announced that El Fureidis was one of the twelve best country houses in the United States.[31] Goodhue may not have regarded the house as entirely his design or one that satisfied his ideas of great architecture, but the project as a whole and the landscape scheme in particular became an important springboard for his architectural career. According to Oliver, the forms of the house "foreshadow the complex eclecticism of Goodhue's mature works: a synthesis of the classical, the romantic, and the vernacular."[32] The house was famous, because the style of architecture with its blend of Roman, Greek, Italian, Spanish, and Persian influences, which Gillespie summed up as "Mediterranean," was the subject of many discussions and established a new trend for the West Coast. A landscape design based on Persian gardens was not only innovative but revolutionary. The use of plain concrete steps, masonry walks, and reflecting pools surrounded by a variety of exotic trees was a radical departure from the traditional green lawns and flower beds that most of California's new inhabitants had brought from their home states. Within a few years residents of Montecito and Los Angeles dared to break the traditional mold and introduce landscape schemes based on Italian villas and Spanish haciendas.[33]

For Goodhue the use of shallow reflecting pools combined with hardscape, intimate courtyards with fountains, and allées lined with Italian cypress, which he had discovered on his Persian journey, became important features in both his residential and secular projects. As made clear in his imaginary essays, Goodhue believed in the integration of landscape and architecture. He had been especially enthralled with the color and beauty of Islamic domes, which were often the centerpieces of city vistas seen from Persian gardens. A domed building bordered or approached by reflecting pools became the centerpiece of several of his future projects: the California Building at the Panama-California Exposition in San Diego; central buildings for the campuses of the California Institute of Technology in Pasadena and Rice University in Houston, Texas; the main church in the city of Tyrone, New Mexico; St. Bartholomew's Church in New York City; and as the first scheme for the Los Angeles Public Library. Sadly, only two domes were built: at the Panama-California Exposition and for St. Bartholomew's Church in New York City.[34] But reflecting pools, in groups of twos or threes, formed the approach to the Los Angeles Library and the National Academy of Sciences in Washington, D.C., and were important elements in the landscape designs for several of the residences, which will be described in later chapters.

farm in upstate New York, where he died on April 26, 1954, at the age of eighty-eight. Having a strong distrust of bankers, he had always deposited his money in many different banks under an array of names. Suffering from memory loss, he was unable to locate his money, and had never trusted anyone else with the information, with the result that he spent his last years unnecessarily poor.[30]

Gillespie wanted to leave his Montecito estate as a park, but it was sold in April 1953 to antique dealers Thad and Jean Foley, who proceeded to sell off the antiques, artwork, and rugs as well as two parcels of land. Many of the rare trees were sold to Disneyland and the Mormon Tabernacle in Salt Lake City. Since then the estate—its size now reduced to fifteen acres—has had several owners and gone through various stages of deterioration and restoration.

El Fureidis was unique when Gillespie took possession of it in 1906, and it remains so today. Despite necessary alterations and modernization, there have been no major demolitions or additions to date to disturb the

Chapter 4

A DIVISION OF LABOR

1902–1911

Each of us came to look on himself as an individual designer
with a definite desire to work things out, each in his own way.

—RALPH ADAMS CRAM[1]

After delaying his wedding for the better part of a year because of the trip with Gillespie, Bertram Goodhue married Lydia Thompson Bryant (1877–1949) on April 8, 1902, in Boston, Massachusetts. His bride, who had been brought up in Kentucky before moving to Boston, was the daughter of James T. Bryant and Helen Adela Mitchell Bryant. In a letter to his half-brother, Wells, Goodhue recalled that though the Bryants "were divorced and scarcely on speaking terms," they "sat apparently holding hands side by side."[2] A local newspaper gave the following report on the ceremony: "Beautiful in its simplicity was the wedding of Miss Lydia Bryant of Pinckney Street, to Bertram Goodhue of Cambridge, which was solemnized at the Church of the Advent, at high noon today. The bride was gowned in a gray traveling suit, with a large black plumed hat, and she carried a bouquet of violets."[3]

She had no attendants and was given away by her father. Goodhue's brother Harry was best man, and Ralph Cram, Frank Ferguson, Edwin Holt, and William Eldredge were ushers.[4] The young couple sailed from New York on April 12 for an extended trip to Europe, which included a visit to Spain and Tangier.

Lydia Goodhue was a good-looking, elegant woman (fig. 4-1). She became a conscientious hostess and shared her husband's love of music and the theater. Though her son, Hugh, recalls that she did not have a grasp of her

husband's architectural philosophy, she loved Bertram deeply and was always supportive of his endeavors and proud of his achievements.[5] She made sure that their social life was commensurate with her husband's work, that they mingled with the right people, and that Goodhue was recognized for the great architect that he became. In a letter to the Reverend Marcus Carroll, Goodhue wrote: "Neither you, nor I, nor any man, understand how completely tied down a mother is by her children. Over and over again I have tried to take Lydia off on little trips with me, to tell the truth, not entirely for her own amusement, but because I find her the greatest help . . . in making people think me a good architect."[6] After their marriage the Goodhues moved into a small house on Brattle Street, Cambridge, "the sweetest thing of its kind you ever saw."[7]

On his return from Europe, Goodhue completed drawings for a women's college on the Sweet Briar Plantation in Virginia; the site planning and landscape design showed Persian influences with a definitive axial arrangement and the use of reflecting pools. The office had also submitted plans and renderings for a competition to renovate and augment the existing campus of the United States Military Academy at West Point, New York. The winning of this commission (1903–1910) marked a significant point in the careers of Cram, Goodhue, and Ferguson. It was well publicized, and

FIG. 4-1. *Lydia Bryant Goodhue.*

placed the firm on an architectural map that went well beyond ecclesiastical boundaries. A Boston newspaper stated, "The capture of the $5,500,000 contract for the West Point improvements by a Boston firm of architects is another of these incidents that serve to reconcile us to generous expenditures by the government for public improvements."[8]

After requesting that Cram, Goodhue & Ferguson establish an office reasonably near the site for preparation of working drawings and construction supervision, the government accepted a location in New York City. It seemed natural that Goodhue, who had done his training in that city, should be the partner to move and head the new office. The office was opened in 1903, but the Goodhues did not move to New York City until 1905. In the interim, family life began to play an important role in Goodhue's career, with Lydia giving birth on April 11, 1904, to a daughter, Frances Bertram Goodhue, and a year later on April 29, 1905, to a son, Hugh Grosvenor Bryant Goodhue.

The architectural firm now had the challenge of functioning from two separate locations. This led to the partners dividing the responsibilities of a project, or submitting two separate solutions when they were unable to agree on a design. Although West Point was done in the name of the firm and Cram was responsible for the planning and some of the buildings, Goodhue maintained

that it was primarily his work. This seemed an appropriate responsibility, since Goodhue's great-grandfather, Colonel Thomas Grosvenor, had built the first fort on the site. Moreover, his cousin, General Charles Grosvenor, may have used his connections to add the firm's name to the list of competition participants. In a letter to architectural critic Montgomery Schuyler, who was planning an article on the firm's achievements, Goodhue explained the division of the West Point work:

I very much hope you will arrange to make a trip to West Point, where the Chapel and the Chaplain's quarters, the interior of which you should see, presumably can be regarded as my magnum opus.

The Post Headquarters, Cram claimed the other night, but I really feel that I must dispute this claim to some extent. The original plan enclosing a court, the placing of the tower, etc., are his, but the carrying out of the building in all its detail should . . . be credited to me. . . . The Gymnasium, on the other hand, is practically Cram's work in its entirety, though I did go all over the exterior, making modifications in accordance with a request received directly from West Point. Cram made the plan for one of the units for the Cadet Barracks Building. . . . He credits this building to me . . . in spite of this fact; but I am not very proud of it as a complete edifice. The other building[s] so far erected are practically all mine. They are . . . of very minor interest.[9]

53

Regardless of the responsibilities, the West Point design with its Gothic-style buildings rising up from the rocky cliffs and blending with the existing campus was a resounding success (figs. 4-2, C-9, and C-10). In his article, which appeared in the *Architectural Record*, Schuyler wrote: "The chapel is from any point of view the dominant building of West Point" and "fitly crowns and culminates an architectural assemblage which marks most signally the re-entry of Gothic into secular architecture."[10]

Goodhue's letter to Schuyler illustrated some of the difficulties encountered by the partners in separating their responsibilities, and the discrepancies that led to disagreements and increasing resentment. In most of their public commissions, whether they were college campuses or ecclesiastical designs, the input of both partners was required, but once the project was complete, the problem of separating credits continued to cause friction. After the dissolution of the firm in 1914, it became even more difficult to sort out details of their earlier collaborations, with unpleasantness clouding the true picture.[11] Even today, Cram's successor firm, Hoyle, Doran & Berry, is protective of its heritage.

For residential work it was easier to separate the responsibilities. Goodhue's personal friendship and travels with Waldron Gillespie put him in the best position to execute the Montecito design. During the same period (1904–1905), the firm designed a grand mansion in Newport, Rhode Island, for Mrs. John Nicholas Brown (Natalie Bayard Dresser Brown). The Brown family, who had been residents of Rhode Island since the early 1700s, had made a fortune in shipping; they then branched into textiles and founded Brown & Ives. In 1764, John Nicholas Brown's great-grandfather had founded Rhode Island College, which was renamed Brown University in 1804 to honor a large donation by the founder's son. When John Nicholas Brown I and his brother both died in 1900, they left their fortune to John's three-month-old son, who became the richest baby in the world. Following her husband's death, Mrs. Brown commissioned Cram, Goodhue & Ferguson to design Emmanuel Church in 1903 in memory of her husband.

Now, as guardian of the estate of John Nicholas Brown II, she asked the same firm to design a residence. This was primarily Cram's project, because he had the closest connections to the Brown family, having become well acquainted with Harold Brown, John's brother, through mutual contacts in Boston. However, Goodhue notes in a letter to Mrs. Brown that he was involved in the initial design phase:

My dear Mrs. Brown,

Though I had little enough—too little for my own satisfaction—to do with the actual building of your house, yet since its beginnings were with me, I should very much like to possess a set of photographs of it, if such exist.

We have, so far as I know, kept the Boston office supplied with photographs of the work done here but they have not sent us much of anything; indeed, so far as I can remember, nothing at all; which would seem to indicate that any application to them from me would not produce the desired response. . . . If you have prints, especially of the interiors of rooms, I should be very grateful to possess such.

With my sincerest regards to you and your son, who must have grown now into quite a young man.[12]

In spite of the fact that Mrs. Brown was now a widow and had only one child, she wanted a grand mansion that would be in keeping with the European style of the other great estates in Newport built by the Vanderbilts, Astors, and Belmonts. This requirement resulted in approximately 22,000 square feet of living space that included eleven bedrooms, nine baths, two half-baths, seven staff bedrooms, and three staff baths. With eight acres of land the house, appropriately named Harbour Court, was sited on a small rise with 550 feet of waterfront facing Newport Harbor.[13] As described in a real-estate brochure, "The house commands one of the most extraordinary views in America, a panorama of Newport Harbor, and the shining, imperial blue waters of Narragansett Bay dotted with the snapping sails of hundreds of yachts and sea-going vessels"[14] (fig. C-11). According to the construction contract, the cost was $103,000.

For such a prestigious location, the Boston office created a chateau in the style of the French Renaissance, with a multigabled roof, tall chimneys, and classical fenestration. The layout consisted of two main wings built around two sides of an open courtyard with a fountain in the center (fig. 4-3). One wing contained the principal rooms, all large and featuring classical columns, implied pilasters, carved moldings and paneling, elaborate cornices, parquet floors, French doors opening onto a terrace, fireplaces with marble or carved wood surrounds in every room, wall coverings of hand-tooled leather or toile, and grand furnishings. The ambience was stately and rich, and reflected the wealth of the owner.

There were several outbuildings—including a six-car carriage house with apartments above, and stables—all designed in an English Tudor Revival style with a half-timbered second story above a stucco base.[15] Though this might appear to be out of keeping with the style of the main residence, the design recalls the black-and-white houses in the villages along France's Rhine Valley.

Mrs. Brown played a leading role in the philanthropic, civic, and cultural affairs of Newport, and her son, John Nicholas Brown II, eventually became president of the Brown Land Company. He served as Assistant Secretary of the Navy for Air under President Truman in

FIG. 4-2. *West Point Chapel (1903–1910) —pencil sketch by Goodhue.*

World War II.[16] After his mother died in 1950, John divided his time between an estate in Providence and Harbour Court, where his widow, Anne Seddon Kinsolving Brown, lived until her death in 1985.[17] In 1987 the children, who were all dedicated sailors like their father and had always dreamt of making their imposing family estate into a yacht club, drew up an agreement with a syndicate made up mostly of New York Yacht Club members. The club, with headquarters on 44th Street in midtown Manhattan, was delighted to finally have its own on-the-water facility.[18]

In 1905, Cram, Goodhue & Ferguson, with Goodhue as the lead designer, entered a competition for a house in Arden, New York. The client was Edward Henry Harriman (1848–1909), a railroad executive who made his money buying bankrupt railroads and successfully rebuilding them.[19] In 1885 he bought 8,000 acres of woodland in Orange County, New York, to preserve its natural beauty and to build a summer retreat. He called the new area Arden and cut enough trees to allow for the construction of a house on a 1,300-foot-high ridge, lying between the Ramapo River valley on one side and a forest and Cranberry Lake on the other. In addition to a road, a cable railway was constructed to carry building materials and passengers to the top.[20]

It was a dramatic setting, and an ideal challenge for the romantic Goodhue, who had already experimented with similar sites in his fantasy drawings. Cram may have claimed responsibility for all the planning in their early collaborations, but as Oliver pointed out, Goodhue's imaginary designs show that he had a good grasp of siting, planning, and massing,[21] which was confirmed by the Harriman project. The house was laid out in an orthogonal arrangement that followed the contours of the ridge, with the principal rooms—library, great hall, staircase hall, and drawing room—opening onto a terrace leading to a gazebo that afforded a view of the garden and valley below (figs. 4-4 and 4-5). The architectural style was restrained English Gothic Revival, with banks of tall oriel windows, imposing pilasters, and a turreted tower that created the feeling of a castle growing out of the mountain ridge.

Oliver suggested that the Harriman design was reminiscent of some of the houses built around the same time by Frank Lloyd Wright (1867–1959). He cited the Martin House (1904) in Buffalo and Wright's unbuilt projects for the McCormick House (1907) in Lake Forest and the Booth House (1911) in Glencoe, Illinois. The architectural styles may differ, but "in each, a formal order is established by cross axes that unite the rooms of each house internally and integrate the house itself with its landscape."[22]

Unfortunately, Goodhue's dramatic scheme was not the winning design. Harriman, who chose a house in the

FIG. 4-3. *Harbour Court—main entrance.*

FIG. 4-4. *Goodhue's
1905 competition
submission for the
Harriman estate,
Arden, New York.
The Harrimans select-
ed a design by Carrère
& Hastings.*

style of a French chateau by Carrère & Hastings, died in
1909 with little time to enjoy his country retreat, which
his wife occupied until her death in 1933. The estate
served as the Arden Conference Center for Columbia
University until 2005.

Sometime around 1909, Goodhue sketched an alteration to a village hall, built by others in 1842, at Dobbs
Ferry-on-Hudson. The owners at the time were Colonel
Franklin Q. Brown and his wife Ada Eldredge Brown, a
cousin of Bertram. Goodhue's charming sketch was later
published in *A Book of Architectural and Decorative
Drawings* (fig. 4-6). In response to Cecil Brewer's enthusiastic compliments on his work, Goodhue wrote:

> The "Village Inn" was an early indiscretion, though as a
> matter of fact so is practically everything in the book. . . .
> Let me say that half-timber, or black-and-white, or what-
> ever you call it in England, as a method of construction
> has long since been abandoned by me as being not only
> more expensive than masonry but in this climate quite
> worthless, while the "Village Hall" at Dobbs Ferry was a
> $3,000 alteration to a miserable shack, that I did about
> ten years ago for a philanthropically minded cousin. The
> drawing was made one afternoon in a few hours, on a sheet
> of yellow detail paper, and is a great deal better than the

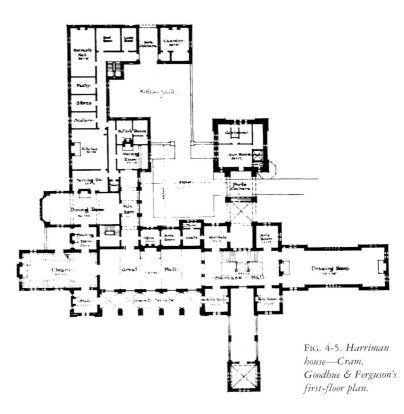

FIG. 4-5. *Harriman
house—Cram,
Goodhue & Ferguson's
first-floor plan.*

FIG. 4-6. *Pen-and-ink drawing for the Village Hall, Dobbs Ferry, New York. Goodhue's sketch (c. 1909) was for a $3,000 alteration to an existing 1842 building.*

building itself, which unfortunately we have to pass every time we go by motor to Briarcliff.[23]

The Browns had asked Goodhue to make a plan for converting their building (the "Village Hall") into a library. The village library, which had been established in 1899, was about to lose its rent-free space in another building. Mrs. Brown also provided rooms in her building for a kindergarten and a mothers' club. Although the library moved into the Brown building in 1909, the construction was not carried out until 1923. At that time, the exterior was altered to reflect the Tudor Revival style designed by Goodhue, presumably to conform to other village structures. The front façade was treated with half-timbering, and the windows were grouped in triplets and divided by heavy mullions. However, the dormers, an important Tudor Revival feature, were never built. In 1951, Colonel Brown donated the building to the village in memory of his wife. By the 1970s the library had outgrown its space, and the village gave serious consideration to replacing the old building with a new, modern structure. But a bond issue to finance the proposal was defeated, and the library made do with minor alterations. Shortly after the turn of the century a new library was built further down the street,[24] and the original Brown building was purchased at auction from the village. The new owners, artist Bruce Richards and his wife Kim Kanatami, after discovering the structure's history, decided to complete Goodhue's original alteration, adding the dormers and rear loggia, which had been omitted in 1923 (fig. C-12).[25] Richards hired Hoyle, Doran & Berry of Boston to execute a renovation that included living quarters, a studio-work-

space, and a gallery. This project provides a significant footnote to Goodhue's work, showing that a sketch for an alteration, drawn in haste one afternoon nearly one hundred years ago, can still be used as the basis for improvements to a structure originally built in 1842.

In 1909, Goodhue designed a house in Waterbury, Connecticut, for Miss Helen Elizabeth Chase (1860–1953), the eldest of six children born to Augustus Sabin Chase and Martha Starkweather Chase.[26] Augustus Chase was born in 1828 in Pomfret, Connecticut, and would have known the Goodhue and Grosvenor families. He began his successful business career in banking but soon embarked on manufacturing. His Waterbury Manufacturing Company, which he established with his eldest son, Henry S. Chase, was exclusively a family enterprise. Family members helped expand the enterprise into other manufacturing companies, which encompassed brass, copper, watches, clocks, buckles, and buttons.[27] Augustus Chase was also one of the original stockholders of the American Printing Company.[28]

In 1890, Augustus Chase moved into a grand Gothic Revival "cottage" mansion called Rose Hill in Hillside, an elegant residential area high above the business district of Waterbury. Rose Hill, which was designed in 1852 by Henry Austin for W. H. Scovill, became a center for family gatherings, concerts, and cultural activities. Chase's eldest daughter, Helen, built a house on part of her parents' property at 155 Grove Street. Helen recorded in her diary the move from the family home: "Aunt Jane [Jane S. Baldwin], cousin Julia [Aunt Jane's daughter] and I came into this house May 10, 1910. The architect was Bertram Grosvenor Goodhue of New York, while he was building the new buildings of Taft School in Watertown, Con. 1909–1910." The move took place on Aunt Jane's eighty-sixth birthday. A year later, Aunt Jane named the house Middlecross.[29] Helen, who had inherited musical skills from her mother, gave regular recitals on a Steinway grand piano in her home until a few months before her death. Helen never married, but used her money and influence to further philanthropic causes in the Waterbury community.[30]

In the early 1900s the residences of Hillside were a mix of Queen Anne, Greek Revival, Italian Villa, and Gothic Revival. In the Connecticut Historic Resources Inventory Miss Chase's house is described as Tudor Revival, but compared with Goodhue's designs to date and with other houses in the area having elaborate decoration, the house was quite plain, with a gabled roof set between two cross gables. The red-brick façade contrasted with the green-gray of the slate roof. Bay windows and a projecting square porch terminating in an arched opening relieved the starkness of the front façade. There was little hint of historical reference, no half-timbering or classical columns, and no dramatic massing. Only the gables and red brick provided an image of an English country house (fig. 4-7). Otherwise the design served as a model for a simpler residential style, which Goodhue developed in later projects.

Unfortunately, the 1970s decline of Waterbury as an important manufacturing center brought about a rapid deterioration in the Hillside district. Residents who had been able to afford large homes moved to the suburbs, and working-class families moved in to mansions now divided into apartments. Helen Chase's house was no exception, and it is now used for both commercial and residential purposes with exterior staircases interrupting the clean lines of the façade.[31] On the garden side an open, arched porch has been filled in, a dormer has been added, the stucco has been neglected, and a plain flat roof supported by four concrete columns has taken the place of an awning to shelter the original arched doorway (fig. 4-8). In the inventory of residences designed by Goodhue, this is the only one to suffer such a calamity.

In a December 1910 letter to William Mead of McKim, Mead & White, regarding his nomination for membership in the Century Club, Goodhue summarized his recent work:

> Fifteen or twenty churches of some magnitude, and though I can claim no particular piety, and am crazy for a skyscraper or two by way of variety, it begins to be evident that church architect I am and must remain, for practically all my work is made up of churches, or is, at least, ecclesiastical in character. There are two pleasant exceptions, however, to this rule, West Point, which, though firm work, is, I suppose I may say, rather more mine than my partners', and the school for Horace Taft, Esq. at

Watertown, Connecticut, which is designed and will be an accomplished fact in two or three years presumably.

As an afterthought he added: "I don't drink enough to produce any effect, never chew, have been known to swear, and smoke inordinately."[32]

The design of the Taft School was executed between 1908 and 1913, and consisted of residential, educational, and recreational facilities. The founder of the school was Horace Taft, brother of the U.S. President William Howard Taft. When Arthur Newman Starin, architect and artist, started his career as an apprentice in Goodhue's New York office, his duty was to sit in the hall by the elevator, greet visitors, and take their cards in to Mr. Goodhue: "One day to my astonishment President Taft stepped off the elevator with two brothers. The office was designing a school for Horace Taft. Needless to say, I didn't have to take their cards in. Mr. Goodhue was in the hall to greet them in no time at all. I just sat glued to my chair, I was so overcome by being in the presence of our President!"[33]

Connections with the Tafts carried over to Helen Chase's project. Helen's brother, Irving Hall Chase, was a trustee of the Taft school, and one of Irving's daughters, Eleanor Kellogg (Helen's niece), married Charles P. Taft, son of President William Taft and nephew of Horace Taft.

To allow for future changes and additions, the school buildings were laid out in a form that would permit easy expansion with a series of gabled wings in an extended H-shaped configuration. A tower over the main lobby identified the center. Courtyards and a wooded landscape softened the severity of the architecture. The sculptural forms of the gabled volumes reflected the influence of Edwin Lutyens, whom Goodhue had met several times on his trips to England and whose work he admired. An English precedent was appropriate for a small private school in New England. The exterior material was brick with precast concrete trimmings. For most of the interior, design was minimal and materials were simple, but oak paneling and ornamental plasterwork were used for important rooms.[34]

In spite of Goodhue's mixed feelings about formal education, he must have found it satisfying to design college campuses and private schools. When reviewing his career, I sometimes wonder what difference a formal education would have made. Would a university program have given his fertile mind opportunities missed in his own reading and apprenticeship training? Would college debates have helped to assuage his tendency to cling to his own opinions and upset clients? With each new architectural success Goodhue yearned for recognition, not just in the form of praise from colleagues but in some type of award. He longed to receive an honorary degree, which some of his contemporaries had already

FIG. 4-7. *Middlecross in 1910—the home of Miss Helen Chase.*

FIG. 4-8. *Middlecross in 2004—converted into apartments and offices.*

received. In June 1910, he wrote to a friend expressing pleasure that Lee Lawrie, the sculptor, had received an honorary doctorate:

He deserves it if anybody does. I am only surprised that so modest a man should be so honored. Perhaps, I am not modest enough. Anyhow, I have given up hopes of having anything of the kind ever happening to me. My partner [Cram], at this very moment probably, is strutting around in his just acquired hood.[35]

Then later that month he wrote to his Canadian friend Percy Nobbs about a successful cathedral (All Saints') that he had completed in 1907 in Halifax, Nova Scotia. He had been assured of an honorary degree by the president of the local college but then learned from the newspapers that

no[t] only had the "Prexy" calmly broken his promise, but that the degree had been given to a rival and what is worse, a very strong Beaux Arts individual.

Cram got a Doctor of Letters from Princeton and you have M.A. tucked in with a lot of other letters after your name. I simply can't afford to walk along looking like an undertaker in a frock coat and silk hat while Cram struts in orange and black. . . . It is a ———— shame but disappointment that comes from the non-attainment of a wholly unworthy ambition is apparently one of the most poignant of its sort.[36]

Finally, on June 28, 1911, Goodhue's ambition was satisfied when he was made an honorary doctor of science by Trinity College, Hartford, Connecticut. Writing to his brother Harry, he explained:

My clothes are, I believe, the same as Cram's, that is, I get a gold tassel on a velvet mortarboard as well as a velvet trimmed silk gown; the only difference between us is that Cram's is lined with the Princeton colours, orange with a black chevron and piped with white, the literary colour, while mine is lined with the Lord knows what,—I have not learned the Trinity colours and piped with yellow, the colour of Science; incidentally my science is pretty yellow in quality.[37]

Goodhue had high hopes, but he was also humble. He was thrilled by the honor and moved by the ceremony: in a letter to the Trinity College president, the Reverend F. S. Luther, he wrote:

It was a great comfort to me to find my little Latin (and it was not so little . . . that old Gen. Russell put me through) coming back to me and even at the time when I was trembling like a leaf, I gathered the pleasant "aproposity" of the use of the college motto.[38]

Goodhue was referring to the phrase "pro patria et ecclesia" in the presenter's speech:

FIG. 4-9. *Bertram Grosvenor Goodhue— Honorary Doctor of Science, Trinity College, Hartford, Connecticut, 1911.*

Hunc virum, praeses reverende, architectum clarissimum, qui pro patria et ecclesia artem suam semper exercebat, ad te duco Bertrandum Grosvenor Goodhue. (Reverend President, I bring to you this man, renowned architect, who always exercised his art in behalf of his country and church, Bertram Grosvenor Goodhue.)[39]

Goodhue's portrait taken in his honorary doctorate gown became his favorite (fig. 4-9). "Lydia says that not only is my hood (lined with baby blue) very becoming but that I behaved myself better and looked better than anybody else."[40]

Nearly a decade later, after receiving the commission to design the Sterling Memorial Library and Graduate School for Yale in 1920, he wrote to a school friend:

You will remember that I am a Connecticuter born and also the scorn with which we were held at Russell's by the University. It is a comfort to feel that now after nearly forty years I should have this opportunity given me. Along with the financial reward that, of course, goes with the work, they have already indicated that they are going to make me a Yale man which I take it means a letter or two after my name.[41]

This would have given Goodhue the greatest satisfaction of all, but fate intervened.

Chapter 5

ANGLOPHILIA

1913–1916

The big house in Long Island is almost done; in fact overdone. . . .
It's certainly big,—almost as big as one of your big English country houses
and even more English than they. . . .

—BERTRAM GROSVENOR GOODHUE[1]

Goodhue had a great love for England and its people. He traveled to the British Isles on numerous occasions, made lifelong friends with several British architects, and frequently employed British workers, either as engineers or architects in his office or as skilled craftsmen able to execute better than anyone else some of the specialized handiwork in his residential designs. One of his closest friends was Cecil Claude Brewer (1871–1918), a renowned architect, who in partnership with Arnold Dunbar Smith (1866–1933) took a leading role in Arts and Crafts organizations and supported cooperation among architects, artists, and craftsmen. Their early work was primarily domestic, based on vernacular traditions.[2] Brewer had hosted Goodhue in London and introduced him to the beauty and architectural features of English country houses. Goodhue and Brewer corresponded frequently, telling each other about their projects, discussing the ups and downs of their lives, and exchanging news of the war activities (World War I). Brewer was a fine watercolorist, and Goodhue regarded his friend's painting of Siena Cathedral, which hung in his New York City office, as one of his most cherished possessions.[3]

At the height of his Gothic Revival period, Goodhue designed several secular and residential projects in what he called his "Anglomania manner," referring to designs inspired by English country houses. The largest and grandest was a mansion for John Aldred on the Gold Coast of Long Island, built between 1913 and 1916.

John E. Aldred came from humble beginnings in Lawrence, Massachusetts, worked as a teenager in textile mills, moved on to banking, and made his money developing hydroelectric power, beginning with a huge power complex on the Shawinigan Falls in Canada. At the zenith of his career, he was either a director or a corporate executive of thirty-seven public utility companies. It is said that his total assets came to over $80 million. In addition to enjoying his wealth, he used it to endow technical training schools.[4]

Sheep and dairy farms and small fishing villages were the only settlements on the northern section of Long Island until 1871, when the Long Island Railroad was extended to Glen Cove, bringing with it summer tourists and a need for resorts and hotels. Summer homes soon became year-round retreats augmented by country clubs, yachting, and duck shooting to attract the wealthy. Between 1900 and 1920, East Coast plutocrats acquired approximately six hundred extensive properties on which they built elaborate mansions, most of them taking their inspirations from Europe and especially England.[5] In the words of Oyster Bay resident and author Monica Randall, "It was the 'Gold Coast' when it glittered, a time of elegance and splendor, gilded ceilings, private yachts, castles surrounded by polo fields, marble pavilions, and formal gardens,"[6] the perfect set-

FIG. 5-1. *Pen-and-ink drawing of the Aldred mansion, garden façade.*

ting for F. Scott Fitzgerald's *Great Gatsby*, and a close rival to Newport, Rhode Island.

In 1910, John Aldred persuaded his friend, lawyer William D. Guthrie, to join him in purchasing 400 acres of land in Locust Valley on the north shore. The setting was peaceful, with rolling hills that flattened out near the coast, winding two-lane roads, and woods filled with locust trees. It was quite customary for new owners to buy up farms to get enough land, but in this case "Mr. Guthrie and I destroyed the village of Lattingtown to get the view we wanted. We tore down all of its 60 houses."[7] In addition, Aldred paid the State of New York $30,000 for the land under the water in order to protect his beach from trespassers.[8]

The Aldreds were of British descent and had a great love of the English countryside and of English architecture. They felt that an English mansion filled with English antiques and art would be a suitable setting to show off their wealth. In their selection of Bertram Goodhue, a reputable New York architect, they also found a passionate Anglophile who was well qualified to execute Aldred's vision "to reproduce as nearly as possible a house of the late Tudor-Elizabethan-Jacobean Period."[9]

Aldred's 117 acres formed an approximate rectangle bordered by a beach and three roads. The house was sited in the center on a man-made rise to permit good views of the gardens, the park, and the ocean (fig. C-13).

Oliver explained that "a Tudor house was a collection of simple gabled volumes." Using such a model "allowed formality—in both rooms and facades—to occur as episodes in an otherwise rambling form." The house was constructed of random-coursed fieldstone with limestone trim and a slate roof. Stone copings emphasized the ends of the gables, and tall, sculptural chimneys added height and elegance.[10] The house was divided into two areas: formal and service. The formal section was in the three-story rectangular mass of the home, with the service area in a gabled wing projecting toward the entry drive. The rectilinear lines of the house were softened by semicircular arches: an arched entry door, an arcaded loggia at one end, and triple arches opening onto a terrace on the garden side (fig. 5-1). Grouped leaded-glass windows contributed to the Tudor ambience, with a stone-ornamented bay emphasizing the center of the house (fig. C-14).

Oak paneling, stone and wood floors, walk-in fireplaces, decorative plaster ceilings, and a massive oak staircase with carved banisters added to the grandeur of the interior. On one side of the foyer was the great hall with a high, beamed ceiling, full-height windows, and a large inglenook fireplace with a carved limestone overmantel. The walls, of plain masonry, originally displayed tapestries above a walnut-paneled wainscot (fig. 5-2). The hall led to a large paneled dining room with a vaulted plaster ceiling decorated with roses and vines execut-

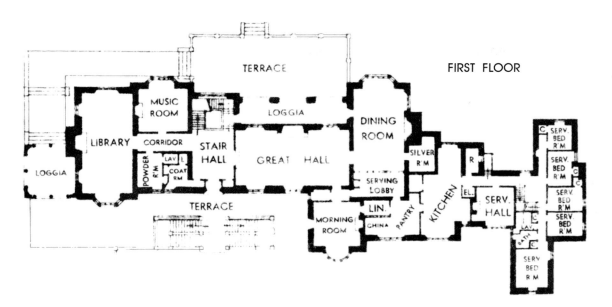

FIG. 5-3. *Aldred
mansion—floor plans.*

ed by English craftsmen (fig. C-17), and a small, rather feminine-style morning room probably used by the ladies when the men stayed at the dinner table to drink brandy and smoke cigars. A music room, cloak and powder rooms, and a large, paneled library with another decorative plaster ceiling were located on the other side of the hall.

Goodhue was not altogether happy with the outcome of this project. He wrote to Cecil Brewer to tell him that the house was almost finished:

> Furthermore, relations are distinctly strained between my client and myself so that he may never let me enter the house after he has paid my last bill. It's . . . almost as big as one of your big English country houses . . . ; but there isn't a place to rest your eye upon quietly, every surface is bedeviled with ornamental low relief plaster or solid English oak panelling, carved to the utmost, or fancy elec-

tric fixtures, or historic examples and "Museum" pieces in the way of furniture.[11]

On the second floor were the Aldreds' separate bedrooms with private baths on one side of the staircase, and guest rooms, a nursery, and servants' rooms beyond a gallery on the other side (fig. 5-3). Goodhue was relieved that at least one bedroom had plain plaster walls and ceiling, but "the last straw came when my client's wife insisted that this particular room should have too its fancy plaster cornice."[12]

The lower floor, only partly below ground, contained Aldred's home office, service areas, storage, a gun room, and a paneled billiard room. Built-in storage cabinets with intricately carved doors lined the corridors.

The Aldreds made approximately thirty visits to England, bringing back wood from Sherwood Forest to

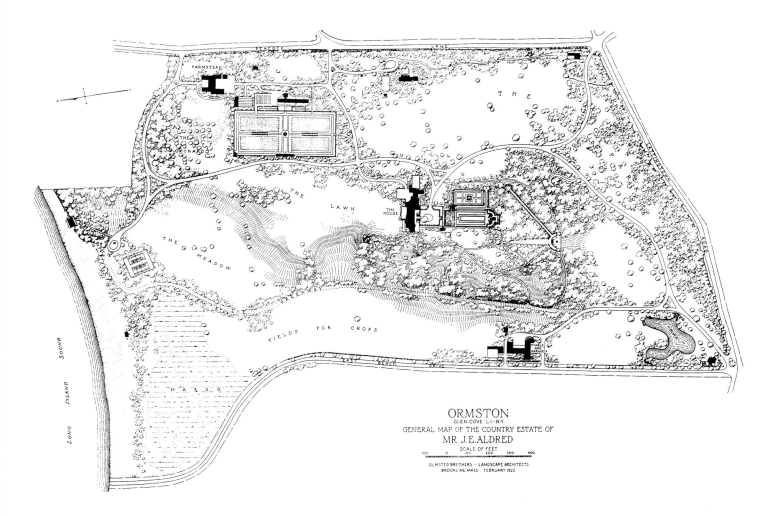

ORMSTON
GLEN COVE · L·I· -N·Y·
GENERAL MAP OF THE COUNTRY ESTATE OF
MR. J. E. ALDRED
SCALE OF FEET
OLMSTED BROTHERS · LANDSCAPE ARCHITECTS
BROOKLINE. MASS · FEBRUARY 1922

FIG. 5-4. *Aldred estate—general landscaping plan by the Olmsted Brothers of Brookline, Massachusetts.*

be used for paneling, stone fireplaces from castles, a walnut organ screen that Goodhue incorporated into the paneling at one end of the great hall, stained-glass window panels, furniture, tapestries, and artwork (fig. C-18).

The Aldreds named their home Ormston, which was Mrs. Aldred's maiden name. The cost of the seventy-four-room house was $3 million, a large sum in those days. Another $200,000 was spent on landscaping, which was done by the Olmsted Brothers of Brookline, Massachusetts (fig. 5-4). John Charles Olmsted (1852–1920) and his half brother Frederick Law Olmsted, Jr. (1870–1957), took over the highly successful landscape architecture practice of their father, Frederick Law Olmsted (1822–1903). Goodhue collaborated on several projects with the Olmsted Brothers and was especially good friends with Frederick Olmsted, Jr.

Mrs. Aldred requested an English setting with formal gardens, brick walks, topiary, statuary, fountains, a rose garden, a rock garden, and a lilac walk arranged around the house. The balance of the property was laid out as a park and planted with rare trees from Europe, including the first Cedars of Lebanon ever transported to the

island. Scattered around the park were guest and gardeners' cottages, stables and garages, greenhouses, an orchard, and a group of tennis courts near the beach. Wrought-iron gates brought from England guarded the two entrances. In contrast to the formal style of the main house, the gatehouses and various outbuildings were designed in a vernacular Tudor style.

Upkeep of the estate was expensive, with thirty-five gardeners employed to keep the grounds immaculate. In their zeal to be thoroughly British, the Aldreds engaged English house servants and chauffeurs (fifteen in all), and every day the "Lord and Lady" of the manor had tea served in a picturesque teahouse a short walk from the front door (fig. C-16).

The owners entertained lavishly. Guests arrived by road and water, and those coming from a distance were invited to stay overnight in the house or a guest cottage. The Aldreds maintained their extravagant lifestyle for twenty-six years until the outbreak of World War II, when several factors coincided to bring about John Aldred's financial ruin. He lost a $50 million investment in a hydroelectric scheme for northern Italy when Italy entered the war, the government's antitrust laws took away his business monopolies, and income and property taxes crippled his assets. He turned the ownership of his estate over to one of his companies and sold his antiques, tapestries, and art collection at auction. The art was originally valued at $500,000 and contained fifteenth- and sixteenth-century religious paintings and altarpieces, a Joshua Reynolds, a Van Cleve, and a Van Dyck. The whole collection went for a paltry $60,000 at a December 1940 auction at the Parke-Bernet Galleries in New York.[13] The next day several Gothic tapestries of the fifteenth and early sixteenth centuries realized $40,000.[14] Accompanied by his distraught wife, John Aldred left his magnificent house, now deprived of its furnishings, and moved into the Garden City Hotel in Garden City. In 1942 the estate, which had cost over $3 million to build, was put up for sale. Now valued at $525,000, it was finally sold in 1944 for $75,000 to the Order of St. Basil the Great for use as St. Josaphat's Monastery.[15]

On October 20, 1942, before giving up his office on the thirtieth floor of 40 Wall Street, Aldred was interviewed by a reporter for the *New York World-Telegram*. He claimed that losing his fortune didn't make him feel like a poor man:

> It depends on what you call poor, on what your sense of value is. It's true that I lost Ormston . . . but when I lost it I lost a lot of responsibilities. A $3,000,000 estate carries obligations. The upkeep was over $100,000 a year. . . . Ormston is out of keeping with the times. I look upon it as an incident in my life—pleasant while it lasted. . . . Money, as money, never meant anything to us. It's useful for what it buys. That's all. The thrill lies in developing new ideas. They can take away my money and my possessions, but they can't take away my memories or the satisfaction I've had in seeing the things I created succeed.[16]

Owing to its purchase by the Basilian religious order and the strict Lattingtown zoning regulations, the former Aldred estate is one of the few intact estates on Long Island. The monks have great respect for the history and architecture of their home, and changes to the house have been minimal (fig. C-15). The rear entry door still has a plaque saying J. E. ALDRED, TRADESMAN'S ENTRANCE, and the original heavily carved billiard table is still in place to provide recreation for the present inhabitants. The paneled great hall makes an ideal gathering place, with religious paintings and icons taking the place of medieval tapestries and art. The elaborate plaster ceiling of the dining room now looks down on refectory tables covered in plastic cloths, and the library serves as a gracious chapel (fig. C-19). The beauty of the formal gardens has long since faded, with swimming pools filled in, statuary depleted, topiary gone, and

lawns in need of grooming, but there is a spirit of peace and seclusion providing an appropriate setting for "learning, prayer and contemplation."[17] Even though Bertram Goodhue was not a religious man, it seems appropriate that a residence designed by one of the greatest church architects should become a monastery.

Starting in 1910 and covering the same period as the Aldred project, Cram, Goodhue & Ferguson, with Goodhue as the design architect, executed four commissions in Duluth, Minnesota: St. Paul's Church, the Kitchi Gammi Club, the Hartley Office Building, and a private home for Cavour Hartley. G. G. Hartley, an influential citizen of Duluth who had business connections in New York City, had most likely suggested the architectural firm as the most qualified to design an English-style church for Duluth's Episcopal congregation. All of the buildings fit comfortably within Goodhue's "Anglomaniac" period but show a progression from the "large and very English—almost too English—house on Long Island"[18] to the less elaborate Tudor Revival designs of the Hartley office building and the Kitchi Gammi Club, and finally to the simplest of English inspirations in Cavour Hartley's house. The club and the office building were essentially residential in character and English in style, and are important entries in Goodhue's Arts and Crafts portfolio.

The Kitchi Gammi Club was established as a private businessman's club, taking its name from the Chippewa name for Lake Superior, which was immortalized in Longfellow's poem, *The Song of Hiawatha*: "By the shores of Gitche Gumee, / By the shining Big-Sea-Water . . ."[19]

As the club was to be a social center and place for relaxation, Goodhue used a residential vocabulary. The building's irregular shape and protruding wing were reminiscent of a Tudor mansion. The exterior materials were brick with stone trim and a gabled roof of graduated slates (fig. C-20). Arthur Starin, the office boy who had been left speechless when President Taft visited Goodhue's office in New York City, had now been promoted to on-site architect to oversee all of the firm's construction in Duluth. Many years later, he recalled how the quality of design that Goodhue had demanded for the club fitted the Arts and Crafts principles that the master promoted. "Every moulding in the stone and woodwork, ornamental plaster . . . was drawn in full size scale in the architect's office."[20] The use of stock items was never considered. Construction techniques followed along the same exacting lines. In spite of the extreme conditions, much of the building was done during the winter by heating the materials (sand and bricks) before they were installed, and letting the concrete slab and fireproofing around the steel frame freeze after it was poured. It was then thawed out when the building could be closed up after the exterior walls and roof were com-

FIG. 5-5. *Pen-and-ink drawing (1913)— front entry of the Cavour Hartley residence.*

pleted. Only the best craftsmen were used. An English firm made the metal sash for the windows, requiring that a factory workman come from England to measure each opening before the sash could be fabricated. Herman Beitz of Hoboken, New Jersey, used English plasterers for the ornamental plaster ceilings, and Henry Mercer's Moravian Pottery & Tile Company of Doylestown, Pennsylvania, made the decorative tile surrounds for the fireplaces.[21]

The cost of the club's construction in 1912 was over $300,000. Oliver commented that the building "combines ceremonial spaces, private guest rooms, and service facilities in a beautifully composed plan."[22] The second-floor dining room, which featured wood paneling, an open timber roof, and a musician's gallery, might have been modeled on a dining hall in one of the colleges of Oxford or Cambridge University.[23] The Olmsted Brothers were the landscape architects, and the interior designer was Francis H. Bacon (1856–1940) of Boston. In a letter to Mrs. Frederic Paine, Goodhue wrote: "I hope . . . you will approve what Bacon and I have done in the way of furniture and decorations in the ladies' portion."[24] Goodhue selected most of the furniture, which is still in use today. He also created the designs for the exterior lamps to light the entry door and terrace steps, and andirons and fireplace tools for the interior. The club has been described as "one of the most significant buildings ever built in Duluth and is every bit as attractive today as it was upon its completion."[25]

G. G. Hartley, who was chairman of the building committee for the church and club projects, was sufficiently impressed by Goodhue's work to ask him to design an office building for himself and a house for his son, Cavour.

Guilford Graham Hartley grew up in New Brunswick, Canada, where he learned the ethics of hard work from his overly strict father. His career included logging, farming, and mineral exploration. After settling in Duluth, he organized the conversion of two street-railway companies from mule power to electrical power and oversaw the building of the Interstate Bridge to link the cities of Duluth and Superior. To further his causes he bought the *Duluth News-Tribune* and became deeply involved in Duluth affairs.[26]

Goodhue's office building for Hartley was set on a narrow thirty-foot-deep lot at 840 E. Superior Street: "Propped between Superior Street and the railroad tracks thirty feet below, it rises up off wooden pilings to a height of four stories and takes fullest advantage of its narrow dimensions by hanging out over the front lot line. A stairhall projects about two feet over the sidewalk on Superior Street."[27] The style of the building followed the English precedent of the Kitchi Gammi Club, with a gabled roof covered in graduated slates to accommodate its slope, and groups of leaded-glass windows. However, Goodhue adjusted the historic vocabulary in order to fit the building into the restrictive space of the lot. The interiors featured paneling, and most of the major rooms had walk-in fireplaces. Parts of the building are now leased to other businesses, but the Hartley Trust Office is still housed there.

Guilford Hartley and his wife, Caroline E. Woodward Hartley, had three daughters and two sons. The older son was Cavour, who attended Yale before joining the family mining business as an engineer. He was active in mining management and real estate until his retirement in 1971. He served with the Duluth National Guard on the Mexican border in 1916 as well as being a soldier in France during World War I and a sailor in World War II. Like his father, he loved the outdoors and supported many wildlife causes.[28]

Cavour was only twenty-three when Goodhue designed his house, "which is not a large one, being built for a pair of nesting doves. [It] is to be on a curious triangular shaped piece of land of about ten acres belonging to Hartley père."[29] Goodhue was writing to Frederick Olmsted, Jr., to ask that his men review the land and make suggestions for its development. The senior Hartley planned "to develop these ten acres into say, three or four house sites of which Cavour's will be the first to be occupied."[30] Homes for other members of the Hartley family were eventually built on the balance of the land.

The design of Cavour's 7,000-square-foot house took its inspiration from an English country house, but was simpler than the Tudor Revival style of the Kitchi Gammi Club and the Hartley Office Building, these in turn having fewer frills than the Aldred estate. In a 1913 letter to Guilford Hartley, Goodhue expressed concern because "the two rooms at the end of the second story do not work out very well. For myself I much prefer the single room scheme. If the house were thicker through it would, of course, be much easier to get the two rooms; but on the other hand, I really wish it were longer and thinner even than it is. I hope anyhow that the sketches will serve as a basis for argument and further suggestion."[31] Goodhue's 1913 renderings (figs. 5-5 and 5-6), which he had enclosed with the above letter, show the offset rooms.

From the design completed in 1914, it appears that this offset was eliminated, and in all aspects the house became more streamlined. The medium-gabled roof of graduated slate was pierced by simple, flat-roofed dormers and one secondary gable, which relieved the flatness of the front façade. The fenestration consisted of groups of leaded-glass casement windows with limestone mullions, slightly inset from the red-brick façade. On the front side, clapboard siding defined the gable, and a semicircular arch provided shelter for an arched entry door (fig. 5-7). On the garden side, two simple limestone columns supported a loggia, which served as a summer indoor-outdoor space ideal for bird watching, with a view of Lake Superior beyond the well-planted

FIG. 5-6. *Pen-and-ink drawing (1913)— garden side of the Cavour Hartley residence with offset, which was eliminated in the final construction.*

FIG. 5-7. *Cavour Hartley residence as built—main façade.*

grounds (figs. 5-8 and 5-9). The interior hall and staircase had full-height paneling with finely carved details on the newel post terminating the staircase railing (fig. 5-10). Floors throughout were quarter-sawn oak in random widths. In place of the elaborate all-over designed ceilings of the Aldred mansion, decorative plasterwork was reserved for the cornices framing the ceilings of the hall and main reception rooms, with small areas of plaster decoration centered over the fireplaces of the living and dining rooms (fig. 5-11). Two fireplaces, one the focal point of the living room, another in the master bedroom, had surrounds in blue, green, and white Moravian tiles with yellow lacings.

Goodhue remained respectful of the quality of English architecture, but he was beginning to exclude many of the more elaborate traditional features. The Hartley house set a precedent for other English-inspired houses that Goodhue designed, the 1920 Myler house in Pittsburgh and the 1924 Lloyd-Smith house on Long Island, which are described in chapter 9.

Cavour Hartley lived in his Goodhue-designed home at 3800 East Superior Street until his death in 1986 at the age of ninety-five. Fortunately, changes to the three-story house have been minimal, with the bathrooms and their fixtures remaining intact except for showers added to the bathtubs. The kitchen, which had been furnished with only a stove and sink, has been modernized. The present owner reported that the house was incredibly well built, with first-class construction and no cracks in the ceilings. The owner likened the full basement to a "battleship." The original coal furnace, though not used, is still in place, and the servants' call boxes still work.[32] This standard of excellence for the construction together with the attention to detail in all areas of a house, from the basement machinery to the wood carving, tile work, plaster decoration, door hardware, flooring materials, and light fixtures, was typical of all Goodhue's designs, residential and commercial.

By the end of 1913, Goodhue, having established a good rapport with the Hartleys, and following the success of their projects, still had hopes for more work in the Duluth area. In his previous letter to Frederick Olmsted, Jr., he wrote:

FIG. 5-8. *Cavour Hartley residence as built—garden façade.*

FIG. 5-9. *Loggia used in the summer months for bird watching. Lake Superior can be seen through a gap in the trees.*

FIG. 5-10. *Cavour Hartley residence—paneled interior hall looking through to the living room fireplace with tiled surround. The staircase railing terminates in a finely carved newel post.*

FIG. 5-11. *Cavour Hartley residence—living room fireplace surrounded by Moravian tiles with plaster decoration above the mantel and on the ceiling beams.*

Mr. Hartley's holdings in Duluth are gigantic, hundreds and hundreds of acres. Immediately the other side of the main avenue from which Cavour's house must be approached is a tract of I should think 80 or 100 acres, where I have great hopes of building in the near future a house for the Hartleys that will be a wonder of its kind. Hartley, in addition to everything else, is considerable of a multi-millionaire, and is one of the finest, squarest, most direct and most getalong-withable men I know. . . . Now, he is merely hinting at his house but I feel quite confident that it will come in the near future.[33]

In Goodhue's *A Book of Architectural and Decorative Drawings*, there is a pen-and-ink study for the future Hartley residence entitled "A House on the Shore of Lake Superior" (fig. 5-12). Though Goodhue sent Mr. Hartley tentative 1/16-inch scale plans for the big house, nothing came of it. World War I may have put a damper on building plans, and in 1922 the senior Hartley died. It is also possible that Hartley decided to stay clear of a potentially volatile situation brewing between the Boston and New York architectural offices.

In their correspondence, Goodhue and Hartley had been discussing a house for Mr. and Mrs. Merrill in the Duluth area.[34] Goodhue had done his best to satisfy their needs. Writing to Frederick Olmsted, Jr., he explained, "We were authorized to design a house for them; the plans were made to both Mr. and Mrs. Merrill's entire satisfaction, which means a good deal, for Mrs. Merrill's requirements as to her own bed room were rather more than . . . could have been those of the late Empress Theodora."[35] Goodhue had already completed drawings for an $8,000 garage. To his dismay he learned that the Merrills had spent a month in Boston, where Mrs. Merrill had been in earnest conversation with Cram and was telling everyone that he (Cram) was the "heart, soul and brains of the concern." On the basis of this gossip, Goodhue became convinced that Cram was trying to take clients away from him: "How I long to discover what alchemistical secret Cram has for turning the lead of someone else's client into the gold of clients for himself."[36] Goodhue's attempts to hang on to the Merrill commission were unsuccessful.

Though Goodhue's office records and correspondence make no mention of another residence in the Duluth area, historians and residents of the town believe that Goodhue's work influenced the design of a cottage and barn for Frederic William Paine's Sunrise Terrace farm near Amity Creek. Goodhue and his assistant, Arthur Starin, worked closely with Paine, who was secretary and treasurer of the Kitchi Gammi Club, as well as a member of the building committee and senior warden

of St. Paul's Church. The Paines had traveled in England and admired British architecture. Lawrence Sommer, director emeritus of the Nebraska State Historical Society, who is writing an architectural history of Duluth, suggests that Starin may have been responsible for the Paine buildings.[37] Starin established an architectural practice in Duluth after the Goodhue projects were completed and designed other houses in a similar fashion. The barn was not constructed until 1924.[38] However, no records have been found to confirm these suppositions.

In spite of his professional success and increasing numbers of projects, this was a rough period for Goodhue. In January 1913 concern about his health led to an "electrocardiogrammatic treatment."[39] His doctor wrote: "I congratulate you on getting the Baltimore [Cathedral] job. It really ought to cure your 'heart trouble.' In the words of the cathedral official, 'I therefore pronounce you wedded' to tobacco and suffering from the same. Nothing worse. And medically recommend divorce from the damned fascinating dame Nicotina."[40] From his late teenage years Goodhue had been a heavy smoker and was never able to cure himself of the habit. Moreover, he had a heart murmur. A May 1913 letter to his lawyer revealed that he was having difficulty persuading any company to give him a life insurance policy. Eventually, the New York Life Insurance Company took him on after a doctor "has passed me as some sort of a special risk."[41] But beyond the health problems, he badly needed to resolve the growing conflict with Cram.

FIG. 5-12. *Pen-and-ink drawing of a proposed house on the shore of Lake Superior for Hartley Senior.*

Chapter 6

FROM A CITY-IN-MINIATURE TO A COMPANY TOWN

1911–1918

Within these confines was built a city-in-miniature wherein everything that met the eye and ear
of the visitor [was] meant to recall to mind the glamour and mystery and poetry of the old Spanish days.

—BERTRAM GROSVENOR GOODHUE[1]

In an article for *The Craftsman* entitled "The Home of the Future," Goodhue explained that a national architectural style for America was unlikely to be developed for the following reasons: "We have no typical climate in America, no typical landscape, or for that matter, typical civilization. . . . In the West we find in our architecture the Spanish influence, which is eminently suited to the landscape and climate, in the East we are still dominated by the classical Renaissance, which in turn owes its tradition to Greece."[2]

For his East Coast architecture, Goodhue took his inspirations from Gothic, Tudor, and classical designs, but for his commissions in the western United States, he was able to draw on his knowledge of Spanish Renaissance and Spanish Colonial architecture.

Goodhue began his love affair with Spanish architecture at the age of twenty-two on his first journey through Mexico. After extending his studies during his second Mexican trip in 1899 with Sylvester Baxter and Henry Peabody, Goodhue claimed a superior knowledge of Spanish architecture and was regarded by others as the architect most capable of executing a design in the Spanish manner. In March 1911, Goodhue wrote to Waldron Gillespie: "I am writing on the very edge of leaving for Panama, or rather Colon. We have been appointed by the Secretary of War architects for the new hotel which the Government is to build there, on the strength, I suppose, of our work in Cuba. . . . President

Taft's appointment of us was due entirely to the fact that he wanted some one sympathetic with Spanish work."[3] President Taft was familiar with Goodhue's work at West Point and with his work on the Taft School in Connecticut. Moreover, Goodhue had been able to show off his mastery of Spanish Colonial architecture in the 1905 design for La Santísima Trinidad, procathedral of Havana, a commission obtained with the help of Gillespie, who owned property in Cuba.

Now Goodhue secured an opportunity to further his "Spanish" work by winning the commission for the proposed Panama-California Exposition buildings in San Diego. The project marked an important change in the direction of Goodhue's architecture, generated several residential designs, and influenced the architectural future of California.

Following the completion of the Panama Canal, the citizens of the nearest port on the California coast to the canal seized an opportunity to bring attention and tourists to their city by holding a fair to celebrate the canal's completion. Initially, the city fathers expected that their own talented architect, Irving Gill, would be the architect of the exposition's buildings.

Goodhue learned about the project from his friends the Olmsted Brothers, who had been hired to design the site for the fair. He wrote: "The fact that I am one of the commission that made a thorough examination of the Spanish Colonial architecture of Mexico, and brought

out a book upon it, ought to have some weight."[4] However, the Olmsteds' efforts on behalf of their friend were unsuccessful. Goodhue expressed his disappointment in a letter of December 28, 1910, to Frederick Olmsted, Jr.: "I can't tell you how much I am grieved by your brother's telegram. . . . I suppose it means that they have got some incapable local talent for the job. I am sorry too for the San Diegans because I consider myself quite a shark on the sort of stuff they ought to have and am pretty familiar with Californian conditions."[5]

Determined to succeed, Goodhue asked another friend, architect Elmer Grey, to support his application. Aaron Betsky in a review of Oliver's book on Goodhue complained that the author glossed over Goodhue's "megalomaniacal and disastrous suppression of less forceful architects such as Gill."[6] As it happened, it was Grey who disliked Gill and belittled him. He considered his work to be too modern and devoid of beauty, telling Goodhue that Gill "hasn't a broad enough outlook for such a position as the Exhibition one."[7] Grey also persuaded his former partner, Myron Hunt, that they should withdraw their own names from the competition. Adding to his search for sponsors, Goodhue wrote to his "old and valued friend" the Right Reverend Joseph H. Johnson, Episcopal Bishop of Los Angeles, for whom he was hoping to design a cathedral and a hospital. But Bishop Johnson favored Gill, who had designed two schools for him in San Diego.[8]

Finally, in 1911, Goodhue was invited to San Diego, where he charmed the committee members and was awarded the commission with the title of Advisory and Consulting Architect. Gill was made Associate Architect but soon found that his minimalist ideas were being pushed aside in favor of Goodhue's more ornamental and dramatic Spanish architecture. Goodhue's idea was to design exotic, fantasy buildings for a temporary installation. Gill's philosophy was to create "practical, lasting structures of simple beauty."[9] In 1912, when an opportunity arose to join the Olmsted Brothers in designing the model industrial city of Torrance, south of Los Angeles, Gill withdrew from the San Diego project.[10] Although Goodhue and Gill may not have agreed on the style of architecture appropriate for the fair, it will be made clear later in this chapter that Goodhue respected Gill's work, had counted on his help, and was influenced by the simplicity of his forms.

A 1,400-acre area in City Park—now renamed Balboa Park—was designated as the site of the exposition. The Olmsteds suggested that the buildings be placed on the edge of the park nearest to the city, but Frank Allen, who had been appointed Construction Supervisor, favored a location on a 400-acre mesa in the center of the park. Seeing an opportunity to create a dramatic grouping, Goodhue voted in favor of the central site. Following the rejection of their plan, the Olmsteds felt compelled to withdraw from the project, but they retained no ill will toward Goodhue:

FIG. 6-1. *Pen-and-ink drawing of the permanent buildings for the Panama-California Exposition, San Diego, California, 1911–1915.*

I don't see why the San Diego episode should interfere with our friendship; because, for all we regret your attitude, both I and my brother absolve you of any unfriendliness or unfairness in the matter.

Even from the standpoint of professional things the fact is not altered that you and I are very much in accord in our sympathies in certain directions.[11]

The Olmsteds remained good friends and collaborators for the rest of Goodhue's career.

The design of the fair was to be festive and colorful, with a theme that would "embody at the same time the romance of the past and the promise of the future."[12] This requirement gave Goodhue a chance to exercise his romanticism and build one of his dream cities featuring a picturesque tower and domed building. He felt that the Mission style, favored by Gill and the San Diegans, would be "too limited in its resources."[13] The padres who built the missions lacked both funds and skilled labor, and as a result the buildings were austere and sometimes crude. On the other hand, the Spanish colonists were wealthy and were able to indulge in elaborately decorated buildings constructed with the help of skilled Aztec and Mayan laborers. Therefore, it seemed clear to Goodhue that Spanish Colonial architecture would provide both the excitement that such a project deserved and a style appropriate for a region that had been settled by the Spaniards and had a climate similar to that of Spain.[14]

During his exploration of Mexico, Goodhue discovered that it was a land of domes. Sylvester Baxter explained that the Persians had developed the dome as a building form after seeing dome-shaped huts made of sun-baked bricks in Turkey. In Spain the dome was referred to as *la media-naranja*, or half-orange. The base of the dome was usually octagonal, and the construction was done in a single layer.[15] Spanish architecture was also strongly affected by the long occupation of the Moors, as Clarence Stein, a former member of Goodhue's firm, observed: "From these Oriental invaders the Spaniards derived the great surfaces of blank wall with occasional spots of luxuriant ornament that characterize nearly all their work."[16] In addition, the Moors introduced the use of tile work with many bright colors, as well as the painting and gilding of sculpture and ornament. Goodhue's visit to Persia had intensified his fascination with domes, and wherever an opportunity arose, he tried to introduce a domed building as the centerpiece of his scheme. Unfortunately, his 1909 scheme for a Persian-style domed building and reflecting pools for the William M. Rice Institute (now Rice University) in Houston, Texas, had been rejected in favor of Cram's eclectic Mediterranean design, even though Goodhue's orthogonal arrangement formed the basis of the final campus plan.

Goodhue was responsible for the layout of the San Diego exposition and for the design of the permanent buildings, "the domed-and-towered California State Building,"[17] the Fine Arts Building, and the Botanical Building. These were grouped dramatically at the end of a 1,000-foot-long, 130-foot-high multiple-arch concrete bridge spanning the Cabrillo Canyon (fig. 6-1). A main tree-lined central avenue with secondary axes formed the spine of the arrangement. Plazas bordered by arcades, reflecting pools, and plantings softened the urban ambience. Though the use of one architectural style made it the most unified fair ever built in America, Oliver explained that the plan was "a reflection of his [Goodhue's] belief that valid artistic ideas arise in a laissez-faire manner from the broad dimensions of history and culture."[18]

The façade of the California Building featured an abundance of Churrigueresque ornament incorporating figures from the state's history (fig. 6-2). The dome was covered in green, yellow, blue, and black tiles, with a quotation in Latin from the Vulgate of St. Jerome (Deuteronomy 8:8) around the base. Translated, the words provide an apt description of California: "A land of wheat, and barley, and vineyards, wherein fig-trees, and pomegranates, and oliveyards grow: a land of oil and honey."[19]

The adjacent tower had a simple shaft bursting into flamboyant ornament beneath another tiled dome (fig. C-21). Carleton Winslow, Goodhue's assistant architect and the designer of the temporary buildings after the departure of Gill, described the view from the West Gate: "This, the best first view of the Fair, gives one the impression of a city of Spanish romance, with pearl gray walls and towers and flashes of color from tile domes and roofs, set in the vivid green of the wooded canyon slopes."[20]

After the opening of the fair in 1915, Goodhue expected that only the permanent buildings and reflecting pools would survive, the temporary buildings would be torn down, and the Prado would become the main allée of beautifully laid out public gardens when the fair was over. Goodhue may have been disappointed that this did not happen, but the San Diegans' enchantment with their exposition buildings and their decision to keep them added to Goodhue's reputation. His work at San Diego inspired other California architects and provided them with an architectural model that was historically and climatically appropriate. Kevin Starr, historian and California State Librarian Emeritus, felt that Goodhue's work confirmed and consolidated the architectural traditions of the region, "moving California further along the path upon which it had already set out through its revival of Mediterranean, toward simplicity of line, drama of mass, and harmony with landscape."[21]

By the early 1900s, Cram and Goodhue were becoming renowned for their ecclesiastical work. The success of the firm's designs for West Point in 1904 expanded their fame on the East Coast beyond church architecture, and the San Diego exposition brought Goodhue to the forefront of public architecture on the West Coast. According to Douglass Shand-Tucci, historian of American art and architecture, "By the eve of World War I Cram and Goodhue were arguably the most celebrated partnership in American architecture, having certainly eclipsed McKim, Mead & White."[22] In Shand-Tucci's opinion, the partners respected each other's roles in design commissions and depended on each other's expertise.[23] However, correspondence showed there was growing rancor in their relationship. Not only did Goodhue fear that Cram was stealing his residential clients and taking more than his fair share of credit, he saw signs of his partner encroaching on his New York territory. In 1911, for example, Cram accepted the role of consulting architect for the Cathedral of St. John the Divine in New York City without Goodhue's participation.[24] Since the establishment of two offices in 1904, Goodhue had requested two revisions to their original agreement in order to clarify their responsibilities, one in February 1910 and another in July 1911. For several years the two principals had submitted separate solutions for joint commissions or had been in charge of separate projects, creating their designs as individuals, but with working drawings produced under the name of the firm in either the Boston or the New York office.

According to Cram, St. Thomas Church in New York (1905–1913) was "the last, and I think the best, of the projects on which we worked together in complete unity,"[25] resulting in an impressive Gothic Revival church on the corner of Fifth Avenue and 53rd Street. Shand-Tucci writes, "The great mass of St. Thomas's Church still dominates its urban setting, the last great work of a fabled American architectural partnership"[26] (fig. 6-3). However, a closer examination of the correspondence shows that Cram's remembrance of "complete unity" is questionable. The project caused increasing acrimony between the two offices. In April 1907, Goodhue wrote a long letter to Cram discussing the various aspects of the church design, and concluding with the following: "What seems to me the most serious point in the whole matter is the attitude you, or even you and Ferguson take of dictating to the poor remaining member of the firm what he shall think, not do but actually think. . . . If the Building committee of St. Thomas's parish . . . reject my arrangement and choose yours, not one word of protest will come from me, and I rely upon you . . . to take the same attitude."[27]

Though both offices produced large numbers of alternate plans for St. Thomas, it was Cram's solution that was finally chosen to form the basis for the development of the architectural details by Goodhue. However, the New York office executed the working drawings. The

main feature of the interior is Goodhue's masterpiece, a stunning stone reredos, 80 feet high by 40 feet wide, whose glorious carvings reach from floor to vaulted roof (fig. 6-4). Lee Lawrie, the sculptor of the reredos, wrote: "No other reredos in the world is of such size, nor of comparable design."[28]

After conflicting reports of the roles played in the design of St. Thomas reached the newspapers, Goodhue wrote to E. M. Camp (January 23, 1914), the editor of the *Church News Association*, rejecting Cram's claim that he "determined the plan, the composition, proportion, interior order and the entire organism of the church" because "what the public sees, the architectural mass, that is, its composition, proportion, its ornament and the placing thereof, and the working out of all the minute details of this church is, I am certain, my own work."[29]

The discrepancy over responsibilities was still unresolved at the time of the dedication in 1916. Before the ceremony, Cram wrote a letter to the rector, the Reverend Ernest M. Stires, stressing that in spite of the

FIG. 6-2. *Panama-California Exposition—California State Building with figures from the state's history incorporated into the Churrigueresque design of the façade.*

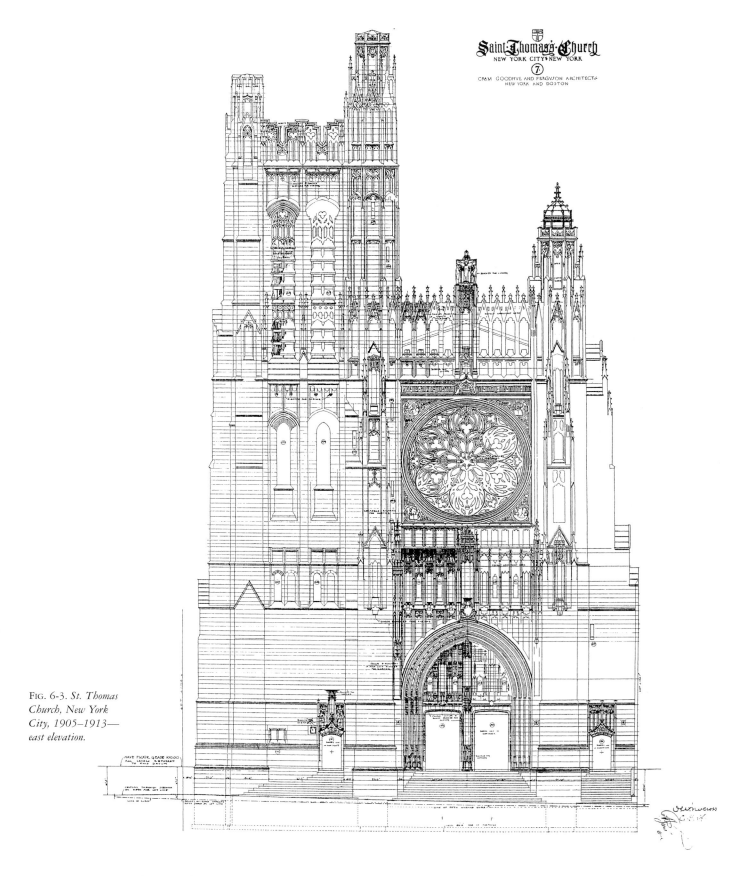

Saint Thomas's Church
NEW YORK CITY • NEW YORK
⑦
CRAM GOODHUE AND FERGUSON ARCHITECTS
NEW YORK AND BOSTON

FIG. 6-3. *St. Thomas Church, New York City, 1905–1913— east elevation.*

FIG. 6-4. *St. Thomas Church—stone reredos designed by Goodhue and sculpted by Lee Lawrie.*

Cram, Goodhue & Ferguson

having determined on a dissolution of partnership

Ralph Adams Cram and Frank William Ferguson

will continue the practice of Architecture as

Cram & Ferguson

at 15 Beacon St. Boston and 33 West 42nd St. New York
while

Bertram Grosvenor Goodhue

will continue the practice of Architecture at

2 West 47th Street, New York

January 1st 1914

January 1, 1914, Bertram G. Goodhue opened his own office in New York City, keeping the studio space that he had designed for all three partners (fig. 6-5). In a letter to Cecil Brewer, Goodhue sounded relieved but nostalgic:

> The breaking with my two partners has been a terrible wrench and though I am happier than I have been for years, there is a certain solemnity about cutting off associations that have lasted so long. Cram and I for nearly a quarter of a century have worked together; we like the same things and the same people and if I could have possibly found a way of keeping on with him and at the same time preserving my self respect, I would have done so. My case, however, was clearly strong and my own belief in the justice of my position and action has been reinforced time and time again since the event by letters and phrases of friends [and] from architects and the like.[32]

Goodhue was pleased to have won his independence, but in spite of becoming increasingly successful, he worried for the rest of his career about winning enough remunerative commissions to provide work for his employees and to support his wife and children. In many letters around this time he expressed his immense relief at reaching the decision to break away, and he received overwhelming support from his colleagues. In August 1913, Goodhue told the Reverend Maurice Britton of New York, "I am feeling happier than at any time for the past five or more years; happy, that is, to find myself standing entirely on my own feet and so to take the discredit of my work rather than to see this forced upon others."[33] In reply, Britton wrote: "As you surmised I had already heard of the dissolution of partnership through the Sunday Times. I am glad you did it, for under the circumstances your best work could never be done."[34] To his brother Ned, Goodhue wrote: "I am as happy as a lark with the rosiest prospects, and feel myself possessed of twice the ability I have had before this, and I stand at last on my own feet."[35]

dissolution of the firm and controversial reports in the newspapers, the design of St. Thomas Church was the work of Cram, Goodhue & Ferguson, and that "if any arrangement has been made whereby Mr. Goodhue is to appear officially, then neither Mr. Ferguson nor I could take our places in the congregation. . . . I am anxious to do nothing that would appear to justify an opinion on the part of the public that any one of the original firm of Cram, Goodhue & Ferguson is, or was, primarily the architect of St. Thomas's."[30]

In July 1913, Goodhue had informed Cram and Ferguson that he wished to dissolve the firm and withdraw from the partnership. An interview on August 30, 1913, for *The Churchman* clarified his position:

> The separation has occurred because I am convinced that the artistic individual mind works to best advantage when alone. With Mr. Cram I worked for ten years or more toward what appeared to be the same artistic ideal. But . . . since the establishment of the office in New York . . . a difference in style has been more and more apparent in the firm's work. In any particular example, architects and most of the clergy have been able to recognize the dominant hand. While Mr. Cram and I recognize equally the practical requirements of the Church in our plans— and the name of these is legion, for they extend even into trifling details—yet in character, I may say in poetic character, the styles we employ are worlds apart.[31]

On December 31, 1913, at 5 P.M., the firm of Cram, Goodhue & Ferguson was officially dissolved, and on

With Ferguson, Goodhue remained the "greatest and closest of personal friends."[36] But the controversy over St. Thomas Church was clear evidence that Goodhue had had a rough time with Cram, who had a hot temper and could be a difficult partner. Goodhue, too, was emotional and at times high-handed and condescending.[37] At one point he said: "Cram has evidently quite gone off the handle. The articles . . . in yesterday evening's Sun and Post are really as misleading as no doubt it was intended they should be. . . . It isn't the sort of thing that I can take up in turn in print, but heart trouble, or no heart trouble, I begin to feel that if R. A. C. ever gets near enough to me for me to try it out, there won't be enough left of him to write to the papers with."[38]

Text continues on page 113.

FIG. C-1. *Ohio University—Konneker Alumni Center (formerly the General Grosvenor mansion).*

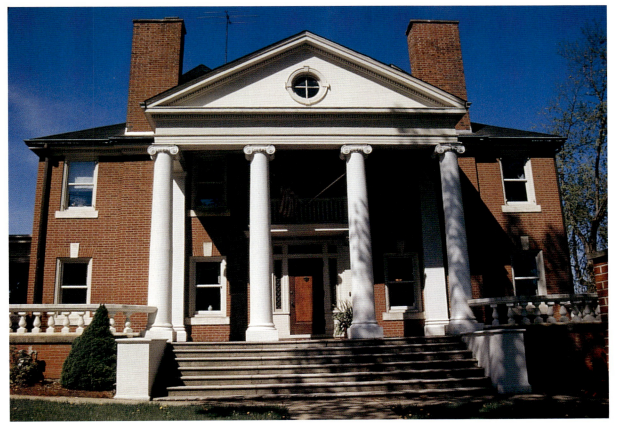

FIG. C-2. *YWCA of Westmoreland County, Pennsylvania (formerly the Huff mansion, remodeled by Cram).*

81

FIG. C-3. *El Fureidis (Gillespie's villa)— garden façade.*

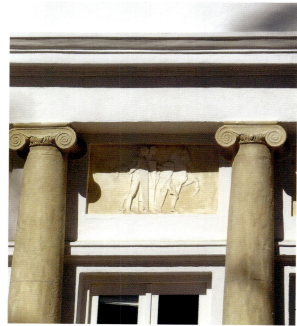

FIG. C-4. *El Fureidis—steps descend to reflecting pools and a colonnaded pavilion.*

FIG. C-5. *Bas-relief by Lee Lawrie depicting scenes from the Arthurian legends.*

FIG. C-6. *A contemporary view of the dining room showing the ceiling frieze painted in gold leaf, and the copper-covered doors.*

FIG. C-7. *Conversation room ceiling. The pattern of spirals, which decorates the domed ceiling, was copied from the Church of St. John Lateran in Rome.*

FIG. C-8. *A lotus casting set in the wall of a fireplace. Gillespie found this treasure in the ancient city of Persepolis.*

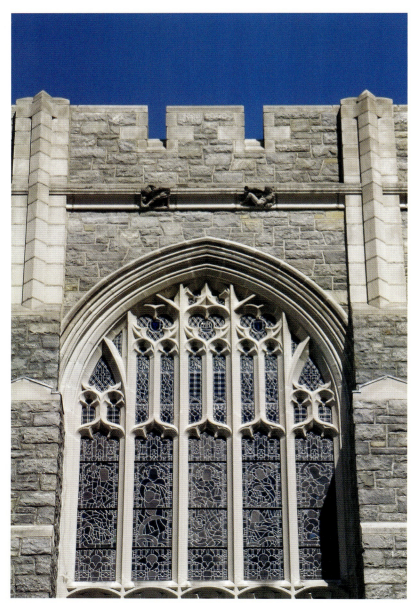

FIG. C-9. *West Point Chapel—window and gargoyle detail.*

FIG. C-10. *West Point Chapel—a carving of a military sword forms a cross over the entry door.*

84

FIG. C-11. *Harbour Court—garden view overlooking Newport Harbor. The John Nicholas Brown estate (1904–1905) became the New York Yacht Club's on-the-water facility in 1987.*

FIG. C-12. *The Village Hall in 2004. The present owners, Bruce Richards and Kim Kanatami, have renovated the building in keeping with Goodhue's original ideas.*

FIG. C-13. *The Aldred estate, Locust Valley, New York, built 1913–1916.*

FIG. C-14. *Aldred mansion—circular driveway and main entrance.*

FIG. C-15. *A wrought-iron gate inside the entry hall of the former Aldred mansion, now St. Josaphat's Monastery.*

FIG. C-16. *The tea-house where tea was served to the "Lord and Lady" of the manor every afternoon.*

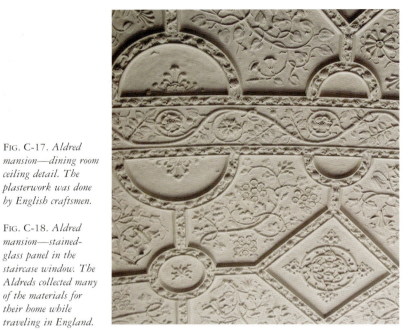

Fig. C-17. *Aldred mansion—dining room ceiling detail. The plasterwork was done by English craftsmen.*

Fig. C-18. *Aldred mansion—stained-glass panel in the staircase window. The Aldreds collected many of the materials for their home while traveling in England.*

Fig. C-19. *The chapel of St. Josaphat's was formerly the library of the Aldred mansion.*

FIG. C-20. *The Kitchi Gammi Club, Duluth, Minnesota, built in 1912.*

FIG. C-21. *Panama-California Exposition—tower with flamboyant ornament and a tiled dome.*

FIG. C-22. *St. Bartholomew's Church, New York City, 1914–1919 (designed by Goodhue with dome and community house completed in 1930 by Mayers, Murray & Phillip, Goodhue's successor firm).*

89

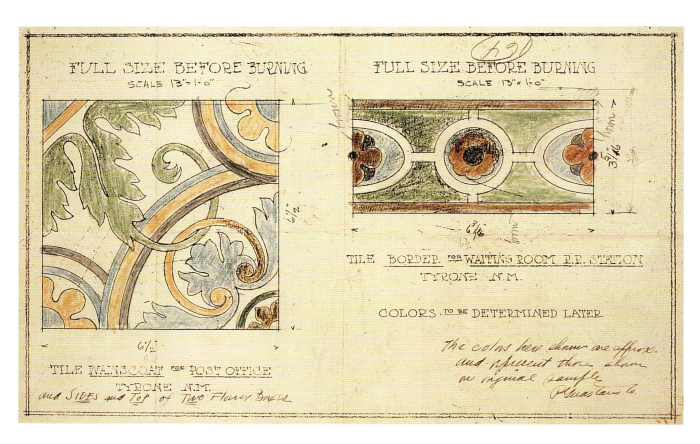

FULL SIZE BEFORE BURNING
SCALE 13"=1'-0"

TILE WAINSCOAT FOR POST OFFICE
TYRONE N.M.
and SIDES and TOP of TWO Flower Boxes

FULL SIZE BEFORE BURNING
SCALE 13"=1'-0"

TILE BORDER FOR WAITING ROOM R.R. STATION
TYRONE N.M.

COLORS TO BE DETERMINED LATER

The colors here shown are approx.
and represent those shown
on original sample
R.Guastavino Co.

FIG. C-23. *Tyrone railroad station waiting room—tile design by the Guastavino company.*

FIG. C-24. *Tyrone—a typical public building with restrained decoration and heavy molding.*

FIG. C-25. *California Institute of Technology (1915–1939)— Goodhue's proposed domed building and reflecting pool. The design was inspired by the approach to the Taj Mahal in India.*

FIG. C-26. *California Institute of Technology— a biology building with a domed porch terminating the arcades.*

FIG. C-27. *The Coppell mansion—living room ceiling detail.*

FIG. C-28. *The Coppell mansion—detail of the living room fireplace. The Latin motto* Bene face ne dubita *means "Do well, doubt not."*

FIG. C-29. *The Coppell mansion—dining room with magnificent* artesonado *ceiling. Doors on either side of the fireplace lead to walk-in safes.*

FIG. C-30. *The Coppell mansion—a bathroom with sylvan glade scene painted on the wall and doors.*

FIG. C-31. *The Coppell mansion—a bathtub with painted side and gold-plated brass plumbing resides in the closet of the present owner.*

93

FIG. C-32. *The Coppell mansion—a reflecting pool on axis with the dining room. The head of Medusa watches over a small fountain at the end of the pool.*

FIG. C-33. *Gary and Norma Cowles, the present owners of the larger part of the Coppell mansion, have reincarnated the spirit of Goodhue's original design.*

FIG. C-34. *Honolulu Academy of Arts, Honolulu, Hawaii, 1922–1927.*

FIG. C-35. *Honolulu Academy of Arts—the Joanna Lau Sullivan Asian Courtyard.*

FIG. C-36. *Dater residence—a curious head forms a waterspout on a wall of the central courtyard.*

FIG. C-37. *Dater residence—a walkway leading to a keyhole room in the garden.*

FIG. C-38. *Dater residence—view of the house from a broad reflecting pool at the bottom of terraced gardens.*

FIG. C-39. *Dater residence—the wall of a small pool still has its original Moroccan tiles, which Goodhue said were laid too evenly.*

FIG. C-40. *Ludington's Val Verde with some of the landscaping changes made by Lockwood de Forest.*

FIG. C-41. *Philip Henry house, Scarborough, New York, 1918.*

FIG. C-42. *Henry house—main entry door.*

FIG. C-43. *Henry house—a stone fountain opposite the entry door.*

FIG. C-44. Myler residence—front view with features reminiscent of postmedieval houses. The 1945 split created a 12-foot space between the two houses.

FIG. C-45. Myler residence—Mrs. Myler's second-floor sitting room, a feature of the 1923 addition.

FIG C-46. Myler residence—on either side of the living room fireplace, implied pilasters feature a carving of a dogwood flower below Ionic capitals.

FIG. C-47. *Myler residence—detail of bookcase in the library now used to display a pottery collection.*

FIG. C-48. *Myler residence—dining room cabinetry with Gothic-arched, leaded-glass doors.*

FIG. C-49. *1333 Bennington—the Mitros were awarded a Certificate of Recognition for a wing that blends perfectly with the original 1920 house and its 1923 addition.*

Fig. C-50. *Kenjockety—detail of the stonework in the front entry porch.*

Fig. C-51. *Kenjockety—bas-relief by Lee Lawrie over the entry porch. The scenes represent activities in the lives of the Lloyd-Smith family below a Latin motto, which translates as "(the house) of Wilton and Marjorie and (their) friends."*

Fig. C-52. *Kenjockety in 2003—except for rebuilding the library and servants' wings, the house has been restored to its former splendor.*

FIG. C-53.
Kenjockety—the entry hall looking toward the front door. Marjorie had the staircase moved to permit a view of Long Island Sound from the entrance.

FIG. C-54.
Kenjockety—view of Long Island Sound from the entry hall.

FIG. C-55.
*Kenjockety—a large
bay window
dramatizes the
broad staircase.*

FIG. C-56.
*Kenjockety—the living
room in 2003.*

FIG. C-57. *A golden Madonna, probably mid-to-late-14th-century Florentine, purchased by Goodhue from a collector in Glasgow.*

FIG. C-58. *Bronze sculpture of a Venus by Lee Lawrie. It was part of a fountain in a passageway linking the living room and library at La Cabaña.*

FIG. C-59. *La Cabaña—the library fireplace features pictorial tiles telling the story of Christopher Columbus discovering the Americas and Spanish sailors trading with an American Indian.*

FIG. C-60. *La Cabaña in 2004 with a recent one-story addition to the right of the photograph..*

FIG. C-61. *Watercolor-and-pastel rendering by Goodhue of his proposed main house on his 12-acre property at Montecito—garden view.*

FIG. C-62. *Watercolor rendering by Goodhue of his proposed Montecito "palace." The front of the house is shown at night. In the bottom left corner of the painting, Goodhue, who did not like to draw figures, wrote, "Figure by Donn Barber under protest."*

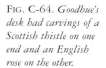

FIG. C-63. *Goodhue's New York reception room in 2003 when it served as a workroom for R. O. Blechman, an illustrator and animated-film maker.*

FIG. C-64. *Goodhue's desk had carvings of a Scottish thistle on one end and an English rose on the other.*

FIG. C-65. *Goodhue's private bathroom had floor-to-ceiling tiles designed by Goodhue and fabricated by the Guastavino company.*

FIG. C-66. *Goodhue's New York office—roof garden with an arcade. A tile, made by the Guastavino company, enlivens a plain wall.*

FIG. C-67. *Rockefeller Memorial Chapel, University of Chicago, 1918–1928.*

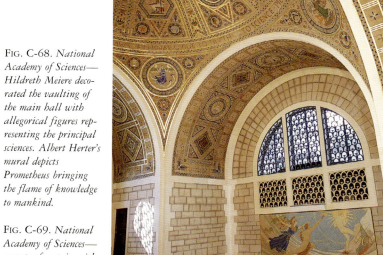
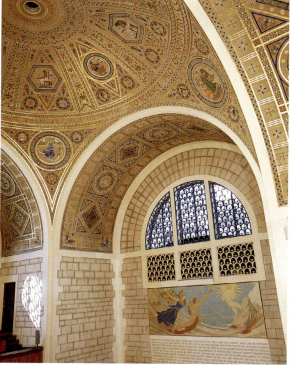

FIG. C-68. *National Academy of Sciences— Hildreth Meiere decorated the vaulting of the main hall with allegorical figures representing the principal sciences. Albert Herter's mural depicts Prometheus bringing the flame of knowledge to mankind.*

FIG. C-69. *National Academy of Sciences— a water fountain with a Greek figure decorating the tile backdrop.*

FIG. C-70. *Nebraska State Capitol—aerial view.*

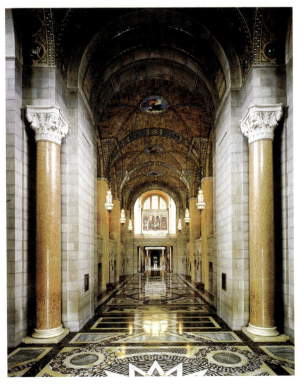

FIG. C-71. *Nebraska State Capitol—interior corridor linking the vestibule to the central rotunda. Hildreth Meiere created the floor mosaics and the Guastavino company designed and built the tiled vaults.*

FIG. C-72. *Nebraska State Capitol—section of the south portal with piers terminating in the figures of the lawgivers Solomon, Julius Caesar, and Justinian above a bas-relief panel depicting the signing of the Declaration of Independence.*

FIG. C-73. *The Los Angeles Public Library sits like a precious stone in a forest of glass skyscrapers.*

FIG. C-74. *Detail of tiled pyramidion and hand holding a golden torch.*

FIG. C-75. *Los Angeles Public Library—the Thinker portrayed as a Greek and the Writer portrayed as an Egyptian watch over the south door.*

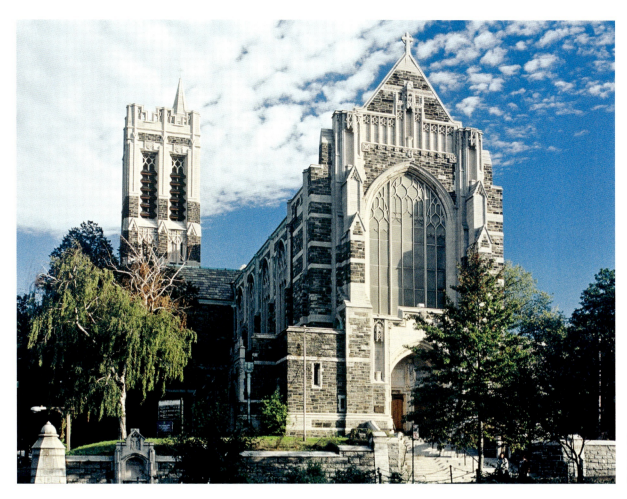

FIG. C-76. *Chapel (now Church) of the Intercession, New York City, 1910–1914.*

FIG. C-77. *Church of the Intercession— detail of tower and spire.*

FIG. C-78. *Tomb of Bertram Grosvenor Goodhue in the Church of the Intercession.*

111

FIG. C-79. A Persian Reminiscence—*a watercolor by Goodhue. In the lower right corner Goodhue wrote a stanza from* The Rubaiyat of Omar Khayyam:

They say the Lion and the Lizard keep
The Courts where Jamshyd gloried and drank deep:
And Bahram, that great Hunter—the Wild Ass
Stamps o'er his Grave, but cannot break his sleep.

Eventually, their relationship mellowed, and exactly one year later Goodhue wrote to Cram: "Now that we are working separately, and by mutual confession both growing stouter in consequence, I am as ready to tell you as anyone . . . that I often miss the stimulation of your companionship and controversion of my ideas, architectural and otherwise, that now pass as law."[39] In 1921, Goodhue even suggested to Cram that they collaborate again in an attempt to do further work at West Point.[40]

After her husband's death, it was to Ralph Cram, his friend and former partner, that Lydia Goodhue turned for help in sorting out the financial and legal difficulties that arose with the successor firm. They exchanged letters as needed, and Cram occasionally visited Lydia in New York. As well as seeking professional help, Lydia shared family news—her daughter was about to have a baby and she would become a grandmother—and took an interest in Cram's personal and professional life. The correspondence ended in July 1929 with Lydia's announcement that she was going to marry Ingalls Kimball and the words, "Thank you again for all the trouble you have taken in the last four years to help me straighten out my affairs."[41]

In retrospect, Cram and Goodhue's friendship and partnership, which produced such exciting and wide-ranging products in the early years, was fated to reach a disastrous climax. Here were two dynamic personalities invested with a wealth of creativity, which in time required space and opportunity to develop independently. Moreover, there was a divergence of ideas: Cram clung to historicism and tradition at the same time that Goodhue was searching for a new architectural language and exploring new forms of expression. Although Goodhue's newly acquired independence marked an important change in his career, his architectural development went through an experimental and uncertain period.[42]

Goodhue's success in San Diego led to several important projects in the western United States and Hawaii: a complex of buildings consisting of an opera house, an agricultural college, and the Union Railway Station for Riverside, California (1915);[43] a campus for the California Institute of Technology (called Throop College of Technology until 1920) (1915–1939); a Marine Corps base and naval air station in San Diego (1918); two colleges and a museum in Honolulu (1917–1927); and a company town at Tyrone, New Mexico (1914–1918).

Observing Irving Gill's work in San Diego may have left more of a mark on Goodhue than he could admit. In a letter to Elmer Grey, Goodhue wrote:

As for Gill, while I don't, by any means, coincide with all his views, and not at all with his theory that ornament is unnecessary, I do think that he has produced some of the most thoughtful work done in the California of today, and that for the average architect, his theories are far safer to follow than mine.[44]

A letter to George Horsefield, one of his employees then serving in the army in India, elaborated on the new direction that his architecture was taking:

You would be amused to see the sort of designs we are making here for my two government jobs, an Aviation Group and Marine Base at San Diego and the mining town for The Phelps Dodge Corporation at Tyrone, New Mexico. There's not an ounce of ornament anywhere, nothing but plaster walls . . . with tile or flat parapetted roofs, things, in fact, that would do just as well in southern India at any rate as in San Diego and that are not unlike the English cantonments I remember seeing at such places as Madras.[45]

Goodhue went on to explain that in his search for freer forms of expression, even his ecclesiastical architecture on the East Coast was taking a new path:

You speak of a Gothicless life as something you hate to contemplate. Here we are taking up such a life from preference. God knows St. Bartholomew's is anything but Gothic indeed when completed, if ever, and with its roc's egg hanging from its central dome, it will look more like Arabian Nights or the last act of Parsifal than any Christian Church.[46]

An existing Romanesque-style triple portal set the tone for the church's theme. Goodhue was delighted to break out of his Gothic mold and develop a design that incorporated Byzantine and Italian Romanesque, using San Marco of Venice as a model (fig. C-22).

During this intensely busy period, Goodhue threw himself with enthusiasm into city planning. His first contact with the Phelps-Dodge family had been in 1893 when, in partnership with Cram and Wentworth, he had participated in the design competition for Walter Phelps Dodge's residence in Simsbury, Connecticut (see chapter 2). In 1885 the Phelps-Dodge family's successful enterprises branched into copper mining with the purchase of the highly lucrative Copper Queen Mine near Bisbee, Arizona. Within fifteen years the company led the Southwest in copper production, and by 1909 they led the world.

In 1911, Walter Douglas, a graduate of Columbia University's School of Mines, succeeded his father as general manager of the Phelps Dodge mining operation and became president of the American Mining Congress. Douglas had a home in New York City and commuted to the Southwest in his privately owned railway car. With unionization hovering on the horizon, he was increasingly concerned about the relationship between management and labor. When labor disputes became more frequent and the hiring of Mexicans grew unpopular in Arizona, Douglas decided to start mining in New Mexico, where Phelps Dodge already owned most of the

FIG. 6-6. *Plan and
perspective of Tyrone,
New Mexico,
1914–1918.*

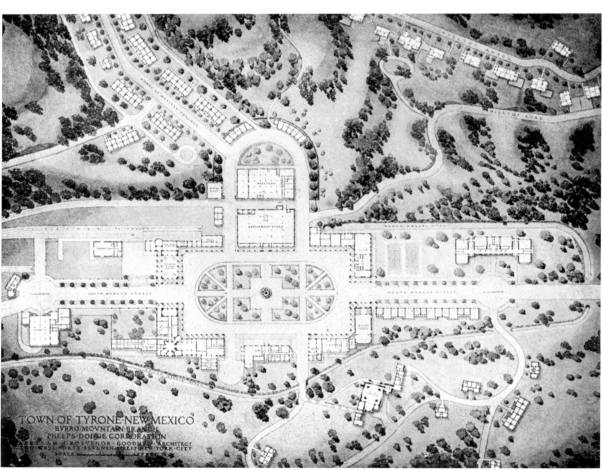

TOWN OF TYRONE NEW MEXICO
BVRRO MOVNTAIN BRANCH
PHELPS DODGE CORPORATION
BERTRAM G·ROSVENOR·GOODHVE·ARCHITECT
170 WEST FORTY SEVENTH STREET NEW YORK CITY
SCALE

copper interests. He felt that improving conditions for the workers would "create a positive public image for the mining industry."[47]

Encouraged by his wife, he devised the idea of building a company town. Already aware of Goodhue's work in New York City and his recent success in San Diego, Douglas invited him to visit New Mexico and consider creating an entire town in Tyrone. This would be Goodhue's first independent project and a perfect opportunity for him to put into practice his desire to do urban planning. While working on architectural projects in Duluth, Goodhue had written to Frederick Olmsted, Jr.: "Duluth is a fine town; it needs a city planner, in fact needs two to cover both sides of its development. . . . I can think of no one more fitted to fill these two positions than F.L.O. and B.G.G."[48]

The small community of Tyrone sat in a narrow valley of the Burro Mountains in southwest New Mexico at an altitude of 6,000 feet. The landscape was typical of the area, windswept and wild with narrow canyons between undulating hills covered in juniper, piñon, live oak, and prickly cacti. The nearest town was Silver City, twelve miles away.[49] Fortunately, a railway that extended to the head of the valley served the existing settlement, but any new development would need to be as self-sufficient as possible.

Goodhue and his wife Lydia spent several weeks with the Douglases traveling in their private railway car through New Mexico. They became good friends, exchanging books and investment tips, and in 1918 Goodhue designed a weekend retreat for the Douglases in the Hudson Valley (see chapter 8).

Tyrone provided Goodhue with another opportunity to use his "Spanish manner" that would fit "the climate, landscape and cultural background"[50] of New Mexico. In contrast to the elaborate Spanish Colonial architecture that was Goodhue's model for the Panama-California Exposition, Goodhue felt that a simpler form of Spanish-inspired architecture was appropriate for a workers' town in this remote location. He took great care to study and photograph the Indian adobe structures in and around Taos. Here was the simplicity of form and use of natural materials, adobe and wood, that had inspired Irving Gill's work and would influence Goodhue's future architectural work. Perhaps with Gill's design of the industrial city of Torrance in mind, Goodhue now created the finest mining town ever built by combining Indian adobe forms, stripped-down Spanish Colonial motifs, and Moorish tiles with his own creative ideas. Though the town was never completed and was later abandoned, it received many accolades from the architectural community and served as a model for other mining towns.

The town was divided into two parts: community facilities and housing. Using a Beaux-Arts axial arrange-

ment, Goodhue created a broad central plaza at the intersection of the two main axes (fig. 6-6). The four corners were anchored by the most important buildings: the railroad station and post office; shops and club; bank, shops, and theater; and a hotel across from the railroad station. A general department store with a warehouse behind it flanked one long side of the plaza, with the company offices, bank, and more shops on the other side. Arcades, whose flat roofs could be used for viewing parades and festivities, linked the buildings as well as providing shelter and shade. With its fountain and bandstand, the plaza (140 by 250 feet) created a feeling of openness and provided a space for gatherings, concerts, and festive events. It was an idealized Mexican town firmly controlled by the mining company. Secondary roads led to a hospital, housing for staff and workers, and the mines.

All the community facilities were well equipped: the school could accommodate 500 pupils, the library housed 5,000 volumes, the hospital (built before Goodhue was involved) had two operating rooms and private phones in every room, and the railroad station had "chandeliers, hand-carved benches, a marble drinking fountain and an arcaded outdoor waiting room. Trains were backed into the station, keeping the locomotive smoke out of the shed, and the dust-laden exhaust from the mines was ducted underground away from the town"[51] (fig. C-23). Two churches were planned: a grandiose Roman Catholic church with a dome and tower set on a rise at one end of the town, and another church for the Protestant sects.

The more important buildings had restrained decoration or heavy moldings to emphasize cornices, windows, or doorways (fig. C-24). Otherwise, Goodhue "relied upon the composition of volumes and upon color for interest."[52] He used a palette of pastel shades to relieve the plain wall surfaces: pearl white, pale blue, yellow

FIG. 6-7. *Tyrone— two-room cement houses for the Mexican workers.*

ter. Here was an opportunity for Goodhue to free himself of the requirements imposed by his wealthy clients and create simple, functional housing at a minimum cost. In his article "The Home of the Future," Goodhue explained that America was too rich: "We want money, and then we want to show it in our surroundings, and the result is we do not get the best out of our surroundings because we are not working toward the very best that mankind is capable of. . . . Our houses, many of them, are too big, our surroundings too elaborate and inappropriate. . . . In building the simple house, the plan is the beginning of wisdom. The person building . . . must consider the best way to use every foot of space."[54]

In contrast to companies that only provided plots of land for their workers to build their own shelters—invariably substandard temporary dwellings—Phelps Dodge asked Goodhue to design frugal but well-built housing. For the Mexicans, Goodhue developed four types of housing: a single-family house, a two-room duplex, a three-room duplex, and a twelve-room sixplex. Building materials consisted of hollow clay tile and stucco for the outer walls, wood stud and plaster over metal lath for the interior walls, and cement floors. The style was simple, with flat roofs and deep porches (fig. 6-7). Three-to-six-room houses for the American workers were

FIG. 6-8. *Tyrone—double house with tile roof for the American workers.*

FIG. 6-9. *Tyrone—elevation and floor plans of double house. Some houses were built on slopes.*

buff, pink buff, and pale lavender. This use of color was similar to what Goodhue had observed in Mediterranean countries, Persia, and India, "where the atmosphere provides nuances of light, where color is seen through delicate shadows, through mists, through pearly sunlight."[53]

Whereas the town, set in the narrow valley, was structured and formal, the workers' housing was informal, arranged along the arroyos, which led away from the cen-

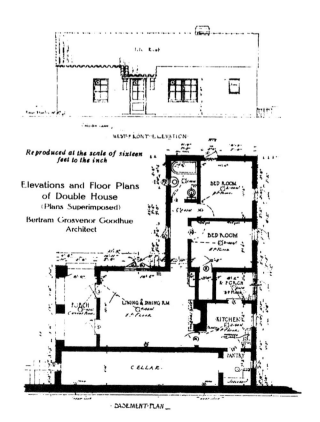

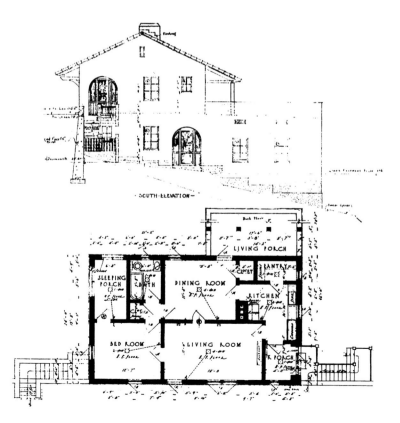

located on a nearby ridge, where the slopes allowed some houses to be constructed on two levels (figs. 6-8 and 6-9). Again the materials were of excellent quality, and the roofs were hipped and tiled. The mining superintendent's house was considerably larger and more elaborate (fig. 6-10).

Goodhue appointed Clarence Stein (1882–1975), one of his best draftsmen and later a successful independent architect and city planner, to oversee the project. Construction began in 1914. Goodhue himself visited the project at least twice a year. Always aware of the importance of creating appropriate landscaping to set off his architecture, Goodhue wrote to Walter Douglas in October 1917:

> The main reason for writing this is to ask you,—and even more important, Mrs. Douglas,—to consider the possibility of carrying a line or two of hydrants . . . around the slopes of the hills behind the various buildings surrounding the Plaza, putting in or developing low shrubbery and a number of big trees. It seems to me that with the Plaza planted and watered, etc. that the buildings will need back-ground as well as fore-ground, and following what I have indicated ought not to be a very expensive process. Of course I do not mean anything very remarkable in the way of specimen plants,—just local stuff,—cotton woods, Arizona Cypress and Scrub Oak will do as well as anything.[55]

Construction proceeded according to plan, and by 1917, 4,000 people had been provided with housing. Though World War I (1914–1918) caused severe restrictions on materials, Tyrone had become the seventh-largest town in New Mexico by 1920. Unfortunately, its rapid development was fated not to last. The war had caused a sharp rise in the price of copper, but this was followed by a slump when the fighting ceased. In April 1921, Phelps Dodge suspended operations and shut down the mines.[56] In the span of a few weeks the population had dwindled to 700, and within a year fewer than 50 people remained in the town. Another factor in this equation was a change in the labor situation in Arizona. The unrest and demonstrations, which had been so unsettling before the war, had dissipated, allowing Phelps Dodge to resume control both economically and politically. Furthermore, the Arizona mines produced a much higher yield of copper, giving the company directors little guilt in abandoning "the most expensive mining town ever built."[57]

With such an auspicious beginning, an ample budget, and the personal support of Walter Douglas, Goodhue had expected that Tyrone would become a major entry in his portfolio. He was certain that with introductions through Douglas to the heads of other mining companies, he would soon have the opportunity to create more mining towns. One possibility was a town in a desert setting with palm trees where Goodhue could utilize design motifs inspired by North African architecture. Sadly, this did not happen. Margaret Crawford, Professor of Urban Design and Planning Theory at the Harvard Graduate School of Design, summarized the situation: "What might have been a major achievement in Goodhue's career turned into a footnote. Goodhue's superb architecture and planning, rather than being, as he assumed, the goal of the project, were simply by-products of Phelps Dodge's need for control over the conditions of production."[58]

During the next forty years the unfinished town, with its romantic decay,[59] became a tourist site·visited by architects who lauded every aspect of its plan, design, and model housing. In the 1960s, Phelps Dodge reopened the mine but changed the method of extraction to open-pit, which scarred the landscape, polluted the atmosphere, and served as a death knell for the city of Tyrone. Most of Goodhue's buildings were demolished. Only the post office was moved to present-day Tyrone, which is located five miles closer to Silver City.[60] Otherwise there are only magazine articles, photographs, and a few remnants to remind us of Goodhue's first and last urban planning triumph.

FIG. 6-10. *Tyrone— elevations and floor plan of mining superintendent's house.*

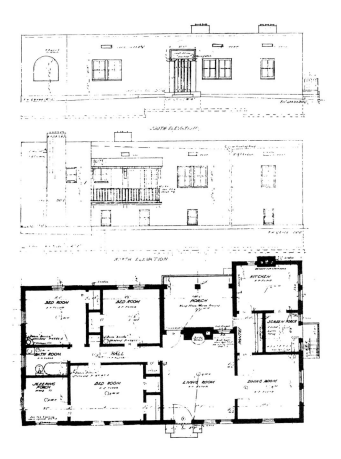

Chapter 7

GOODHUE'S SPANISH MANNER

1915–1924

In the West we find in our architecture the Spanish influence, which is eminently suited to the landscape and climate.

—BERTRAM GROSVENOR GOODHUE[1]

IN MANY ASPECTS Goodhue's master plan for Throop College in Pasadena, California, followed along the same lines as the mining town of Tyrone, New Mexico. When astronomer George Ellery Hale joined Amos Throop's Board of Trustees in 1907, he persuaded them to change the direction of their nascent school from manual arts training to science and engineering.[2] Hale's vision included a campus with a unified architecture in a style appropriate for the region. He felt that the master plan already being developed by local architects Myron Hunt (1868–1952) and Elmer Grey (1872–1963) was lacking in excitement, but after seeing the Panama-California Exposition in San Diego, Hale recognized its designer as a genius:

> I discovered Bertram Goodhue when I first looked across the great causeway that leads to the San Diego Exposition. This superb creation, so Spanish in feeling—yet so rarely equalled in Spain—with its stately approach, its walls springing from the hillside, its welcoming gateway, its soaring tower, and its resplendent dome, foretelling all the southern privacy and charm of the courts that lie beyond, reveals much of its author. . . .
>
> Seeing this, and realizing at once that its creator was a pure genius, I urged the trustees of the California Institute of Technology . . . to profit by their opportunity.[3]

Goodhue's work for Throop College began in 1915, and his architectural firm continued to develop the mas-

ter plan until 1939. In 1910, Throop College had moved from a collection of downtown buildings to a 22-acre area of open land and orange groves, which trustee Arthur Fleming had bought and given to the school. Goodhue's 1917 plan expanded the axial arrangement begun by Hunt and Grey, and was similar to the layout of Tyrone. His Spanish theme, which was based on Renaissance designs in central and southern Spain combined with the adobe forms of the American Southwest, included a central courtyard at the intersection of the two major axes, plain rectilinear buildings linked by arcades to serve the varying academic needs of the school, large expanses of plain walls set off by a restrained use of Churrigueresque ornament to emphasize doors, towers, or groups of windows, and tile work to introduce color and excitement. Courtyards, fountains, reflecting pools, and plantings would add to the Spanish atmosphere and form a parklike setting. Unhappy with the design and the lack of grandeur of Hunt and Grey's Pasadena Hall (later renamed Throop Hall), Goodhue designed a Memorial Building with a resplendent blue-tiled dome to be sited on the opposite side of the central square to Throop Hall. Similar to the domed building in Balboa Park, this would be the centerpiece of the campus, visible from every corner (fig. C-25). The approach from the west would consist of a long courtyard with a reflecting pool down its central axis and cypress trees planted alongside the bordering arcades. Goodhue's plan was

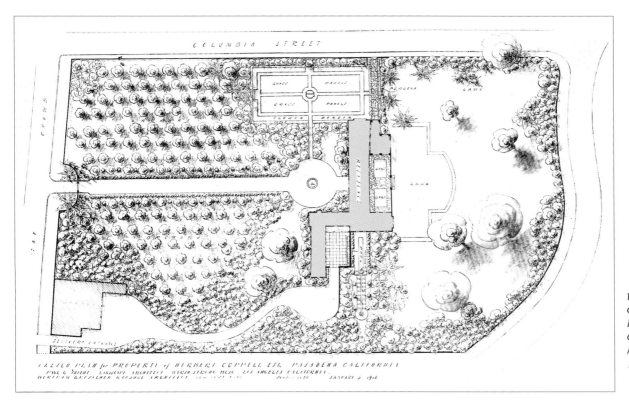

FIG. 7-1. *The Herbert Coppell estate, Pasadena, California—plan of house and property, 1915.*

based on the approach to the Taj Mahal in India, which he had visited on his overseas tour with Waldron Gillespie.[4] Like his romantic concept for Rice Institute in Texas, Goodhue's vision of a central domed building and reflecting pool was never realized, but the academic buildings, the background elements, became the nucleus of a physical environment that is considered to be one of the finest in the United States (fig. C-26).

In addition to the civic, educational, and government projects that emanated from the San Diego exposition, Goodhue's popularity extended to residential commissions. In the spring of 1915, New York financier Herbert Coppell and his wife, Georgia Estelle Myers Coppell, purchased 4.6 acres of pristine land on the border of Pasadena and South Pasadena and commissioned Bertram Goodhue to design a winter home. The property ran along the eastern edge of the Arroyo Seco and was bordered by Arroyo Drive (now Boulevard), Columbia Place, and Grand Avenue (fig. 7-1). At that time Orange Grove Boulevard and Grand Avenue were the elite residential areas of Pasadena. Mrs. Coppell's sister, Mrs. John S. Cravens, lived on the corner of Orange Grove Avenue and Madeline Drive. According to an article in the *Pasadena Star-News* of April 17, 1915, the Coppells had visited Mr. and Mrs. Cravens in the winter of 1914 and "fell so in love with the climate and attractions of the Crown City that the decision to build a winter home here resulted."[5]

Herbert Coppell was one of eight children. He grew up in the Cotswold area of Tenafly, New Jersey, where his parents had a large estate and were regular attendees at the Church of the Atonement. His father, George Coppell, was a prominent railroad man and a senior member of Maitland, Coppell & Company, a New York banking and brokerage firm founded in 1796.[6] Herbert was educated at St. John's School, in Ossining, New York, and at Harvard College. He graduated in 1896 and went straight into the family business, becoming a partner in 1899 and a member of the New York Stock Exchange in 1920.[7] He also had extensive interests in coal and iron in the Great Lakes region. He married Georgia (Georgie) Myers, who had inherited a large fortune from her father, George S. Myers, a partner in the Liggett & Myers Tobacco Company. After their marriage the Herbert Coppells lived in New York City, with other homes in Tenafly, New Jersey; Easthampton, New York; and Pasadena, California.

The Coppells bought their Pasadena land from Alonzo Phillips, paying $18,000 for it. They already knew of Goodhue's reputation in New York City and were entranced by his design for the Panama-California Exposition, feeling that a Spanish Colonial theme was appropriate for their winter retreat in California. Though they had only one child, a son of Mrs. Coppell by a previous marriage, they asked Goodhue to design a 16,000-square-foot, twenty-eight-room mansion.

FIG. 7-2. *The Coppell mansion—main entrance featuring Churrigueresque decoration.*

FIG. 7-3. *The Coppell mansion—original garden façade.*

FIG. 7-4. *The Coppell mansion—a painting by Magnasco in a polychromed-gilt frame hung above the living room fireplace.*

The overall plan was an elongated zigzag (fig. 7-1). The main section consisted of a long, narrow rectangle parallel to Grand Avenue, with the entry hall and living room lit by floor-to-ceiling windows on both sides. At one end a short wing housing the dining room extended to the garden side. A flat-roofed section linked the dining room to the servants' wing, which in turn angled back so that it was parallel to the main house. A hipped Spanish-tile roof covered the main house with the flat-roofed servants' quarters being balanced by a flat-roofed section at the living room end. The exterior walls were made of clay tile covered in stucco, pinkish buff in color, with horizontal molding linking the tops of the second-story windows. The cornice featured quatrefoil windows at significant locations. In addition to arched first-floor windows and wrought-iron balconies and grilles, flamboyant Churrigueresque decoration around the central doors, on both the entry and garden sides, gave the house its Spanish character (figs. 7-2 and 7-3).

The understated grandeur of the exterior belied the richness of the interior reception rooms. The main feature of the entry hall was a double marble staircase with wrought-iron balustrade. At one end, the hall led into a 60-by-25-foot drawing room with a teakwood floor and a beamed ceiling of warm-brown mahogany with carved

FIG. 7-5. *The Coppell mansion—a parterre of lawns separated by red-brick pathways was part of the original landscaping scheme. The pathways still exist.*

FIG. 7-6. *The Coppell mansion—a rose-covered pergola led from Columbia Place to the house.*

brackets and subtle decoration (fig. C-27). A large fire-place at the far end had a carved stone surround and mantel, above which an elaborate polychromed-gilt frame encased a landscape painting by Alessandro Magnasco (figs. C-28 and 7-4). Goodhue himself helped Mrs. Coppell find this painting, the only one to grace the walls of the house. In September 1916, Goodhue wrote to his wife: "Tomorrow night as it happens I expect to spend at the Coppells'. We went around looking at various pictures today without finding anything absolutely satisfactory for her living room mantel-piece. . . . A very great collector, a friend of the Coppells, lives in Englewood. He has, it seems, a number of pictures down in his basement that he will sell so I am going out to have a look at these with the hope that we can find something appropriate."[8]

At the other side of the entry hall was a reception area used as a gathering place for cocktails. In the center of this space, a rectangular basin of verde marble contained a fountain with a figure of a woman by English sculptor Marie Apel (1880–1970). The dining room, with its elaborately gilded and coffered *artesonado*[9] ceiling, black-and-white marble floor, and oversized walk-in fireplace lined with Guastavino tiles interspersed with a scattering of old Spanish pictorial tiles, was the grandest room of the house (fig. C-29). The proportions—50 by 25 feet with a 12-foot ceiling—were ideal for large or small groups. A 7-foot space above the ceiling functioned like the sounding board of a musical instrument, creating excellent acoustics. Goodhue told Cecil Brewer: "The dining room ceiling and the living room mantel in especial [are,] to my mind, not only gorgeous, but successfully so."[10]

On the second floor were six master bedrooms, each with its own bathroom. Here the interior décor featured French Renaissance accents to provide grace and lightness to the bedrooms. The principal bedrooms had beds set up on platforms and bathrooms with sylvan glade scenes painted on the walls and the sides of the bathtubs (figs. C-30 and C-31). All plumbing fixtures were solid brass with gold plating.

The service wing consisted of the kitchen, pantry, servants' dining room, three manservant's bedrooms and one bathroom downstairs, and five maid's bedrooms and bath on the second floor, as well as a sewing room and a linen room. A full basement contained furnaces, water heaters, laundry, wine cellar, and ample storage space. A separate garage was located away from the main house at the end of a service driveway off Grand Avenue. It could accommodate twelve cars with turntable and washing platform, as well as four men's bedrooms and one bathroom on the upper level. The butler was privileged to have his own small cottage adjacent to the garage.

Goodhue worked with Paul Thiene, the head nurseryman for the Panama-California Exposition, to devel-

FIG. 7-7. *The Coppell mansion—a Persian-style water garden is aligned with the reflecting pool on the other side of the tiled wall fountain where water trickles through Pan's pipes.*

op a landscape architecture that combined a European layout and California plantings with Persian pools. Thiene (1880–1971) had immigrated to America from his native Germany in 1903 and been employed by the Olmsted Brothers before moving to San Diego.

Unlike most large homes in the area, the Coppell property was enclosed by a 16-foot-high wall, which was camouflaged by foliage. The gates at the main entrance off Grand opened onto a long driveway bordered by cypress and orange trees. At the south end of the house red-brick walkways divided a formal parterre of manicured lawns (fig. 7-5). A long pergola, leading from a small gate on Columbia Place to the house, was covered by climbing roses that provided a sheltered viewing arbor for afternoon tea (fig. 7-6). On axis with the dining room wing were elegant cypress trees bordering a long, shallow reflecting pool. This terminated in a small fountain with the head of Medusa forming the waterspout (fig. C-32). On the other side of Medusa, water ran over Pan's pipes against a backdrop of colorful tiles into a basin, which overflowed into a narrow channel descending between shallow steps covered in Arroyo boulders to a circular basin at the end (fig. 7-7). Here the Spanish Colonial architecture merged with a Persian-style water garden, a smaller version of the scheme that Goodhue had designed for the Gillespie estate in Montecito.

FIG. 7-8. *A scene from the Lasky company's* Wealth *was filmed under the pergola of the Coppell mansion in 1920.*

The Coppells, probably introduced by Mr. and Mrs. Cravens, soon found a place in Pasadena society and hosted lavish parties during their winter visits. They traveled west in their own private railway car, bringing most of their servants with them. They called their California home Mi Sueño (My Dream). The estimated construction cost was $70,000, with an added $10,000 invested in the garage. However, a 1950 article stated that the total cost exceeded $500,000.[11] On completion the Coppell place was the largest house in the area. Goodhue referred to it as "quite a palace," and a 1920 article in *Arts and Decoration* reported that "Pasadena is, after all, a suburb of the already large and constantly growing city of Los Angeles. 'Mi Sueno'. . . must not be regarded as a country house in the exact sense, rather it is a palace, of limited size, to be sure, but still a palace, similar to that which a Florentine of the Renaissance might have built in the immediate outskirts of the city."[12] This palace and its grounds also attracted the movie industry. Scenes for the film *Wealth*, made by the Lasky company and starring Ethel Clayton with a small supporting cast of seven, were filmed at the Coppell estate in 1920 (fig. 7-8).[13]

Herbert Coppell caught pneumonia and died on October 30, 1931. Two years earlier, the Coppells had given their Pasadena home to Mrs. Coppell's son, George Myers Church. After graduating from Princeton, Church joined his stepfather's firm, Maitland, Coppell & Company. The firm was dissolved in 1932, a year after Herbert Coppell's death. Church then moved into the oil business and became president of the Crane Oil Corporation. He and his second wife, Augusta Hahl Badgley Church, lived in Fort Worth, Texas, but spent the winters in Pasadena. Church was a renowned tennis player, winning intercollegiate championships and holding a high rank nationally. He served in both world wars, but poor health forced him to leave the Air Force in 1942. He died on January 16, 1946, at the age of fifty-six.[14] For several years his widow retained ownership of

the Pasadena property, renting it out and struggling with the cost of upkeep and increasing property taxes. By 1949 the house was vacant.

In 1950 the real estate firms of Bleier & Scharf and William Wilson decided to break up the property into smaller lots in order to save the house from being torn down or converted into apartments, as was happening elsewhere in Pasadena. The east side facing Grand Avenue was divided into six lots and called Churchill Place, with much of the original landscaping left undisturbed. The garage, which had its own entrance from Grand, was reconstructed as a single-family home. The west side was divided into two lots with new entrances from Columbia Place and Arroyo Boulevard. But how could the residence itself be split? Unfortunately, the most feasible solution was to cut the house into two parts by removing the magnificent entry doors (the heart of the design), the two-story entry hall, and the marble staircase, thus ruining the integrity of the architecture.

Fortunately, further attempts to subdivide the larger half of the house were unsuccessful. But the property remained unappreciated until Gary and Norma Cowles fell in love with Goodhue's Spanish masterpiece and teamed up with Erik Evens of KAA Design Group, Los Angeles, to do an extensive remodel and restoration. Many of the 1950s changes were reworked to make better use of the space. The former dining room, now the living room, is still the main feature of the house, with its ceiling brought back to its former splendor.

Melinda Taylor, known for her Walt Disney Concert Hall garden, created an appropriate landscaping scheme. The reflecting pool was relined with Italian mosaic tiles, and the fountains and Persian watercourse were restored (fig. C-33).

Owners of the smaller half of the house have built an addition without detracting from the original structure. Thus both parts of Coppell's winter mansion have become ideal living spaces for two families. At the time of its completion, Goodhue's Spanish mansion received much attention, which he hoped would lead to future domestic commissions.

In stark contrast to the Coppell residence but developed at the same time, Goodhue designed a castle on a rugged hilltop near Brewster, New York, for his good friend Dr. Frederick Peterson (fig. 7-9). In a 1916 letter to Peterson, Goodhue wrote: "Thank you tremendously for the beautiful old Chinese painting which I shall prize very much indeed; though I am a little embarrassed by the thought that it may be regarded as a quid pro quo for the castle sketches, for which certainly nothing of the sort was looked for. As I am sure I explained, the castle drawings were merely the result of a sudden impulse brought about by the generally ideal character of the whole possible operation."[15]

Goodhue had found the hillside site a perfect setting for one of his medieval dream castles and had created a drawing that was featured later in several exhibits. In a book on architectural drawings, Deborah Nevins, nationally recognized landscape designer and landscape historian, wrote that "the rendering demonstrates the power of a drawing to create mood. . . . Associations between the sublime nature of Gothic architecture and an ominous air of mystery are evoked here through Goodhue's masterful graphic technique."[16] Oliver described the proposed house as "a craggy sculptured mass in total command of the landscape, backdropped by the big blaze of a brilliant dawn sky. The drawing is full of precisely the sublime, mysterious and powerful atmosphere one associates with the architect's buildings"[17] (figs. 7-10 and 7-11). Once again the carefully drawn plans demonstrate Goodhue's mastery of site planning and his ability to mass the volumes to take full advantage of the topography.

In June 1916, Goodhue wrote to Eugene Klapp in Cuba about a possible house for a Mr. Untermeyer, saying, however, that he should probably decline any further commissions, as "a lot of new and important jobs have come in lately, especially in the way of houses, so I find myself with a couple of million dollars' worth of this sort of thing and several very multimillionairish clients."[18] These included another "magnificent palace" in California for a Mrs. Clark of San Mateo,[19] and the development of a fifteen-acre site overlooking the Arroyo Seco south of Columbia Street and the Coppell property, for John North Willys, a leader in the automobile industry and head of the Willys-Overland Company. An article in the *Pasadena Star-News* of July 29, 1916, announced that Bertram Goodhue, "a recognized

authority on Spanish colonial architecture as found in the older cities of Mexico and as amplified in his work for the San Diego exposition, . . . is to plan a mansion which will be one of the greatest additions to Pasadena architecture built in many years. . . . The new residence is not to be noted so much for the number of its rooms as for their size and the massive type of construction which will be used."[20] The article stated that Willys was expecting to spend $200,000 on the house alone, and that Clarence P. Day, a civil engineer and landscape architect, had already traveled to Goodhue's office in New York to submit a map of the site that included the "spread and height of every tree."[21] In April of the same year, Goodhue had written to Mrs. William Graham of Montecito, who was well acquainted with John Willys, about the proposed project: "As you prophesied, I distinctly liked my—I suppose I may safely say—new client, and his property, though strange enough to be very difficult, is quite wonderfully beautiful. He evidently intends to have the house and gardens commensurate with the property and with his purse, and I, for my part, am going to see to it that he gets what he wants if I have the ability to do so."[22]

However, none of these residential projects materialized. The now famous architect was stretching himself almost beyond his control. From 1914 on, he was designing and managing commissions all across America and beyond its shores to Hawaii.

In April 1917, Goodhue wrote to C. Peake Anderson, one of his former British employees, now fighting in the European war:

You will be interested to learn that the last batch of commissions that have reached the office have come from a

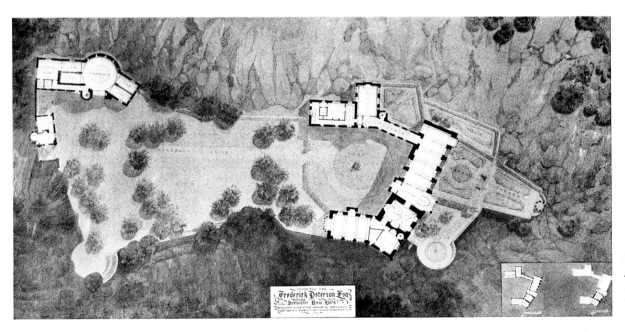

FIG. 7-9. *Proposed site plan and residence for Dr. Frederick Peterson, Brewster, New York, 1916.*

FIG. 7-10. *Pen-and-pencil sketch of the Peterson residence (mislabeled for a show a "House in Westchester, New York"). The design recalls Goodhue's medieval dream castles.*

FIG. 7-11. *Alternate view of the Peterson residence (also mislabeled)*

126 *Goodhue's Spanish Manner*

long way off indeed, i.e. Honolulu. Of course, they are vague as yet, but there is an awful lot of them,—three colleges, the covering of a city block with a store and office building, fixing up the City of Honolulu with a sea wall like the Chiaja at Naples, a church, couple of private houses, etc. It is too good to be true that I shall get them all, but I have named a price for going out and have my points looked over, and they have accepted.[23]

Goodhue sailed to Hawaii with his family in July 1917. To Cecil Brewer he wrote:

Although I was here for a few hours seventeen years ago I had forgotten how wonderful it all is as to its climate and natural beauty. The nights are always cool and there is always a breeze that tempers even the hottest part of the day.[24]

The possibility of several projects in Hawaii gave Goodhue an opportunity to explore further his idea of an architecture suited to its surroundings. As he explained in his 1916 article "The Home of the Future," a unified architectural style was not feasible for the mainland of America because the climate and light conditions were too varied.[25] However, here was a group of tropical islands, which in Goodhue's opinion lacked good design or even competent construction, a situation calling for the introduction of an architectural style that would fit the climate and the landscape. He also saw a chance to develop a simpler version of the Spanish theme that he had used for the company town in Tyrone and the cam-

pus for the California Institute of Technology. He told Brewer that he was not sure how his ideas for a specifically Hawaiian architecture would go over:

I have found only one person here who "gets me" and all the others look at me with a pitying expression and go off and build wood bungalows with gingerbread all over them, or else houses as near "like mother used to make" in New England as Japanese laborers, imported Oregon Pine and a very poor grade of cement will permit.[26]

Brewer was not in good health, and Goodhue hoped he could persuade him to come to the better climate of Hawaii and even be his Hawaiian representative. He told his friend about his block plans for two colleges: the Kamehameha Institute, founded by the Bishop family, and Oahu College, the oldest school in the Islands. Goodhue hoped to persuade the trustees of the Kamehameha Institute to sell their present land with its "dreadful buildings, set down in a perfectly haphazard fashion,"[27] and move to the outskirts of the city with money in hand to build a new campus from scratch. Staying within a reasonable budget for Oahu College was going to be a challenge. He feared that his plans would be too expensive, except for the Auditorium (the main building), which was to be "the gift of another rich native . . . by the name of Dillingham. It won't cost over $100,000, if that, but it will be the first building I shall have to do . . . and an opportunity for me to win my local architectural 'spurs.'"[28] He was also expecting to design "a private house of some pretensions,"[29] a project he was confident he could do well and use as an example of his new style of architecture.

Although excited by the prospect of so many commissions, Goodhue expressed concern to Ruth Baldwin, now Mrs. Leo Pierson: "I never can live up to the reputation that seems to have preceded me. I am cocky enough to think I am a good architect, distinctly better than most, but I am no architectural Mahatma, and can't perform miracles."[30] He goes on to describe the various architectural styles that pervaded Hawaii, beginning with the missionary buildings: "churches houses and everything else [made] out of coral and curious native wood. Following them came the bracket style, then the jig-saw, then the post centennial, Queen Anne, Mission and all the others. . . . And now, here am I supposed to be able with a wave of my magic wand to fix everything up, overnight so to speak. Schools, houses, parks, civic centers, water gates and the Lord knows what not."[31]

Goodhue's family was enjoying the beach at Waikiki, but he was anxious to get back to the mainland and his office in New York. In November 1917, he sent his block plans for the Kamehameha Institute, to be followed by plans for Oahu College. To back up the ideas that he had proposed while in Honolulu, Goodhue prepared some drawings, based on picture postcards, showing the town as he thought it ought to look: blocks of simple, undecorated Spanish-style buildings with open arcades at street level to provide shade. Heavy moldings defined the ground level and cornices, relieving the plainness of the stucco facades (fig. 7-12). He told T. A. Jaggar, Jr., of the Hawaiian Volcano Observatory, that he had sent "prints of half dozen drawings of possible and impossible Honolulu and Island buildings that will, I'm sure, create a good deal of talk."[32] The drawings were similar to his scheme for the Dater house in Montecito, California, which he was working on at the same time.

In May 1918, another letter to Ruth Baldwin explained that a second proposed trip to Hawaii had been canceled:

> When I told them last summer that I believed the proper thing in the way of buildings for them would be absolute simplicity in the way of white-washed masonry walls and tile roofs my word seemed to sink into their hearts but when I sent them out sketches illustrative of my theories they promptly turned and rent me. The average American certainly likes "spinach" and plenty of it. This doesn't mean that my commissions there have altogether faded away into thin air but merely that instead of being greeted with hugs so to speak, everything I send them is now regarded with suspicion and weighed gravely before being approved. One of the two colleges is all right and the other one I am sure will be. Meanwhile I am to cool my heels with what patience I can until the following summer.[33]

At the same time, Goodhue also expressed his disappointment to Cecil Brewer:

> I am broken hearted . . . they could not stand the simplicity I had advocated verbally. I am sorry because I am sure I am right and that simple white walled buildings with tile roofs and no, or practically no, ornamental features whatsoever would be the rightest thing for them.[34]

Goodhue went on to explain that Louis Christian Mullgardt (1866–1942), an Arts and Crafts architect from San Francisco, had already made some designs for four commercial buildings in Honolulu "that clearly pleased the populace much better. Mullgardt is a fine fellow and a good architect; anyhow his buildings, one of which is going to be built, are loaded with soi-disant 'spinach.'"[35] The Hawaiians were finding it hard to believe that Goodhue, who came so highly recommended and whose decorative Spanish work at San Diego they so admired, would now advocate a Spanish style devoid of ornament. Goodhue went into more detail in a letter to Waldron Gillespie:

> Clearly I made my design too plain for them. The Corinthian taste developed by the grandchildren of Connecticut missionaries is something awful and the transition from a "cozy" grass house to a post-centennial bungalow is, after all, a perfectly natural one.[36]

Nonetheless, Goodhue's ideas, which were too radical and thus premature for the Hawaiians in 1917, did eventually influence the architecture of the islands. Six years later, in 1923, Goodhue was invited back to design a building for the Honolulu Academy of Arts, a museum that was the dream of Anna Rice Cooke, the daughter of New England missionaries, who grew up learning to appreciate art. Following her marriage to Charles Montague Cooke, Anna started an art collection that soon outgrew her home. With the help of her daughter, her daughter-in-law, and an art teacher, Cooke catalogued and researched her pieces and envisioned a museum where they could be displayed for the education and enjoyment of children. In 1922 she obtained a charter from the Territory of Hawaii, and, along with a generous endowment, she and her family donated their home and land as the site of the museum. Perhaps recalling Goodhue's previous visit and presentation, Cooke hired him to help fulfill her vision of a center that would reflect the unique attributes of Hawaii's multicultural makeup. The architect was told: "The completed building should represent in stone the story of the islands. It should be neither prosaic nor exotic but simple, preferably Hawaiian in tone."[37]

Goodhue's solution was a series of galleries and classrooms grouped around open courts. Mrs. Cooke was pleased with the plan but felt that the exterior and an

Oriental tower were too ornate. Three family members involved with the project left for the mainland to discuss the changes with Goodhue's firm.[38] Hardie Phillip, principal architect of the Goodhue Associates, simplified the design in accordance with Mrs. Cooke's wishes, and the museum was completed in December 1926 (figs. C-34 and C-35). In an issue of the *Museum News* published following the dedication on April 8, 1927, the building is described as "a low whitewashed stone structure, with a gently sloping roof of grey tile. It has a main and several smaller courts, so that the visitor in passing from one gallery to another obtains glimpses of these open spaces, tastefully provided with shrubs and trees. The Spanish and Chinese courts have been arranged and planted with appropriate plants and one contains a fountain, the other a pool. A part of the garden outside the building has been arranged in English and Colonial fashion."[39]

The local chapter of the American Institute of Architects named the museum Hawaii's best building. It is now listed as a state and national historic site. The project gave Goodhue the opportunity to use his earlier ideas to establish an architecture that could become identified with the islands, using a classical plan and massing but with simple, clean lines, free of unnecessary decoration. Tragically, it was too late for him to enjoy the rewards. If only he could have known that during the next several decades many Hawaiian buildings would be created in the architectural style that he had felt was appropriate for this island group.

The "house of some pretensions" that he had referred to in his earlier letter to Brewer was a residence for Harold Castle in Kailua, Oahu. Castle was a friend of Goodhue's naval brother, Ned, and was involved with the Oahu College project. His father had obtained a large tract of land, the Kaneohe Ranch property, which was used for cattle grazing. The Castles' house was to be located on 22 acres, 500 feet above sea level, at the foot of the Ko'olau Range, with breathtaking views all around. Goodhue had begun designing the house in 1917, hoping that the built product would serve as an example of the new ideas that he was advocating for the nonresidential buildings that he was expecting to build in Honolulu. The design consisted of a Spanish-style two-story house in keeping with his philosophy of simple forms with minimal decoration that would be appropriate for the environmental conditions of Kailua (fig. 7-13). One-story, flat-roofed cubes with white stucco walls and arched openings framed the main block of the house, which had two stories under a tiled hipped roof. The upstairs rooms had floor-to-ceiling shuttered doors opening onto a wooden balcony running the length of the house. Indigenous materials were used for the stone walls and woodwork, and a large reflecting pool united the house with its landscape.

FIG. 7-13. *Residence for Harold Castle, Kailua, Oahu, 1923–1927.*

Although the final execution of the design was delayed, the Goodhue Associates completed the project in 1927. Harry Bent of Los Angeles, who was sent by the New York firm to supervise the construction, was responsible for finalizing the design of the wood trim. The balcony railing was made of redwood, which had been soaked in salt water, then carved and chipped to make it look old.

After World War II, Castle and his wife Alice decided that the house was too large for a couple whose children had left home; so, in September 1946, they sold the house and land to the Roman Catholic bishop of Honolulu for use as St. Stephen's Seminary. Over the years, a dormitory, classrooms, a chapel, and an auditorium have been added to the property.[40] Once again, a Goodhue domestic design has become an ecclesiastical center in an ideal setting for prayer, study, and contemplation.

Goodhue's influence on Hawaiian architecture continued as his firm executed several more projects, which included commercial buildings in a simplified Spanish Colonial style and a 26,000-square-foot residence for Governor George Robert Carter on the 10-acre Lihiwai (meaning "water's edge") estate in Honolulu.[41] The grand house was designed by Hardie Phillip in a Spanish Colonial style with Chinese overtones. Hawaii's National Register Inventory described it as "one of the most outstanding examples of Hawaiian architecture of the 1920s" and "probably the largest and finest private residence ever constructed in Hawaii."[42] The grounds were superbly landscaped with native plants, natural streams, Chinese bridges, and Persian-style reflecting pools. These Hawaiian buildings stand as a legacy from Bertram Goodhue, who could envision an architectural style in keeping with the environment and culture of the islands and had the courage to present his ideas, knowing at the time that the people might be too conservative to accept them.

Chapter 8

A SIMPLER ARCHITECTURE

1916–1918

Beautiful architecture is just as much in my mind a matter of inspiration as poetry, painting,
or sculpture; in fact, I believe all art to be a varied expression of the one great impulse toward beauty.

—BERTRAM GROSVENOR GOODHUE[1]

On his way to and from Hawaii, Goodhue would stop in California to oversee his West Coast projects, visit his friends in Montecito, and check on the construction of an expensive new clubhouse for the Santa Barbara Country Club, a commission that Waldron Gillespie had probably obtained for his architect friend. The club, which is now the Montecito Country Club, was sited on a hill just west of Hot Springs Road and today is still clearly visible as you drive along Cabrillo Boulevard by the beach. Dominated by an elegant, 90-foot-tall tower, the façade of simple arches below a line of clerestory vertical windows terminating in a tiled roof looked like an abbey following the slope of the hill.[2] Goodhue told Gillespie that the design, even when on display in the old clubhouse, evoked from onlookers "little Santa Barbarian touches like this: 'It looks like a church tumbling down hill.'"[3] Though the architect had embarked on his simpler architectural phase, he felt that "Spanish" was most appropriate for a town settled by the Spanish missionaries, and one where the climate was conducive to a Mediterranean building style. But he limited the decoration on the clubhouse to some curvilinear moldings defining the base and the opening of the tower. The result was simple elegance in a monastic vein.

At the same time, Goodhue had the opportunity to explore further the ideas that he was advocating for Hawaii in a residential design for Henry Dater, a cousin of Waldron Gillespie. Goodhue had originally made a preliminary pen-and-ink drawing for a proposed house for Dater (fig. 8-1) in 1902 when he first started work on Gillespie's estate. Henry Dater, Jr., had followed in his father's footsteps as a coffee trader, and also benefited from a substantial inheritance and ownership of the family estate above the Harlem River in New York. In 1896 he purchased a 10-acre property along Sycamore Canyon Road in Montecito bordering on his cousin Waldron's estate. Henry and his wife, Mary Hays Dater, became seasonal visitors to California and were soon immersed in Santa Barbara social life. Occasionally, they stayed at El Fureidis (the "Gillespie Place") where Mrs. Dater, known as Molly by her friends, would host some of Waldron's lavish parties. They also liked to vacation in Europe, especially France, but with the onset of hostilities in Europe their travels were curtailed, creating an opportunity to build on their Montecito land.[4]

Goodhue's 1902 design for the Daters had a hipped roof and simple arched openings leading to a loggia on the first level. At one end a single-story section abutted a tall tower, which gave prominence to the structure. All the roofs were tiled, and the general feeling was of a Spanish country house. In a 1915 letter responding to Dater's request for "a blue print of the pool and steps," Goodhue reminded him:

> You have for the past eight or ten years wholly and completely declined to pay my extremely reasonable bill for a

FIG. 8-1. *Goodhue's
1902 pen-and-ink
sketch for the proposed
Henry Dater residence,
Montecito, California.*

drawing made for you, and even regarded the idea of payment as a joke. I trust you will appreciate my "goodness and kindness" at its very full value.

I am glad you wrote me for this print because it enables me to say, ungoverned by the fact that you and I are distinctly great friends, that the bill originally sent did not begin to cover the cost to me of doing the work.[5]

Thirteen years after Goodhue's initial sketch, his architecture, both secular and domestic, had moved through a series of progressions to a point where he was ready to break with traditional forms and embark on a plainer style. Though his design for the Herbert Coppell residence in Pasadena included some of the decorative elements that were a part of his Spanish Colonial work at the Panama-California Exposition in San Diego, Goodhue's concurrent projects—the mining town at Tyrone, New Mexico, the campus of the California Institute of Technology, and schematics for buildings in Hawaii—incorporated simple adobe cubes with minimal decoration. In a 1915 letter to Lieutenant Colonel John D. Moore, a former employee, he thanked him "for the magazine with the beautiful North African houses. . . . The North African work may come in very handy here in the not too distant future."[6] Goodhue's design for the Dater house represents a major step toward the simpler architecture that he felt would be especially appropriate for Hawaii. In a 1916 letter to Moore he wrote: "The copy of 'Country Life' you sent me is proving

most useful. We are now beginning sketches for a house based in spirit at least on the North African style to be built in Montecito, California. Of course, not so extensive as the Moroccan example nor, I am afraid, anything like so well built; but still with a liberal use of irregular plastered walls and Tunisian and San Diego tile."[7]

Like Gillespie's Roman-style villa, Goodhue organized Dater's house around a central court, 55 by 27 feet in size (fig. 8-2). A driveway, passing under the servants' wing—an appendage to the main block—brought a visitor to the west entrance. The entrance door opened into a long hallway with windows looking onto the inner courtyard, a reception room and lavatory at one end, and a men's coatroom at the other. The staircase hall was on the south side of the courtyard, and a service hall led past the kitchen and pantry to a large dining room on the north side. The east-facing wing comprised a spacious living room in the center with library at one end and breakfast room at the other. The organization was superb and the detailing simple. The rooms, with their well-balanced proportions, created a feeling of openness and graciousness without pretension.

The exterior featured simple flat-roofed cubes with softened edges and textured buff-colored stucco (fig. 8-3). Only the three two-story sections had tiled hipped roofs. Fenestration was simple, with arched openings on the garden side. A flat-roofed loggia with simple arches featuring wood grilles in the tympanums sheltered a sec-

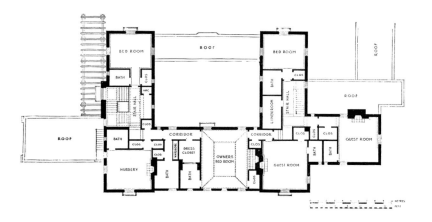

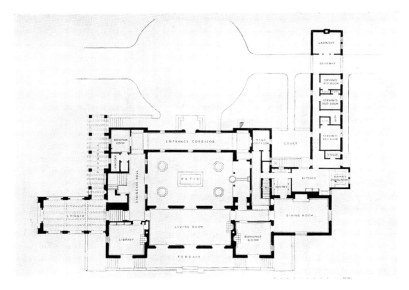

TOP
FIG. 8-2. *Dater residence, 1915–1918—floor plans: top, second floor; bottom, first floor.*

ABOVE
FIG. 8-3. *Dater residence— main entrance.*

ondary entrance on the south side (fig. 8-4). This was reserved for family members and close friends. From the motor court, visitors would walk down a few steps and follow a pergola to the private entry. The central courtyard was "resplendent with Moroccan tiles,"[8] which bordered planters and a small pool (fig. 8-5). On one wall, water spouted from sculptured heads into a narrow channel leading to the central pool (fig. C-36). Goodhue employed Charles Gibbs Adams (1884–1953), who was known for innovative landscape designs using native plants, to help him create a landscape scheme that blended Persian water elements with California plants, trees, and shrubbery. At the corners of a U-shaped walkway Goodhue located "keyhole rooms"—circular seating areas surrounded by walls and hedges with small entrances (fig. C-37). Everywhere small fountains and shallow rivulets of water, reminiscent of Persia, added to the beauty and serenity of the outdoors. On the east side, a paved patio bordered the house where guests could enjoy a view of terraced gardens descending to a broad reflecting pool at the bottom (fig. C-38).[9]

In general, Goodhue was pleased with the progress and quality of construction, and sent annual reports to Gillespie. In April 1917 he wrote:

> while he [Henry Dater] is a poor correspondent, his contractors are excellent, not only as correspondents but as builders, and are clearly endeavoring to do a thoroughly good piece of work; indeed, I expect to find his house much better than I had supposed possible in California.[10]

A year later he wrote: "It's wonderful to have you like it," but in response to a comment about the doors of the main rooms, he expressed concern that

> the painter and grainer let himself loose on the graining, until the doors look more like Italian walnut than the real thing would. Mr. Guastavino was here this morning and agreed that you were probably right in your criticism of the blue tiles in the pool, but you will remember that this tile cost, all of it, less than $1.00 per ft. and so can't be expected to quite reflect the blue sky of Isfahan.[11]

For his residential work Goodhue used two major tile companies: the Moravian Pottery & Tile Works of Pennsylvania, whose origins are outlined in chapter 10, and the Guastavino company, a New York firm that Goodhue and Cram used extensively for the vaulting of their many churches. The latter company made most of Goodhue's decorative tiles featuring Persian or Tunisian designs. The Guastavinos were Rafael I and Rafael II, father and son. Rafael I began his career as an architect in Barcelona, where he "pioneered the adaptation of a centuries-old building technology, the Catalan vault, a fireproof method of construction in which courses of tile are laminated with mortar." After moving with his son

FIG. 8-4. *Dater residence—a loggia with simple arches served as a secondary entrance.*

FIG. 8-5. *Dater residence—original view of the central courtyard with Moroccan tiles lining an alcove, and bordering a pool and planters.*

to New York in 1881, he established the Guastavino Fireproof Construction Company, whose work strongly influenced American architecture.[12]

In May 1918 Goodhue wrote again to Gillespie:

Harry's house really must be pretty good and the photographs Messrs. Snook & Kenyon sent me of the tile work in the court give a surprising effect of the North African work from which they were derived. Of course the fact that they are laid too evenly, which I understand they are, doesn't show in the photographs. I only wish I could be right there now to place the furniture and stuff that has been sent out. I am sure Harry will put it in precisely the wrong place and that I'll have to go through a sort of house moving process for him when I arrive in July[13] [fig. C-39].

Unlike Frank Lloyd Wright, Goodhue did not design built-in seating or uncomfortable furniture for his clients, but for some buildings, such as the Kitchi Gammi Club in Duluth, he worked with a reputable interior designer and designed some of the accessories himself. Whenever possible he liked to help his residential clients shop for the right furnishings and art. For Harry he had found mantelpieces in Mexico, and "an old Italian picture of a rather more than life size cupid. . . . If I can get it at any reasonable price, I think I'd like to make a present of it to Harry, for anything more appropriate to his character and general career I can't imagine, though he's getting to be a rather elderly and decrepit cupid." (Henry Dater was reputed to have a roving eye.) Goodhue had been buying furniture for the Daters but was concerned that they "are so devoid of the little trifling impedimenta that serve to make a house livable."[14] The house was finished in 1918, and the new owners called their home Días Felices (Happy Days).

In spite of a design with which Goodhue was justifiably pleased, the Daters used their Montecito retreat for only a few years before selling it in May 1925. A month later, to Goodhue's credit, the house survived a major earthquake without damage. The architect was fully aware of the importance of specifying the right construction for varying conditions, and on one of his trips to Hawaii he had asked T. A. Jaggar, Jr., director of the Hawaiian Volcano Observatory, about appropriate construction for earthquake-prone areas. In reply, Jaggar had offered to help at any time: "I believe that the influence of architects and engineers in earthquake countries like California can do more to protect life and property than any other one control. The earthquake question is brought home to the average intellect so seldom that it is hard to keep before the public the necessity for eternal vigilance and the utmost caution in building."[15]

From their earliest days as church builders, Cram and Goodhue had always hired the best engineers to make sure their buildings were sound and stable. The most important members of Goodhue's staff in his New York office were the engineers, who were usually Scotsmen. Goodhue's residential buildings were just as well constructed as his ecclesiastical and secular structures. Houses had solid foundations and full basements. The walls were usually made of clay tile and covered with whatever skin was appropriate for the region. All the details, exterior and interior, were carefully drafted and supervised. Goodhue himself was not able to supervise every detail, but he always appointed a site architect to oversee the construction.

The new owner of Días Felices was Charles Ludington (1866–1927), vice president and treasurer of the Curtis Publishing Company (publisher of the *Saturday Evening Post* and the *Ladies' Home Journal*). After moving to California in 1925, he purchased the Dater estate, but died two years later, leaving the house and land to his son, Wright.

With the help of Lockwood de Forest (1896–1949), whom he had met at the Thacher School for Boys in Ojai, Wright, who was an avid art collector and patron of the arts, made many changes to the estate, including renaming it Val Verde (Green Valley). Lockwood de Forest, whose father was a well-known landscape painter, interior designer, and partner for a while of Louis C. Tiffany, studied landscape architecture at Harvard University and established his own practice in Santa Barbara and Montecito in 1920.[16]

Most of the changes to the property took the form of additions to accommodate Ludington's art collection, and landscaping to complement the pseudo-Roman theme for the interior devised by Ludington's theatrical friends.[17] In the 1930s a new garden and reflecting pools were added on an axis with the north and south sides of the main house (fig. C-40). To bring some cohesion to this mélange, groups of square columns (fifty-six in all) were clustered at either end of the reflecting pools. Furthermore, the arched loggia was taken down to make room for some of the Roman columns, and the main features of the interior courtyard were destroyed: the carved capitals of the columns were removed, and all the Moroccan tiles were replaced with inferior ceramics. On the inside the original plan and form of the house remained intact, but the terra-cotta floors and staircase steps, so typical of Southwest architecture, were painted black to strengthen the Roman theme (fig. 8-6). We are left to wonder how Goodhue would have reacted to the changes. At best, he would have blamed them on a typical misunderstanding of good architecture by the crazy people of California; at worst, he would have used some unprintable language.

In 1956, Florence Heath Horton (known as Bunny), heiress of the Chicago Bridge & Iron Company, purchased the estate as a wedding gift for her new husband,

Warren Austin, who was Ludington's doctor.[18] After his wife died, Dr. Austin decided to turn his house and grounds into a museum as a memorial to his wife.[19]

Unfortunately, Austin's wish triggered a still unresolved conflict between the County Planning Commission and the residents of Montecito, who continue to resist the opening of the house and gardens to the public because of dangerous traffic conditions and the impact of a public institution on their bucolic neighborhood.[20] Meanwhile the Austin Val Verde Foundation struggles to maintain the property. We can only hope for a solution that will keep what remains of Goodhue's masterpiece intact. As stated in a letter to the *Santa Barbara News-Press,* "Warren Austin recognized that Val Verde is an exceptional work of art. It is one of America's great gardens, and the house that it embraces is a landmark of West Coast regional architectural style."[21] The design of the house played a significant role in Goodhue's career, establishing unequivocally an architectural style devoid of historicism.

This project was followed in 1918 by a related design for a house on the East Coast for a Mr. and Mrs. Philip Henry (fig. C-41). In a letter to Cecil Brewer, Goodhue expressed delight that he had the chance to create more modest houses for less money:

> I have two much smaller, and, breathe it gently lest my plutocratic clients should hear, to my mind much more successful houses under construction,—one in . . . Montecito, for my friend, Henry Dater, Esq., that is costing, house, electric fixtures, furniture, rugs, everything,—less than $50,000.00,—that I think you would characterize . . . as rather North African . . . and the other for Mrs. Philip Henry, of Scarborough-on-Hudson, that is a sort of Eastern and Anglicized version of the same thing. Both are cemented. The California example on hollow tile, and the Eastern example in the form of thin, rough-cement-cast on an irregular stone wall. The California is of tile, and the Eastern roof of what you Britons call "stone slate." Both are simple,—but dearer to my heart than palaces,—even though the commissions do not have so many ciphers.[22]

Scarborough-on-Hudson, named for a well-known seaside resort on the east coast of Yorkshire, England, is 30 miles north of Manhattan with a convenient train service to the city. In the early 1900s it was a rural community of farms, small villages, and a few palatial estates belonging to the Rockefellers, Astors, Vanderbilts, and Vanderlips. It was common practice for businessmen living in New York City either to own land or to rent riverfront cottages to escape the heat of the city in the summer months. In 1913, Goodhue himself bought a 30-acre farm on the border of Scarborough, Briarcliff, and Ossining, which he used as a weekend and summer retreat (described in chapter 10).

The river, which provided an important means of transport, is at its widest (three miles across) as it flows past Scarborough. Most of the opposite shore is parkland purchased by the Rockefellers, so that they could enjoy a pristine view of the Palisades from Kykuit, their estate between Scarborough and Tarrytown.

Linden Circle, where the Henry house was built, had been laid out by Frederick Law Olmsted, Sr. (1822–1903), and had been part of Beechwood, the Vanderlip estate. Frank Arthur Vanderlip (1864–1937) was born in Aurora, Illinois, the son of a blacksmith and farmer. After a stint as a reporter and financial editor, he was selected by President McKinley to be Assistant Secretary of the Treasury. In 1901 he joined the National City Bank of New York City as vice president, and in 1909 he was appointed president. Under Vanderlip's presidency, National City Bank became one of the nation's outstanding financial institutions.[23] In 1906 the bank joined forces with Speyer & Company to finance and oversee the building of a railroad in Bolivia, a vital means of transportation for that landlocked country.

FIG. 8-6. *Dater residence—Ludington had the original terra-cotta flooring of the hall and staircase painted black to reinforce his "Roman" theme.*

FIG. 8-7. *Philip
Henry house,
Scarborough,
New York—
garden view.*

James Speyer, an international banker, also had a country estate near the Vanderlips.

Vanderlip chose engineer Philip Henry to manage the railroad project. Henry's wife, Clover, was the sister of Vanderlip's wife, Narcissa Cox Vanderlip, a suffragist, social feminist, and philanthropist.[24] Henry, as a client and employee of National City Bank, met the requirements of the by-laws of Linden Circle, which stated that residents must be either vice presidents or clients of the bank.

The connection with Goodhue was probably twofold. First, Vanderlip would have known about his work in San Diego after he bought 16,000 acres of ranch land on the Palos Verdes Peninsula, just south of Los Angeles, which he planned to convert into one of the most exclusive residential areas in the country. Second, it is quite likely that Henry had asked Goodhue to design a house reminiscent of the Spanish Colonial architecture with which he had become familiar during his travels in South America.

Linden Circle contained homes in all the traditional East Coast styles: French Colonial, Tudor Revival, and clapboard English cottages. Into this typical eastern milieu Goodhue dared to introduce a simple, unadorned, boldly massed, stone house, shockingly different from its neighbors (fig. C-41). Even today it stands out as stark, rustic, and stunningly haunting. The walls are made of Manhattan schist laid in horizontal bedding planes. This local schist, which forms Manhattan's bedrock and was available in abundance after the excavation of the New York subway, is a charcoal-colored rock dominated by shiny, mirrorlike flakes of mica. The rock formation was originally a mud composed of clay minerals. As the mud became buried by more mud, geological processes caused recrystallization that generated a layer cake of parallel glittering micas, studded with occasional plums of red garnet. Goodhue, who liked to use native materials, probably felt that the roughness of the schist was perfect for a rural retreat in the woods and would add interest to a house devoid of architectural detailing or decoration.

The cubistic forms of the house, softened by semicircular arches forming a loggia on the garden side, reflect the Dater estate (fig. 8-7). The main entrance is an unimposing arched doorway made more rustic by the rough-cut brickwork. A niche was created around a small staircase window on one side to balance the window on the other side (fig. C-42). Opposite the door, a stone fountain provides a delicate, soothing gurgle sometimes muffled by the sound of rustling leaves as breezes blow through the surrounding beech trees (fig. C-43). Appropriately, the house was named La Paz (Peace).

To provide a contrast to the severity of the exterior, Goodhue created a warm, inviting interior blending English, Spanish, and North African elements. The house was featured in the February 1920 issue of *House Beautiful* in an article that included floor plans and a detailed description of the interior.[25] The opening remarks of the article, which discuss the relationship between architect and client, are of particular interest in reviewing Goodhue's domestic designs:

> We have always believed that the genuine domestic work in any country is that which results from the influence upon the architect of the personality and particular needs of the owner: the architect keeps the owner in line with good tradition and restrains personality from overflowing into personal idiosyncrasy; and the owner prevents the architect from designing a merely puristic house. Such co-operation . . . results in the best work only when the architect is a man of genius and his client is an individual of wide general culture.[26]

Architectural critics, especially of residential work, often forget that the designer does not have the freedom to create an ideal living space without regard to the occupant. The owner, for whom the residence is being built, should have the right to influence the architectural design. Without question Goodhue was a genius, and in the Henrys he found the perfect client. The *House Beautiful* article quotes Goodhue as follows:

> The architect wishes to record here his sense of deep obligation to Mrs. Henry. Clients are frequently . . . unsympathetic; but Mrs. Henry's taste in furniture and pictures seems to me to have been unerringly good, and, though I aided and abetted her in much that she bought, almost as much again she ferreted out and purchased herself.[27]

This must have been especially satisfying to Goodhue, who, as stated before, liked to be involved in every detail of his designs, including making sure that the interior was appropriately furnished.

The interior plan of the Henry house reflected the sloping ground on which it was built (fig. 8-8). The entry vestibule and landing were five steps above the level of the first-floor rooms, and the dining room, pantry, and kitchen were two steps lower. As in many of Goodhue's designs, the principal space of the house was the great hall, which had arched openings, a painted beamed ceiling of Oregon pine, a floor of irregular slate flags, and a

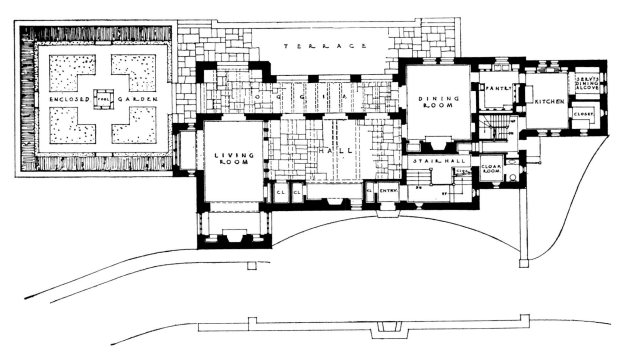

FIG. 8-8. *Henry house—original first-floor and garden plan.*

fireplace with a dominant stone mantel and space above for some important painting. Varying tones of the finishes added interest: lightly tinted walls contrasted with the darkness of the ceiling beams and stone floor (fig. 8-9). The hall led into the living room, which continued the theme of the great hall but was smaller and more intimate (fig. 8-10). Of particular interest was the fireplace with its stone bracketed lintel and brick surround, and "above this an elaborate and amusing mantelshelf in oak. The bosses at each end represent two youthful figures apparently warming their hands at the fire below."[28] Light poured into the room from a large, leaded window looking onto an enclosed garden with a parterre of flower beds forming a square around a central tiled fountain. At the opposite end of the great room was the dining room, with a large window framing a view of the river. Here the mantel breast of the fireplace had bricks set into a chevron design and a carved lintel with five scenes from

the life of Henry Hudson, particularly appropriate for the location of the house (fig. 8-11). The Irving & Casson–A. H. Davenport Company, Goodhue's master wood-carvers, executed all the woodwork, and the Edward Schroeder Lamp Works fabricated the lighting fixtures. Goodhue credited Howard E. Watkins with the design of the fixtures and explained that "they are very different from the usual thing, the two hanging lanterns in the great hall being of pewter, touched with color and gold, with pieces of clear glass, also treated in the same fashion as the pewter, separating the actual lamps."[29]

The upstairs consisted of four bedrooms, three bathrooms, and a servants' wing with three bedrooms and one bathroom (fig. 8-12). In addition, there were several porches, two designated for sleeping. Throughout the upstairs, a lighter effect was achieved by painting or modeling the plaster walls and ceilings. The two principal bedrooms featured fireplaces with antique mantels.

Goodhue explained that he was delighted to have created a rather exotic bathroom for his client:

> Though the baths are for the most part precisely similar to those in any other house, in that adjoining the owner's rooms, the architect has permitted himself, and has been graciously permitted by the owner, to indulge himself in a bit of fancy that after all, is not unreasonable. The room is domed, with an alabaster lamp hanging from its apex, and wainscoted with Tunisian tile. . . . However the effect may be roughly classed as somewhat Oriental, there's no absence of the most extreme practicality.[30]

The romantic architect had also designed a Roman bathing room for Gillespie's house in Montecito. The *House Beautiful* article noted that part of the success of the Henry project was due to "the co-operative idea. Not because the architect has in any way resigned his mastership; but rather because he has had the insight to call out in his assistants as in his client their several abilities to help; and he has had the generosity to acknowledge the help that has been given."[31]

Tragically, a fire swept through the house in 1947, leaving the stone shell intact but gutting the interior, which was rebuilt without the charm and detailing of the original. Sol Stein (of Stein & Day), author, editor, and publisher, was one of the later occupants of this unusual structure. Another writer, John Cheever, helped to immortalize the house as the Warburtons' home in his short story "The Housebreaker of Shady Hill." He wrote, "In the dim night light that came in at the windows, the house looked like a shell, a nautilus, shaped to contain itself."[32]

After the strange fortress had caught her fancy, the present owner, Roberta Arena, had bought a nearby

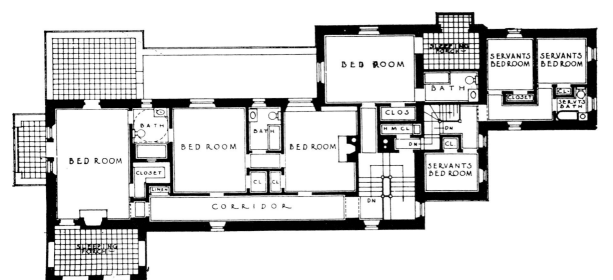

TOP
FIG. 8-10. *Henry house—original living room with a carved mantelshelf supported by bosses representing two figures warming their hands at the fire.*

ABOVE
FIG. 8-11. *Henry house—dining room fireplace with a carved lintel featuring scenes from the life of Henry Hudson.*

LEFT
FIG. 8-12. *Henry house—original second-floor plan.*

FIG. 8-13. Pen-and-
ink sketch of proposed
house for Mr. and
Mrs. Walter Douglas,
Scarborough, New
York, 1918 (misla-
beled "Peterson
Residence").

house so that she would be on the spot when Sol Stein was ready to sell. After finalizing the purchase from Stein, she tore down her interim abode to permit an unobstructed view of the river. Her future plans—now made feasible with my discovery of the layout in the *House Beautiful* article—include restoring the Henry house's original interior.

According to Goodhue's correspondence, he had designed another house in 1918 for Walter Douglas, the general manager of the Phelps Dodge mining operation in Tyrone, New Mexico. Douglas had a home in New York City, and the two families often dined and went to the theater together. In fact, Goodhue had sponsored Douglas for membership in the Century and Grolier clubs, two of the most prestigious clubs in New York.[33]

The Douglases' house was to be situated on another of the Linden Circle lots. The land, which was steeply sloped, was adjacent to the Philip Henry house but with an entrance on

Revolutionary Road.[34] It would be, like Goodhue's own farm, a weekend retreat from New York City. To judge from Goodhue's description of it in a letter to John Moore, it was to be in the same rustic vein as the Henry house:

I have a house and garden with terraces at Scarboro in Westchester County. It's somewhat Lindebergish—I am afraid even more in the 1900–1905 manner of your friend Sir Edwin Lutyens, though by no means so splendid as his clients usually demand, being built of almost anything handy, split stone from pasture walls, second-hand brick with a little terra cotta and the like, all whitewashed with a wobbly and irregular slate roof. Mrs. Douglas says it's to be a week-end cottage and as farmhousy as possible, but she doesn't really mean it because already she is snooping around after genuine old English oak furniture and whispers when her husband isn't listening of linen-fold panel-ing, etc. She wants, in fact, about as much of a farm house as Marie Antoinette at the petit Trianon.[35]

Although there is no record of the house being built, two drawings by Goodhue help us visualize this charming country retreat[36] (figs. 8-13 and 8-14).

The design of these two houses must have given Goodhue great satisfaction, because they fulfilled much of what he wrote about in his essay "The Home of the Future." The houses were moderate in size and price, the antithesis of the grand mansions that he had designed in California and Long Island. The plans were sound and every square foot of space well used. Goodhue used local materials and applied them in such a way that the individuality of the craftsmen who did the work was retained. In his essay, he stressed the importance of freedom of expression both for the architect and for the artisans who did the work. "I am confident that the home of the future must be made beautiful by freedom of thought in the artist, by freedom also in the people who cooperate with his work." Even

though "the house of the future will surpass all other forms of domestic architecture in that it will be the most sanitary, the most fireproof, the most comfortable," Goodhue feared that the search for beauty would become subservient to the need to build cheaply and sell at the highest price. As a result, "all freshness and originality of treatment, all beauty of spontaneity is lost. It is difficult to get a workman to do anything that is not of the ordinary." He despaired of the role of the unions, which "have no respect for skill, no respect for art. . . . We will not accept the standards of the trade unions forever, however important the trade unions may have been in the development of our business system."[37] Goodhue's concerns went unheeded. We look back at the period between the two world wars and envy the homeowners, who enjoyed the kind of craftsmanship that Goodhue advocated and practiced in all his designs.

FIG. 8-14. *Alternate view of the Douglas house set up on a rise, supported by walls and terraces (also mislabeled "Peterson Residence")*

Chapter 9

PITTSBURGH PICTURESQUE AND LONG ISLAND TUDOR

1919–1924

It seems to me as we look into the future of domestic architecture, we must find for many years to come a great variety of individual expression—houses suited to each State and to each individual in the State.

—BERTRAM GROSVENOR GOODHUE[1]

In 1919 Goodhue was commissioned by Mrs. William Myler to design a house in a Pittsburgh neighborhood for herself and her married daughter and family.[2] Mrs. Myler and her recently deceased husband would have met Goodhue when he was designing the First Baptist Church on North Bellefield Avenue and Bayard Street. This project (1909–1912), executed by the New York office of Cram, Goodhue & Ferguson, was one of Goodhue's most important buildings. Critics of the time commended him for successfully reworking traditional Gothic forms in the context of the contemporary needs of the church. George Edgell, in his book *The American Architecture of To-day*, wrote, "As one studies this monumental work, one feels more and more that American Gothic has originality and beauty and that the modern work shows an understanding and deliberate deviation from historic form thoroughly assimilated."[3] A more recent commentator, Pittsburgh historian James Van Trump, said, "The general mass has a moulded sculptural quality . . . and the well-calculated relationship between the large area of glass and the solids makes for a composition of great airiness, liveliness, and verve."[4] The exterior of the church was striking for its smooth limestone walls and 182-foot-high green copper-clad flèche, reminiscent of French Gothic. In 1920, Mrs. Myler commissioned Goodhue to design an elaborately carved pulpit in memory of her husband.

At the beginning of the twentieth century, Pittsburgh, at the confluence of the Allegheny and Monongahela rivers, which form the Ohio, was well established as the center of the steel industry. Van Trump described it as both beautiful and ugly: "What old Pittsburgher does not remember those spectacular nights when, at 'pouring time' in the steel mills, half the sky was suffused with a throbbing curtain of light."[5] The rivers, which provided an essential means of transportation, separated the city into many diverse sections, scattered up and down the hilly topography. Van Trump called Pittsburgh "a collection of wandering towns which have taken squatter's rights and lodged themselves helter-skelter among the sheltering ridges."[6]

The urban architecture was predominantly Richardsonian Romanesque intermingled with Renaissance. In many of the residential communities that were populated by diverse nationalities, housing evolved in a variety of styles. Without a rail line or major industry, the development of Squirrel Hill, where the Myler house was located, lagged behind that of other areas. Between 1910 and 1930, the neighborhood began to change. Electric trolley lines were built and the Boulevard of the Allies opened, improving connections with the city. This was soon followed by construction along tree-lined streets of large, sturdy houses in different architectural modes—Tudor Revival, Colonial

Revival, Shingle, and Craftsman. Mrs. Myler's property consisted of two parcels on Bennington Avenue that had been part of James Murdoch's original farmland.[7]

William Albert Myler (1851–1918), whose career began in the wholesale dry goods business, moved rapidly through the ranks to become a well-known and successful Pittsburgh businessman. He was a director or officer of several manufacturing companies, eventually becoming secretary and treasurer of the Standard Sanitary Manufacturing Company, the forerunner of American Standard, which is now the world's largest producer of bathroom and kitchen fixtures.[8] He married Mary I. K. Dennison, and the couple had two daughters. The Mylers lived in a large townhouse in Pittsburgh until William's death on July 25, 1918. They also had a summer home in Patterson Heights, Beaver Falls.[9]

After the loss of her husband, Mrs. Myler decided to move to one of the newest suburbs of Pittsburgh and share a house with her daughter Mary and her husband, Frank Kier, and their two children, aged nine and six years. Mrs. Myler asked Goodhue to draw up plans for a house, which upon completion cost $86,250.[10] Outwardly, it was to look like a single house, but in fact it would be two individual residences.[11] In this way, Mrs. Myler could enjoy her privacy but remain close to her daughter's family and allay her loneliness.

Goodhue's solution was to create an L-shaped house sheltering a good-sized common garden (figs. 9-1 and 9-2). The daughter and her family were to inhabit the larger section of the house at 1331 Bennington. A wing, extending along the side of the garden, contained the dining room and kitchen. The main part of the house was parallel to the street, with entry vestibule, hall, library, and a great room bordered by a long gallery and porch on the garden side, linking the two parts. The second floor was divided into servants' quarters and a guest room over the kitchen-dining wing, parents' and children's bedrooms facing the front, and a sleeping porch looking onto the garden. The third floor consisted of a nursemaid's bedroom and a children's playroom.

At first, Mrs. Myler's segment at 1333 Bennington consisted only of a small entry leading directly into the living room and staircase, with a bay-windowed library facing the garden. There were two bedrooms and a bathroom upstairs. Mrs. Myler had easy access to her daughter's portion through the long gallery and presumably shared the great room on occasion. In 1923, perhaps tired of dining with her daughter and family, Mrs. Myler asked Goodhue to design a two-story addition to her house at a cost of $25,000 (fig. 9-2).[12] This provided her with her own dining room, kitchen, and charming upstairs sitting room with a vaulted, beamed ceiling and a bay window reminiscent of Goodhue's attic studio in his New York townhouse (fig. C-45).

FIG. 9-1. *Myler residence, Pittsburgh, Pennsylvania, 1919. Photograph of the double house from the garden side before the 1923 addition.*

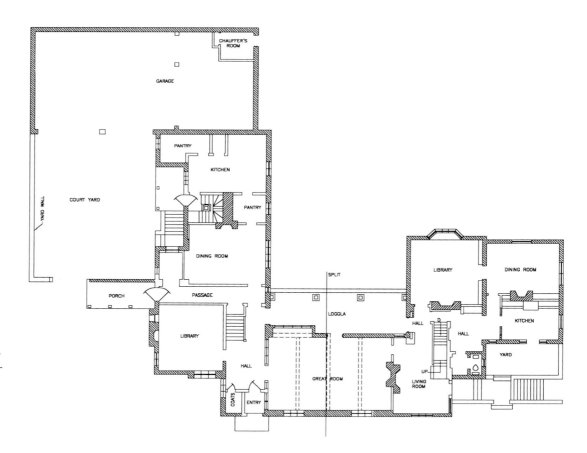

FIG. 9-2. *Myler residence—original first-floor plan showing 1923 addition and location of the 1945 division.*

Both houses had a full basement and third floor. The original room-sized coal furnace and a wall of five laundry sinks, representing William Myler's manufacturing company, still exist on the daughter's side. In addition, all the bathrooms were fitted with Standard Sanitary plumbing fixtures, including an example of an early shower in the master bathroom. Mrs. Myler's basement had a sitting room and a separate entrance for the servants.

The architectural style of the house has been called "Picturesque." It is reminiscent of the postmedieval houses with steeply gabled roofs that were a dominant influence on Goodhue's childhood.[13] In place of clapboard, the base is brick, laid in an English bond with an overhanging second floor clad in overlapping cypress clapboard and supported by a cornice with turned spindles (fig. C-44). Windows are small, leaded, and scattered in singles, doubles, triples, and quadruples, with large bay windows on the garden side.

The interior provides a superb example of Goodhue's utilization of the best craftsmen and his attention to detail. The major rooms have fireplaces in Renaissance, Tudor Revival, and Adamesque styles built of stone, a variety of marbles, and carved wood. Carved moldings with egg-and-dart, acanthus leaf, rope, and abacus bead

designs surround a grand fireplace that was the central feature of the great room. A dogwood flower sits below the Ionic capitals that frame this same fireplace (fig. C-46). In the library implied pilasters with fluted shafts separate arched bookcases decorated with carvings of fruit and vine (fig. C-47). The dining rooms in both halves of the house have built-in cabinets with Gothic-arched, leaded-glass doors (fig. C-48). Attention to detail is also evident in the hand-carved chamfered corners of the paneling in Mrs. Myler's upstairs sitting room.

This beautiful interior was unfinished when four anonymous members of the Pittsburgh Architectural Club wrote a scathing criticism of the house's design in their publication, *The Charette*, in 1921. The harshness of their review might in part have reflected their resentment of an out-of-towner designing a church and residence in *their* town. The author of "Impression the Fourth" was a trifle kinder:

The Goodhue house is in many respects most interesting; the component parts are in the main excellent, except the porch in the court which is commonplace and unlovely in itself and a discordant note in the ensemble. Perhaps the best portion of the entire building is the service wing from the northeast; the mass is very satisfactory, the detail

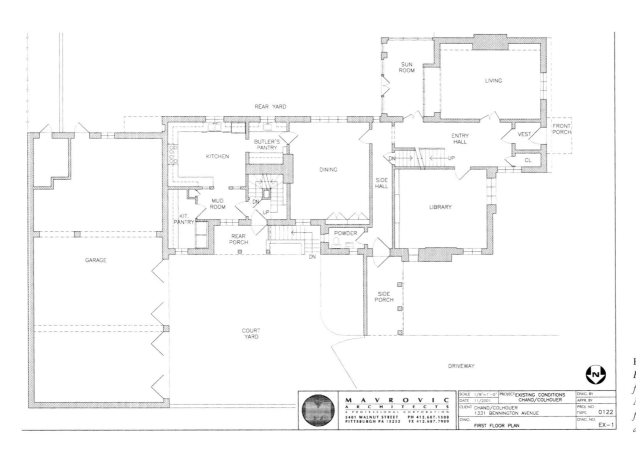

FIG. 9-3. *1331 Bennington—first-floor plan revised by Mavrovic Architects for owners Riz Chand and Laura Colhouer.*

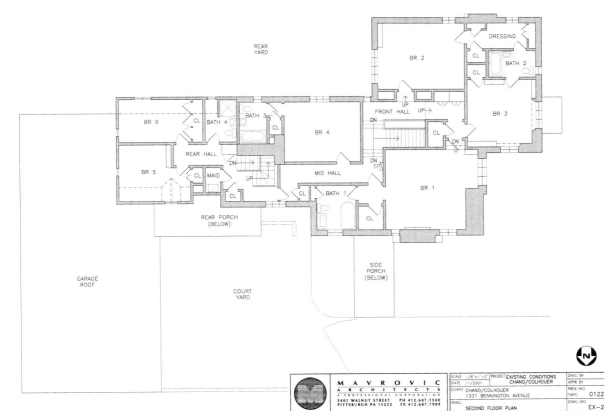

FIG. 9-4. *1331 Bennington—revised second-floor plan.*

full of charm and the materials and their handling most interesting. But the building as a whole does not impress one as architecture. It is too false and as one gazes at the fabric of beautiful materials put together with the finest workmanship, one can not but regret that the architect did not take his inspiration from the spirit of our honest, simple farmer forefathers rather than the forms they left behind them.[14]

In 1927, the double residence was sold to Mary Alice Brown Painter, who sold the property to Agnes Hobart Hower in 1945. The idea of splitting the house into two parts was considered as early as 1936, but nothing was done until 1945 when Agnes and Edwin Hower finalized the plans so that Agnes's father, Harold P. Hobart, and his second wife could occupy 1333 Bennington. In the end, three-quarters of the beamed great room was demolished to make a twelve-foot space between the two houses (see fig. C-44). This left sufficient square footage for a living room at 1331 Bennington where the great room's magnificent fireplace was reinstalled. The balance of Mary Kier's home was easily adapted to a comfortable new residence of 6,300 square feet (figs. 9-3 and 9-4). Laura Colhouer and her husband, Riz Chand, owners of 1331 Bennington at the time of the researching of this book, succeeded in incorporating appropriate modernizations in the kitchen, bathrooms, and servants' quarters while restoring their section to its original splendor.

Mrs. Myler's house, referred to in the neighborhood as the "Butler's Quarters," remained small and cozy until the present owners bought it in 1991 and found an architect, Gerald Lee Morosco, sympathetic to Goodhue's architecture and detailing. He created a new interior and addition suited to the needs of his clients. The City of Pittsburgh and the Historic Review Commission awarded the owners, Robert and Concetta Mitro, a Certificate of Recognition "for the excellent design of the addition to the residential building located at 1333 Bennington Avenue." The new wing blends seamlessly with the original 1920 house and its 1923 addition (fig. C-49).

Although a photograph of this late example of Goodhue's East Coast residential work, taken before the 1923 addition, was published in the Whitaker memorial volume[15] (fig. 9-1), the existence of the house seems otherwise to have been overlooked, nor does Goodhue mention it in any of his correspondence. At the time of its design he was immersed in developing a simpler architecture. He had succeeded in creating an "Eastern and Anglicized version"[16] of the Daters' North African house for the Henrys in Scarborough. But Philip Henry was an engineer who was attuned to Spanish architecture, and it is unlikely that such a stark house would have appealed to the conservative wife of a Pittsburgh businessman. Although Goodhue had wondered whether

it was feasible, or even desirable, to develop an architecture that could be characterized as American, he had resigned himself to designing in a variety of regional styles because America lacked a typical climate, unified civilization, or common form of artistic expression.[17] He probably felt that a version of a New England country house would suit his client and provide a contrast to the mix of traditional European styles in the neighborhood. However, mindful of the criticism of his peers, we are left to wonder whether the design was executed in a hurry, squeezed in between the architect's more important nonresidential commissions. Architectural historian Walter Kidney summed up the findings of the Charette authors in a 1994 article in the Pittsburgh History & Landmarks Foundation's PHLF News:

> The house . . . is contrivedly picturesque, with steep roofs, jutting clapboard second floors, and very random fenestration. The four critics more or less agreed . . . that the plan was convenient, that the exterior was a mishmash of forms and styles, and that the whole thing was a not-very-good work by a great architect. . . . Even apart from changes, it is a rather restless design.[18]

Nonetheless, the once double house is now two separate, charming houses displaying a quality of design, construction, and materials that is rarely reproduced today.

Since Goodhue was fully committed to his ecclesiastical and secular projects, three years passed before he began work in 1923 on another residential commission. On April 21, 1924, Goodhue wrote to Mrs. Wilton Lloyd-Smith:

> Here I am just back from California. . . . Mr. Murray has delighted me with the information that your plan is at last satisfactory—or, at any rate, satisfactory enough for you, after the manner of all clients, to want to get the house built by next week, Thursday. Of course this is impossible. I should say that the process of making working drawings and specifications and enough details to start on would take not less than four months; sorry, but it can't be helped.[19]

The letter continues with the question of making arrangements to get together with the Lloyd-Smiths, either for a picnic on the site of the proposed Long Island home, which Marjorie had suggested to Goodhue's wife Lydia, or for a meeting in New York. However, Goodhue was tied up with other commitments: "I must be in Washington to help Mr. Coolidge to his throne at the dedication of the National Academy of Sciences—something your father is going to, too."[20] The dedication of one of Goodhue's most important projects was scheduled for April 25, 1924, the architect's fifty-fifth birthday. Goodhue's letter to Marjorie continues:

But can't you somehow manage to get in here and go over the final drawings at 1/8 inch scale so that we can start at the regular scale of 1/4 inch to a foot? It would be better to do this with Mr. Murray and me. Of course I realize that if we all meet in the evening at your apartment, decisions would be sharper and better and much more accelerated—thanks to the liquid accompaniment provided by Wilton; but after all, business is business.[21]

The next day, April 22, 1924, Goodhue sent a brief note to Wilton: "We are authorizing the making of an eighth-inch scale model of the exterior of your house at a cost of $500, and are proceeding with the working drawings at the scale of one-quarter inch to the foot."[22] He added that they were now due one-fifth of their commission, which came to $6,000.

Like many wealthy New Yorkers, the Lloyd-Smiths, who owned a three-story penthouse in Gracie Square overlooking the East River, had decided to build a weekend and summer retreat on Long Island. Their choice of architect resulted more from Goodhue's California work than from his fame as a leading New York architect. Wilton Lloyd-Smith's wife, Marjorie, was the only daughter of Arthur H. Fleming, a wealthy resident of

Pasadena with interests in lumber and mining companies, and a trustee of the California Institute of Technology, for which Goodhue was the master architect. Marjorie recalled, "Father insisted that we have Bertram Goodhue as our architect."[23] Because her father had indicated that the house would be a gift, Marjorie and her husband could hardly object.

In spite of a strict upbringing following the death of her mother when she was only ten, Marjorie had persuaded her father to approve her marriage to Wilton Lloyd-Smith[24] on August 25, 1917, just eight weeks before he left with his Second U.S. Cavalry regiment to fight in France. On his return he attended Harvard Law School and later joined the firm of Cotton & Franklin, where he soon became a partner. He was an active Republican, was on the board of several companies, joined the most prestigious clubs in New York, loved to hunt, flew his own airplanes, bred dogs, and, like Marjorie, had a love of music and an ability to sing. He became a trustee of the American Museum of Natural History and gave the museum several of his best hunting specimens.[25]

In 1923, Lloyd-Smith bought 101 acres on the westerly edge of Lloyd's Neck.[26] An article in a New York

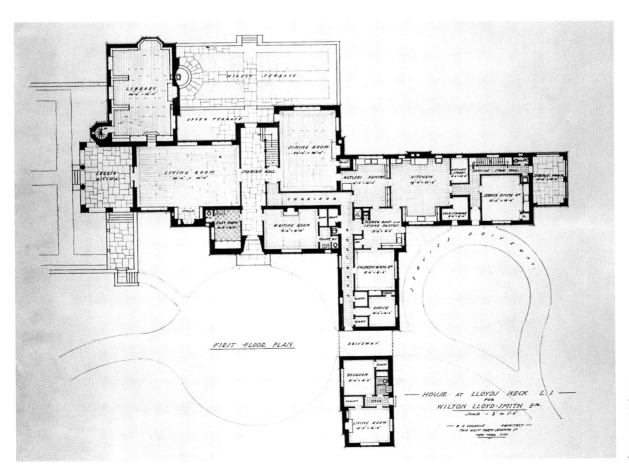

FIG. 9-5. *The Lloyd-Smith estate, Lloyd's Neck, Long Island, New York, 1923–1926—first-floor plan.*

newspaper, *The Sun and the Globe*, described the property: "It has a frontage of about half a mile on Cold Spring Harbor, and is covered by woodland which nurserymen consider to be the finest now standing on Long Island. . . . In the immediate vicinity are the estates of Marshall Field, W. J. Matheson, Donald Scott, J. Herbert Johnston, Roland R. Conklin, Francis M. Weld, and A. G. Milbank."[27] Thus situated among elite neighbors on the prestigious Gold Coast of Long Island, the Lloyd-Smiths joined the best clubs and enjoyed all the amenities of wealthy country living. Using the services of a "Nomenclator" agency, they chose to call their new home Kenjockety, an Indian name meaning "away from the masses." Laura Lee Rogers, who had published an article in *Country Life* entitled "Naming the Country Home," wrote to Mrs. Lloyd-Smith: "The ideal name expresses the individuality of the home, indeed is a mental picture of it."[28] For the Lloyd-Smiths and their four daughters,[29] Kenjockety was the most special of all their homes. Daughter Diane wrote: "Kenjockety was the sort of place where you could be cozy even if you were all by yourself."[30] It provided a place of enchantment where the young girls could ride, play tennis, swim, and boat, and each have her own dog. The chil-

dren were permitted to bring their dogs into the dining room, where each dog sat or lay obediently in its own spot against the wall.

Goodhue sited the main part of the three-story house overlooking Long Island Sound, with sufficient space for a gracious lawn and gardens descending gradually to the edge of a 100-foot-high cliff (figs. 9-5 and 9-6). A mile-long drive through dense woods led to a turnaround circle and the main entry, which passed under part of the service-wing appendage, a typical feature of Goodhue's large estates. The style of the house was simplified Tudor—more rustic and less ostentatious than the Aldred mansion but considerably larger and more complex than the Hartley house. Viewed from the bottom of the cliff, the mass of the house had a high gabled roof with cross gables, tall chimneys, and partial half-timbering assembled in the spirit of Edwin Lutyens's English country-house designs (fig. 9-6). At one end, a protruding wing housed the library; and at the other, a long wing in line with the main house accommodated the kitchen and part of the service area (fig. 9-7). The roof was slate and the façade red brick in an English bond, pierced by groups of bay or flat leaded-glass windows. As with the Aldred and Hartley residences, arches in the

Fig. 9-7. A view of Kenjockety taken from the cliff above the Long Island Sound soon after completion. The library wing on the right and the servants' wing on the left were demolished by the owner who bought the property from Marjorie Lloyd-Smith.

loggia and entryway softened the rectilinear lines of the structure. In contrast to the red-brick walls, the arch of the entry porch was accented by sandstone cut in such a way that it revealed its geological features and natural colors (fig. C-50). On the underside of the bay window overhanging the entry porch, the Lloyd-Smiths had commissioned Lee Lawrie to design a lead-cast bas-relief (fig. C-51). The design comprised scenes of a family fishing, sailing, camping, playing with dogs, and hunting below a Latin inscription that read WILTONIS ET MARJO-RIAE ET AMICORUM ([the house] of Wilton and Marjorie and [their] friends) and LLOYD'S NECK AD 1926. In addition to the main house, the property included a garage for twelve cars with a chauffeur's apartment, a superintendent's cottage, and a tall tower housing the water tank.

In 1923, at Goodhue's suggestion, Marjorie had sent him a long list of her requirements for the house. The document is a good example of the challenging demands of a residential client. Like her father, Marjorie was well organized and thorough, and her document should have been of great help to her architect. The first page consisted of a list of rooms on each floor followed by two pages giving detailed requirements for each area. Here are some excerpts:

GROUND FLOOR

I think it would be nice to have a terrace in front of the house and also a terrace on the opposite side, with the playroom underneath the back terrace.

The ladies' dressing room is to be more of a writing and reception room with a lavatory off, which can readily be turned into a dressing room when there is entertainment.

Lavatory on the other side is to have a large coat closet to be used for all sorts of extra coats, and all the odds and ends needed in the country, such as rubbers, raincoats, galoshes, decoys for duck-shooting, tennis rackets, golf bags, etc. etc. It might be wiser to have two closets, one for just coats and the other for the odds and ends.

It would be nice to have doors instead of windows in the dining-room to the terrace. . . . I would like the dining-room to be white, the living room green and the library paneled pine, perhaps walnut.

SECOND FLOOR

I should like to have our suite and the children's rooms close together.

The den Wilton would use a great deal, keeping in it all his choice fishing rods, guns, law-books, fishing books—his holy of holies, where he could bring men to smoke after dinner if he wishes—at least special men [fig. 9-8].

FIG. 9-8. Kenjockety—
Wilton's den, where he
kept his guns, fishing
rods, and trophies.
A portrait of Marjorie
hangs amid the
collection of antlers.

Our bathroom would need to be pretty large, and, as already mentioned, with blue tiling, a large tub and large shower bath. Also, of course, a fireplace.

We want but one sleeping porch, and that for the children.

Fireplaces in just as many of the rooms as possible.

The playroom ought to be large enough to have a billiard table in it, also to have a small stage and plenty of room for games, dancing etc.[31]

Even after the plans had been finalized and approved, Marjorie made several changes to the design. She wanted more light and, therefore, had the windows enlarged or made into French doors. She also improved Goodhue's large central hall, which separated the living area from the dining and service wing, by moving the staircase to the opposite side to permit a wonderful vista from the front door through the hall to the terrace door and Long Island Sound beyond (figs. C-53 and C-54). Daughter Diane recalled her mother's gift for interior design and how she created a warm and welcoming interior.

Marjorie's memory of the "lovely green hall that was all paneled wood and that Nielson [the Lloyd-Smiths' majordomo] polished within an inch of his life"[32] provides a picture of Goodhue's characteristic paneling used for the principal spaces. But unlike the Hartley and Myler houses, Kenjockety's interior lacked the touch of his intricate detailing and signature carvings.

A large bay window dramatized the broad staircase, and the walls provided a perfect setting for the finest of Wilton's hunting trophies (figs. C-55 and 9-9). On the second floor Marjorie and Wilton's rooms were above the living room and library wing, while the children's and governess's rooms were over the dining and kitchen areas. Four guest rooms and a special room reserved for Arthur Fleming were situated above the service appendage. The third-floor attic contained two of the children's bedrooms as well as a large cedar-lined storage room "with drawers full of costumes."[33]

Fleming paid approximately $650,000 to build the house and sent one of his most trusted employees,

George H. Raitt, to live on the grounds and oversee the construction. Fleming himself was involved with every detail of the building. He made sure that the house was as fireproof as possible by having the walls constructed of terra-cotta tile and having fire hoses located on each floor. Appropriate and cost-saving materials were used—in some cases lumber from Fleming's own operations. Chimneys were designed in such a manner as to permit a smokeless fire, and electrical plates in wet locations were ceramic, not metal. Raitt wrote frequent reports to Fleming, who in turn wrote long lists of instructions and questions. Building operations began in 1925 and were completed in the summer of 1926. The result was an 18,000-square-foot house of impeccable construction.

Although the Goodhue Associates made suggestions for the initial layout of the gardens, Marjorie eventually employed the Cambridge, Massachusetts, firm of Warren H. Manning to design the formal gardens and make some necessary changes to the extensive wood-

land. Warren Manning (1860–1938) had spent eight years working for Frederick Law Olmsted, Sr., before establishing his own business in 1896. He was involved in the landscape design of Kenjockety for five years, from 1924 to 1929, where he exercised his skill at developing a successful plan based on the local environmental and soil conditions. After the initial design and planting, he made annual visits and wrote long letters with detailed instructions for Marjorie Lloyd-Smith and her head gardener concerning new plantings, the moving of plants and trees, and ideas for the children to follow. During this period Manning added a teahouse and a children's garden, built a tennis court, and "developed a trail system to connect buildings, gardens and shores . . . as well as introduced plant life, and wild life habitations for the four-footers, and two-footers of which the Duck Pens are of special interest now."[34] Because Wilton was an avid bird hunter and raised his own ducks, a special bridge was constructed over the driveway to provide safe passage to Lake Caumsett, just below the house.

FIG. 9-9. *Kenjockety— the staircase walls were a perfect place for Wilton's finest trophies, including a tiger that appears to be walking out of the wall.*

Fig. 9-10. *Rendering for Rensselaer Society of Engineers Club House.*

Manning also recommended ways to accommodate 160 or more cars when the Lloyd-Smiths had large parties.[35] In 1929, he advised them to locate the horse barns and kennels (for which two additional acres had been acquired) near each other to facilitate a single administrative control.[36]

What with its size and splendor, Kenjockety was often the scene of elaborate parties. Weekend visits or summer vacations involved a large retinue of chauffeur-driven Rolls-Royces and Hispano-Suizas leaving the city loaded with parents, children, nursemaids, servants, dogs, and provisions. Two servants and the ten gardeners worked full-time at Kenjockety.

The location of the estate made it accessible by seaplane. Wilton and Marshall Field shared one of the first amphibian planes, named the *Rubber Duck*, made by the Grumman company. During the summer months, Wilton commuted to the city by plane, a mere ten-minute journey. One of the pilots (Wilton employed two) would fly him to 28th Street and the East River, where he would disembark at the East River Club and walk to his office. Sometimes the plane would return to Kenjockety to pick up Marjorie and the children for visits to the dentist or city shopping.

For many years Wilton Lloyd-Smith had suffered from undulant fever, probably from drinking unpasteurized

milk on one of his hunting trips. He never recovered. Frequent fevers and pains in his joints led to alcoholism and depression, and in 1940 he committed suicide. After his death, Marjorie continued using the house until 1952, mostly for the sake of the children. She "circulated around a great deal,"[37] spent time in Antigua, where she had property, and eventually married Knight Woolley in 1957.

In 1953, Kenjockety was sold for $125,000 to an attorney, Prentice Brower, who subdivided most of the acreage and destroyed the integrity of the house by removing the library wing and servants' quarters beyond the kitchen (fig. C-52). Between 1963 and 1969, the property was owned by Edouard Cournand, president of Lanvin perfumes, and his wife. After the Cournands' deaths, their daughter gave the house to an order of Jesuits, who sold off everything of value but did not take up residence. The next owner was Robin Gibb of the Bee Gees. He made some disastrous "modernizations," even though he used the house only as a stopover between estates in England and Florida.[38] The present owners, Paula and Bruce Rice, have spent twenty years restoring the home's original features, and Paula has re-created an appropriate landscaping scheme in the spirit of the original. Except for the previously demolished areas (the two wings, the garage, and the water tower), the property (now six acres) has been reclaimed as a magical retreat

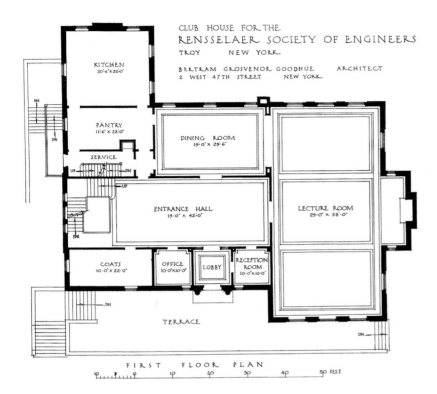

KITCHEN
20'-6" x 22'-0"

PANTRY
11'-6" x 22'-0"

SERVICE

DINING ROOM
19'-0" x 29'-6"

ENTRANCE HALL
19'-0" x 42'-0"

LECTURE ROOM
29'-0" x 58'-0"

COATS
10'-0" x 22'-0"

OFFICE
10'-0"x10'-0"

LOBBY

RECEPTION ROOM
10'-0"x10'-0"

TERRACE

FIRST   FLOOR   PLAN

Fig. 9-11. *Rensselaer Society of Engineers Club House— first-floor plan.*

"away from the masses" and a fitting tribute to Bertram Goodhue (figs. C-52 and C-56).

In 1923 and 1924, while he was working on the Lloyd-Smith residence, Goodhue was preparing a design for a fraternity house for the Rensselaer Society of Engineers at the Rensselaer Polytechnic Institute in Troy, New York. The society had been founded in 1866 as the Pi Eta Scientific Society. Stephen Van Rensselaer established the Rensselaer School in 1824 for instruction in science and civil engineering. In 1861 the school became the Rensselaer Polytechnic Institute and is now a technological university encompassing Schools of Architecture, Science, and Engineering, a School of Humanities and Social Sciences, a School of Management and Technology, and an Information Technology Program.

Goodhue designed a large, three-story, flat-roofed rectangular house with approximately 20,000 square feet and an offset or "wing" on one side (fig. 9-10). The style was restrained classical, with the first floor faced in stone and the upper two floors of brick. Architectural details consisted of horizontal molding defining the first floor and the cornice, a columned entry porch, and arched floor-to-ceiling windows in the wing. The front façade opened onto a balustraded terrace.

The entrance lobby led into a spacious central hall, with a lecture room filling the wing on one side, a staircase on the other side, and a dining room and service areas in the rear (fig. 9-11). The second floor was made up of a large central study hall, a library, a drafting room, and private study rooms. The third floor had one large open dormitory with thirty beds over the lecture-hall wing with the balance of the space divided between small dressing cubicles and bathroom facilities.[39]

In the final construction some of the architectural refinements were eliminated, and over the years changes have been made to the living areas of the upper floors. But according to member Rob Steere, "the public rooms of the first floor remain greatly unchanged. . . . People are often in awe of the size and magnitude of the house."[40]

Taking into account Goodhue's heavy schedule, one wonders how he became involved in this commission. He may have felt some connection with the city of Troy because his mother attended the Troy Female Seminary, or it is possible that one of his engineers graduated from the institute. It would certainly have served as a nice design and planning project for a younger member of his firm well supervised by the "boss." Although this is not comparable to the private residences designed by Goodhue, it is worth noting for its architectural style and its role as a valued student clubhouse.

Chapter 10

GOODHUE'S OWN ABODES

1908–1924

What we get most, perhaps, from Mr. Goodhue's house is the impression that beauty
is preeminently a livable quality. Beauty may be truth, and of course it is:
but it's pleasant to realize anew that beauty is also a warm, friendly companion.

—ROBERT CRAIGHEAD[1]

It must be every architect's dream to design and build his own house, and the intensely creative Goodhue was no exception. An examination of Goodhue's own residences will provide the reader with a meaningful review of his architectural development and his Arts and Crafts aesthetics, as well as a closer look at the private life of this fascinating man.

In the earlier years of his career Goodhue lacked the money to build from scratch, but he made radical alterations and additions to every place he lived. After their wedding in 1902, Goodhue and his wife, Lydia, moved to a charming little house on Brattle Street, Cambridge,[2] but their stay here was relatively short. Following the appointment of Goodhue to head his firm's New York City office, the Goodhues purchased a townhouse in 1905 at 106 East 74th Street. However, before they could move in, the interior of the house was "entirely burned out together with all the stuff from my 'far sea faring' Persia and the like. . . . Fortunately the family things, furniture, etc. we did not have at the time so they were saved."[3] It is possible that Goodhue was already planning to renovate the townhouse, but the fire would have given him the perfect excuse to virtually gut the building and redesign it to suit his architectural ideas and the needs of his growing family. The alteration application was to "build walls, staircase, foundation" for a cost of $10,000.[4] However, the final cost exceeded this estimate. In a 1913 letter asking for an evaluation of the

house with a view to putting it on the market, Goodhue wrote: "I spent . . . quite a considerable sum in building the house over, and as all the contractors and subcontractors did the work for approximately 'cost,' I suppose it is safe to assume that what cost me a little over $18,000, would have cost one of my clients perhaps $25,000."[5] Before moving into their rebuilt home in 1906, the Goodhues took temporary lodgings at 23 Fifth Avenue.[6]

The 1905–1906 townhouse renovation was well documented in Robert Craighead's article in the February 1916 issue of *House Beautiful* magazine. Cognizant of the limitations of city living ("in the city we are often confined to a plot resembling half a small suspender or a piece of pie"),[7] the author commended Goodhue for meeting the challenge and creating an efficient and charming abode on a footprint that was only 18 feet wide and 74 feet deep.

Goodhue took a typical New York high-stooped brownstone, a style of house Henry James described "as being cut out of chocolate,"[8] and turned the façade into something strikingly different: a simplified version of English Tudor with a bank of oriel windows accented in stone and Gothic details (fig. 10-1). As in his ecclesiastical work, Goodhue succeeded in extracting a few essential elements of medieval architecture to imbue his own home with a Gothic spirit "seen in the carved bosses of the cornice, the patterning in the brick work, and the character of the wrought-iron railings and the entrance gate."[9]

He changed the entrance from the usual "walk-up" flight of stairs to a three-step flight descending from the sidewalk through a wrought-iron gate set in a stone arch, which was separated from the bay window above by a running band of leaves and rosettes (fig. 10-2). The interior five floors were organized around a central core made up of the staircase, hall, bathrooms, and closets, leaving the balance of the space for main rooms front and back (fig. 10-3). The lowest level consisted of a square entrance hall with the kitchen at the back of the house and a service corridor leading to a secondary entrance at the front. The first-floor area was taken up with a dining room at the rear and a drawing room/library at the front. The second floor was made up of the master bedroom with a five-light leaded-glass bay window matching the window of the drawing room below, and a nursery looking out the back. The front part of the third floor and part of the fourth were dedicated to Goodhue's home workroom, with the servants' bedrooms completing the balance of the top floor.

The interior design provided many examples of work by members of the Arts and Crafts Movement such as wallpaper, tile work, modeled ceiling plaster, wood paneling, stained-glass window panels, light fixtures, and hand-carved wooden figures. The entry hall was paneled in gumwood and off-white enamel, with a wall of Moravian tiles made by Henry Mercer of Doylestown, Pennsylvania, surrounding a welcoming fireplace. The

white tiles of the original floor were stained a dull yellow, and its black lozenges replaced with green tiles with an unusual fylfot design that Goodhue had found in Persepolis.[10] As well as using Mercer, or Moravian, tiles for his townhouse and later a cottage in Montecito, Goodhue used products from the same tile works in several of his clients' residences. Henry Chapman Mercer (1856–1930) was an important leader in the Arts and Crafts Movement. After graduating from Harvard he studied law before turning his attention to archaeology. The discovery of old Pennsylvania German pottery led him to the craft of tile work. In 1899 he began producing architectural tiles of the highest quality. Beginning in 1908 he built his home, a factory—the Moravian Pottery & Tile Works—and the Mercer Museum. The factory, which was modeled on the Spanish mission churches of California, is still in operation today.[11]

For his townhouse furniture Goodhue was able to use treasured pieces brought by his mother from their Pomfret home to Cambridge and inherited by him at her death in 1906. These were combined with artifacts and art that he had collected on his travels, and a few choice items that he had designed or actually made himself. The main focus of the house was the drawing room, which also served as a library, with built-in bookcases on either side of a fireplace that featured a single row of Persian-style tiles made by Goodhue himself, working every evening for three weeks (fig. 10-4). Door-height

FIG. 10-1. *Goodhue's townhouse at 106 East 74th Street, New York City. The renovation created a façade strikingly different from those of its brownstone neighbors.*

FIG. 10-2. *Goodhue's townhouse—front entrance three steps down from the sidewalk.*

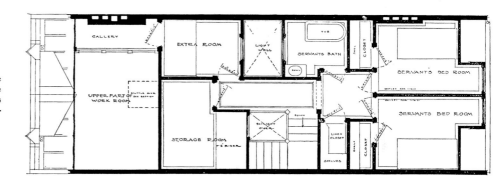

The top floor contains the servants' bedrooms and the upper part of Mr. Goodhue's workroom, which is two stories in height.

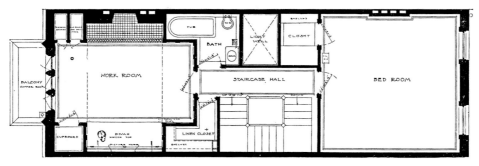

The front part of the third floor is given over to Mr. Goodhue's own personal workroom.

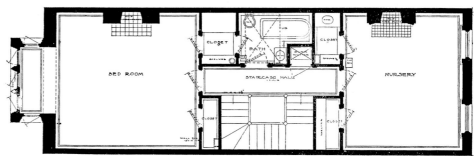

The whole of the second floor and rear of the third floor are taken up by bedrooms, bath, etc.

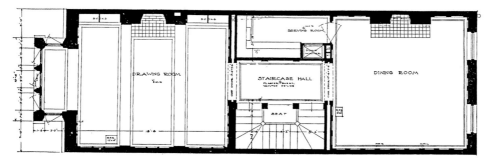

The first floor is given over to the living-room and dining-room.

Entrance hall and service quarters.

FIG. 10-3. *Goodhue's townhouse—interior floor plans.*

Fig. 10-4. *Goodhue's townhouse—drawing room with fireplace surrounded by a row of Persian-style tiles designed and made by Goodhue.*

chestnut paneling covered the walls with ceiling beams of the same material. The frieze above the paneling was papered in a William Morris–style design. According to Goodhue, all the wallpapers in the house came from England, the one in the dining room being designed by Heywood Sumner. "While the duty on wallpaper into this country is only 25%, I must warn you that I was quite staggered by its cost in both the dining room and the library."[12] The furnishings included a Martha Washington rocking chair, also known as a "lolling chair," and an upright piano whose case Goodhue had designed (fig. 10-5). Above the keyboard was a Latin inscription in "Gothic riband letters,"[13] reading as follows: JONAS CHICKERING ME FECIT, BELTRAMUS GROSVENOR GOODHUE VESTIVIT ME, DEUS AUTEM ANIMAM IN ME SPIRAVIT ANNO SALUTIS MCMVII (Jonas Chickering made me, Bertram Grosvenor Goodhue clothed me, while God breathed a soul into me in the year of salvation 1907).[14] Because of space limitations the Goodhues had chosen an upright piano over a grand, but its owner had disguised a mundane article of furniture with a

beautiful case with specially designed hardware (fig. 10-6). He had even exchanged "the black vulcanized rubber and white celluloid keys of commerce. Instead they are of boxwood and coromandel."[15] Goodhue told his friend Percy Nobbs about his piano: "Though I did design it, I regard it as one of the wonders of the world. It is a shame that I am not a finished pianist instead of a bungling, play-by-ear amateur."[16]

Adjacent to the bay window stood a grandfather clock that had belonged originally to Colonel Thomas Grosvenor (Bertram's great-grandfather) (fig. 10-7). The clock traveled back and forth between several homes of the Grosvenor family, to Ohio and back, and to New York and back. It now resides in South Carolina in the home of Thomas Hamilton, General Charles Grosvenor's great-great-grandson.[17]

The earth-tone colors of the room provided a warm, cozy setting. Books and paintings added life and color to the walls, and Oriental rugs enriched the floors. In the dining room "the plaster ceiling was richly modeled,"[18] the walls paneled, and the moldings painted green to

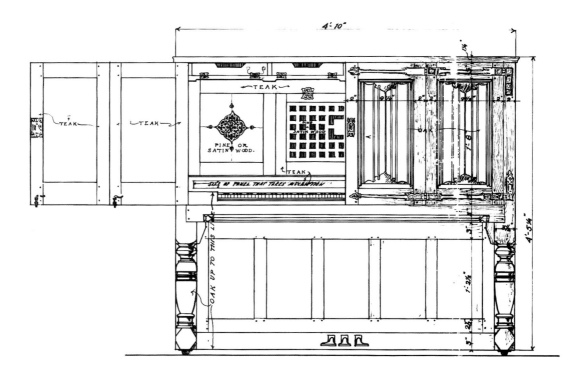

FIG. 10-5. *Pen-and-ink drawing of an upright piano case designed by Goodhue.*

FIG. 10-6. *Goodhue's townhouse—the upright piano in a corner of the drawing room.*

OPPOSITE
FIG. 10-7. *Goodhue's townhouse—bay window with the well-traveled grandfather clock at one side.*

match the Moravian tiles surrounding the fireplace.

Craighead's article stated that Goodhue's workroom was really a "glorified garret"[19] (fig. 10-8). Perhaps recalling the attic space of his Pomfret home, Goodhue could seclude himself and nurture his creative thinking, surrounded by art treasures, rapiers and guns, and hunting trophies. Light was provided by a triple window "leaded with diamond quarries. The center light is a patch of color by Mr. Harry E. Goodhue. It is a representation of the Emperor Charlemagne returning from Roncesvalles, with a quotation from the old French 'Song of Roland.'"[20] The medieval theme was enhanced by tiles incised with "knights, dragons, and centaurs in armor"[21] set among the Moravian tiles surrounding a simple fireplace opening. The andirons, which were designed by Goodhue, resided for many years in his son's home in Pasadena (figs. 10-9 and 10-10). Supporting the newel posts of the musician's gallery railing were figures by Johannes Kirchmayer (1860–1930), a Bavarian immigrant who became one of the foremost woodcarvers in America, was an important member of the Arts and Crafts Movement of Boston, and executed intricate wood carvings for many of Cram's and Goodhue's church designs. One figure represented Design seated at a writing board; the other figure represented Handicraft

his effort to explain his own beliefs, he wrote:

> For myself I regard Buddha's "Wheel of the Law" as quite as exemplary a document as the "Sermon on the Mount"—furthermore I cannot see—and have not been able to see since I was nineteen—how any Creed can be other than a personal one.
>
> You may infer from all this that I am an irreligious person but I don't think so. At any rate I have always enjoyed the designing and building of churches more than anything else because of the idea or ideal behind such.[26]

In his essay on Goodhue in the Whitaker volume, Hartley Burr Alexander quoted Goodhue as saying, "If there is a God—and there is—he, she, or it, are human pronouns, and not to be applied."[27]

Whatever his inner beliefs, Goodhue maintained that his own morality and principles had been formed without the aid of religion. Theodore Price, the father of one of his children's friends, clearly expressed what he regarded as the dichotomy of Goodhue's views:

> Your life and your character is . . . so much at variance with your attitude toward Christianity that I cannot help resenting your inconsistency.
>
> You devote your life to making the truth and beauty of Christianity architecturally articulate and yet you are continually assailing them.
>
> You send your boy to a church school because I think you realize you could not find the moral atmosphere that is there provided under agnostic auspices and yet you resent an effort to bring him affirmatively within the ranks of those whose enthusiasm for religion has made St. Paul's what it is and provided the very environment in which you have been glad to place him.
>
> You are generous, kind and good and I venture to believe, though I do not know, that a Christian ancestry has made you the man you are.[28]

Goodhue composed a reply to Price but never mailed it. Here is an excerpt:

> But neither life nor character, nor decency, nor truth, nor any of the virtues have anything to do with Christianity or indeed with any religion. Practically every principle of pure morality was well known, better expressed, and by those who were familiar with them, as well practiced before the Christian era as they have been since.[29]

Goodhue may not have followed any religion or believed in the teachings of the church, but he had a vast knowledge of church history, architecture, and ritual, and a love for religious paintings. Valuable and sentimental acquisitions from his travels adorned the walls of his home. A large canvas, the *Adoration of the Magi*, painted in 1602 by a Peruvian, Juan Coello, filled a wall at one end of his attic studio; a painting of St. Anthony

in the form of a medieval carpenter kneeling on a sawhorse. Sculptures of angels holding models of churches had been made into bronze light fixtures by Lee Lawrie (fig. 10-11). The heart of the space was a "great table or desk" with a "drawing board on it, bare when we saw it save for immemorial marks and scratches and the charrings from uncounted generations of cigarettes." Craighead saw this table as "the plain of creation,"[22] where many creative battles would have been fought and won.

Goodhue's selection of art, mostly religious, was indicative of the contradictory nature of his personality. It was well known that Goodhue considered himself "anti-religious and strongly anti-Catholic."[23] Yet, according to Christine Smith, he was "a deeply spiritual man" who was extremely reticent about revealing his inner self and private beliefs.[24] Goodhue wrote several letters to the Reverend Samuel Drury, headmaster of St. Paul's School, about his son Hugh attending confirmation classes.[25] In

of Padua holding the infant Christ in his arms, the purchase of which was recorded in *Mexican Memories* (recounting his first trip to Mexico),[30] had a place of honor over the mantel in the living room where it had been carefully framed to fit the space; near the front window "the gold ground of an old Madonna, evidently very early Sienese, shame[d] all modern gold"[31] (fig. C-57). Various Flemish and Italian Adorations, more Madonnas, and "a good old copy of an Adoration by Bernhaerdt van Orley,"[32] as well as his own paintings, completed Goodhue's art collection (fig. 10-12).

Goodhue's most prized wall hanging was probably Colonel Thomas Grosvenor's certificate of membership in the Society of the Cincinnati, signed by General George Washington.[33] The society was formed in 1783 and took its name from the Roman citizen-soldier Lucius Quinctius Cincinnatus.[34] The inscription on the certificate states that the society was "instituted by the Officers of the American Army, at the Period of its Dissolution, as well to commemorate the great Event which gave Independence to North America, as for the laudable Purpose of inculcating the Duty of laying down in Peace Arms assumed for public Defence, and of uniting in Acts of brotherly Affection, and Bonds of perpetual Friendship, the Members constituting the same." Goodhue was invited to join the Connecticut branch in 1911, but he was not sure if he "could establish any right to membership"[35] because only direct male or collateral male descendants could inherit the certificate, medals, and other honors of the society. He was also concerned that it was too expensive.

In February 1915 the secretary, Bryce Metcalf, again asked Goodhue to consider membership. This time Goodhue, who really yearned for the honor, decided to

ABOVE
FIG. 10-9. *Goodhue's townhouse—above the fireplace are carved figures of Design and Handicraft supporting the newel posts of the gallery railing.*

FAR LEFT
FIG. 10-10. *Andirons designed by Goodhue are still in the family.*

LEFT
FIG. 10-11. *A bronze light fixture made by Lee Lawrie for Goodhue's workroom.*

give it a try. Little did he know that it would take him a year and a half to obtain waivers from all the "lost heirs," who had a prior right because they were more direct descendants of Thomas Grosvenor.[36]

In July 1916, Bryce Metcalf informed Goodhue that he had been "duly elected an hereditary member of the Society in right of Colonel Thomas Grosvenor"[37] at the annual meeting held on July 4, 1916, in Hartford, Connecticut. The annual cost of membership was $250. In February 1917, Goodhue attended his first dinner, describing the occasion in a letter to Cecil Brewer: "Last night I dined with the Cincinnati Society, it being the 185th birthday of its first President, to wit, the late General Washington."[38] He went on to explain to his English friend the origins of the society:

> It was founded by General Washington and his officers, and is restricted to the eldest sons of the eldest sons of the original members unless, as in my own case, this line has died out, and those more nearly in succession waive their rights.
>
> It has been assailed ever since its beginning as un-American and tending to establish a noble caste. However this may be, those of us who belong are tremendously proud, and it certainly is as fine a body of men . . . as anyone could wish to see.[39]

Back in 1911, at the age of six, Goodhue's son had developed a nervous twitching in his shoulder following a mild case of scarlet fever. A New York specialist recommended country air, and in the midst of the Christmas season poor Hugh (called Hugo by his family) was dispatched to Westchester County to stay with a local doctor and his family. This was followed by a trip to Bermuda with his mother. Much to the relief of his parents, his condition soon improved.[40] However, the experience added to Goodhue's concerns for the health of his family, and he decided they would all benefit from more time spent in the country. After renting property on the Palisades for several summer seasons, Goodhue decided to buy a country place.

In May 1913 he began inquiring about property belonging to a Mary Collyer on the border of Briarcliff and Ossining[41] in the Hudson Valley area of New York State not far from the river. Goodhue's lawyer, Henry Gennert, had reservations about the purchase because of a "lost heir," making it difficult to obtain clear title. However, by November 1913, Goodhue was the new owner. In a letter to his client, Gennert explained that "the property consists of about thirty or thirty-two acres of land situated on both sides of the road leading from Ossining to Chappaqua."[42]

Goodhue sent Cecil Brewer a vivid description of his "lordly domain":

It is at Briarcliff, about thirty miles north of here, reachable in about an hour by train and in almost the same time by motor; consists of thirty odd acres . . . with a good little brook, a piece of woodland and bully house site 500' up and the like; also on a little triangle of land across the highway a stupid old house dating from about 1820, clapboarded and green blinded, which I am now engaged in patching up and adding to. It will contain a large living room, dining room, kitchen, pantry, store room, one large and one small servant's bed room, servants' bath, servants' porch, large veranda on the ground floor, and five bedrooms, two baths and a dressing room for Madame on the next. It will never be pretty but should be comfortable and some day I will build a Breweresque Fives-Courtsy type of house I really long for and cannot live without.[43]

Goodhue was referring to Brewer's design of a house in Pinner, Middlesex, called the Fives Court. The client, furniture designer Ambrose Heal, was an exercise fanatic and insisted on having a lawn-tennis court and a court for fives (a British handball game).[44]

Before Goodhue could begin work on the ambitious alterations outlined in his letter to Brewer, he had to deal with a water problem. A water and sewage company reported, "The dug well just west of the farm house contains contaminated surface water, and should not be used for drinking." One solution was an "extension of the village water mains . . . for a distance of about 3700 feet along public roads. The cost of such extension would be for a 4" main about $3,000, exclusive of rock excavation."[45] Goodhue was aghast at the possible expense. Although the previous owners must have become immune to the polluted water, this was not a situation Goodhue could risk. Determined to overcome the limitations of a well that was less than 10 feet deep, Goodhue hired a company to dig deeper in the hopes of finding uncontaminated water. He reported to Brewer:

> Briarcliff isn't proving the unalloyed satisfaction I had expected. . . . Anyhow, with three bathrooms in the house and with two growing children, it became evident that more and better water was needed, the result being an artesian well. For something over 100 feet the drill bored daily through the driest of dry earth and rock at $3.00 per foot. The minute I am sure of water, I am going to go ahead with the house but if the drill is to go much deeper, there won't be any money left to alter the house.[46]

By the time he wrote to Brewer again, the drilling had met with success:

> At 142 feet, behold, there bubbled forth, twenty gallons per minute of something analyzed and absolutely guaranteed to be two parts hydrogen and one of oxygen, with only a trace of wholesome mineral salts. It is a comfort to know that I can offer you not only food and shelter but also an occasional bath when you next come to America.[47]

FIG. 10-13. *Pen-and-ink drawing of Goodhue's proposed country house on the border of Briarcliff and Ossining, New York.*

Goodhue gave more details of the alterations to his cousin Constance:

> It was a very pretty old farmhouse, little more than a shanty. I lifted the roof, put on two porches one on each end with sleeping porches above and a tail for the servant's quarters, tacked wire lath right on to the old clapboards and cemented the whole, etc. Now the house is very comfortable . . . but every vestige of its former attractiveness seems to me to have gone.[48]

Although he termed the house "as ugly as sin," they had "what our millionaire neighbours have not—an adequate supply of water."[49] In 1915, Goodhue purchased an additional strip of 45 feet, which included a garage and other buildings. In spite of not liking farming, he spoke of fooling with the farm for the rest of his life, but despaired of achieving any measure of control over the land:

> My only crops are golden rod, dandelion and Michaelmas daisies. . . . All my stone walls are ruinous and covered with poison ivy, a plant that doesn't touch either Hugo or me. . . . I have a little wood . . . but even here the chestnut trees, that were the chief glory, are all dead, thanks to some eager botanist who, some years ago, introduced some Japanese chestnuts and their "little Fleas" with them.[50]

Goodhue's original ambition had been to tear down the old farmhouse and build a new house. In response to

Brewer's compliments on the 1914 publication of *A Book of Architectural and Decorative Drawings*, he wrote:

> The fear assails me that you have mistaken "A house in Briarcliff" in the "Me book" [i.e., *A Book of Drawings*] for *the* house in Briarcliff. The one in the book represents what I should like to have (and there are plans, elevations, sections and everything else,—enough to obtain an accurate and wholly impossible estimate, of course).[51]

Unfortunately, the plans have not been found, but from the published sketches we see that Goodhue designed a simple and tasteful two-story country house to be built of stone, possibly local Manhattan schist, which he used for the 1918 Philip Henry house in nearby Scarborough described in chapter 8 (figs. 10-13 and 10-14). The roof would have been of slate, the windows leaded with stone mullions and copings. A gently arched entry would probably have been made of limestone, and the balconies or sleeping porches would have had decorative wood or stone balustrades. The style was reminiscent of an English country house, something that his friend Cecil Brewer would have designed. It was unpretentious but elegant, rustic in its materials but refined in its detailing. Above all it would have provided his family and guests with a warm and welcome retreat from the hectic atmosphere of the city. Until this dream could be realized, Goodhue took great pleasure in possessing a comfortable, converted farmhouse furnished with family heirlooms where he and his family could benefit from

Fig. 10-14. *Pen-and-ink drawing of Goodhue's proposed country house—garden view.*

the country air and he could teach his offspring to fish and explore the woods as he had done as a child.

Ever since Goodhue had designed his friend Waldron Gillespie's estate in Montecito, he had been enthralled with that coastal community. Since his San Diego initiation as an architect well versed in Spanish Colonial designs, Goodhue had garnered commissions in Hawaii and a growing number of projects in California. In addition to the Marine base and Naval Air Station for the government in San Diego, Goodhue was in the process of planning a campus for the California Institute of Technology, had begun work on a central library for Los Angeles, had completed working drawings for a cathedral and hospital complex for the Episcopal Diocese of Los Angeles, had been discussing several projects in Riverside,[52] and had completed the Santa Barbara Country Club and the Dater house in Montecito, the Coppell house in Pasadena, and a church in South Pasadena. Not all of these projects came to fruition. Goodhue fell afoul of the Episcopalians over costs, and his contract for the cathedral and hospital was canceled;[53] the Riverside projects never reached the drawing boards. However, there were other clients waiting in the wings.

The work in progress and in the planning stages required many trips to California, or a stop on the West Coast en route to Hawaii, with an occasional holiday for the family added to the schedule. On several occasions the Goodhues stayed at the "Gillespie Place"; other times they took rooms in a hotel resort in Santa Barbara,

or, if Goodhue was on his own, he stayed in Los Angeles, sometimes with the Coppells or his Caltech friend Arthur Fleming. However, the dreamer had been envisioning "a sort of Italian-Spanish *podere* on some foothill slope, but nothing is available."[54] Then in the summer of 1918 he found "a very great buy,"[55] which he told Cecil Brewer about in a letter written in August:

> I have bought a real place here, some 12 acres, with quite wonderful 35-year-old planting, with wonderful views, and set precisely where it ought to be, though not quite in accordance with my ideal. . . . In one corner is, or rather was, since it is largely demolished now, an "old adobe." There is sentimental value attached to adobes . . . consequently I am rigging up our old one,—it was actually a stable,—into a cottage by means of a stone addition and some old roof tiles I found on one of the outbuildings. On the ground floor there will be a not very large living room, two bed rooms and bath, a combined kitchen and laundry, pantry, servant's bed room and bath, and the so-called "screen porch"—an absolute necessity in this part of the world,—while upstairs there are two more bedrooms, bath and a store room.[56]

Goodhue tore down an old house on the property, which he referred to as "a terror," and used the lumber in the conversion of the stable into a cottage (fig. 10-16). He raised the roof and virtually rebuilt the structure, as he did for his farmhouse in Briarcliff, adding a servant's bedroom off the kitchen and two separate additions. One addition (to the east of the kitchen) consisted of a stor-

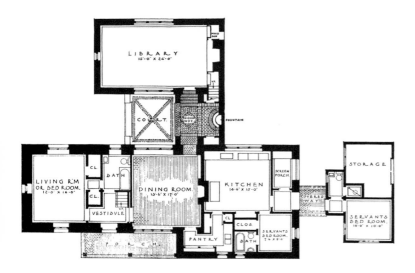

Goodhue's letter to Brewer expressed his delight that the Brewers were finally coming to America. He promised to meet them at the dock, to take them to his country place in Briarcliff, and then to bring them out to Montecito. Brewer had been ill and Goodhue was sure that the trip would do him good, especially the warm, dry climate of California. Sadly, Brewer died in November 1918, before the planned visit could materialize.

In the same month a letter to Peake Anderson, one of his former employees, expanded on his excitement at acquiring property in Montecito:

> This summer I bought a very beautiful place at Montecito in California where I have changed the old adobe stable in one corner into a very attractive cottage to occupy while I formalize and correct the present gardens which are dreadful in shape though magnificently planted in old stone pines, cypresses, etc. This cottage I propose to live in while the gardens are in progress and while I build the main house, build, that is, if Allah is good and brings me in commissions enough to pay for it. Of late I have been sitting up way into the night, after my fashion of ten years ago, over the design for this house. It's about 170 ft. long, by about 40 ft. deep, all of whitewashed stone (possibly inside as well as out) and without one particle of ornament beyond a little semi-Spanish wrought iron work. It probably never will be built, but at least it's fun to do and certainly good practice to see how good a design can be made without recourse to ornament to pull things together with.[61]

age room and a second servant's bedroom (fig. 10-15). At the back of the main cottage, Goodhue built a one-story stone structure to serve as a large library. Both additions were linked to the main cottage by covered ways, with a courtyard space between the library wing and the main house. The passage to the library, which Goodhue also referred to as a living room, featured a fountain in a niche with a statue by Lee Lawrie. "It's a pale green bronze Venus, standing in a shell. She's very attractive and her costume indicates distinct readiness to take a bath"[57] (fig. C-58). Goodhue gave Waldron Gillespie more details of the sculpture:

> The other day Lydia and I went around and had a look at the little bronze figure for the wall fountain that comes in the covered recess between the present dining room and the new room. Personally I am wholly delighted with it. Lawrie's theory was that the figure, though representing quite frankly a Venus . . . should not attempt to rival the glories of the best Classic period but should rather look as though she had been dug up in Spain, the product of the last period of the Roman occupation, hence her wrists and ankles are a trifle heavier than would be the case were she the real thing.[58]

The library itself had a coffered ceiling (fig. 10-17) and a fireplace surrounded by Moravian tiles interspersed with pictorial tiles telling the story of Christopher Columbus discovering the Americas (fig. C-59). On either side of the fireplace were built-in bookcases, with one bookcase that pivoted to reveal a hidden staircase to the roof. The furnishings were mostly antique: "I have been ransacking antique shops, including my own house, for its furnishings which now are either on their way or about to be shipped."[59] Goodhue named his cottage La Cabaña at least temporarily, he told Ruth Baldwin (fig. C-60).[60]

Writing to Clarence Stein, one of the many graduates of the New York studio who went on to establish successful practices of their own, Goodhue reported on the activities of the office "while the boss himself has taken to drawing again (to preposterous hours at night) on a possible (or rather quite impossible) palace for himself at Montecito"[62] (fig. C-61).

The architect's late-night sessions produced several alternate floor plans, notations of dimensions and calculations,[63] and two stunning renderings in watercolor and pastels. The day scene showed two simple cubes or wings, linked by an arcaded wall framing a tiled-roof center section. On the first floor three arched doors opened onto a patio with a reflecting pool aligned with the central axis of the house and bordered by pathways and flower beds. In contrast to this presumed garden elevation, a night-scene rendering illustrated the more formal front view with the house elevated on a plinth (fig. C-62).[64] The first floor retained the arched-window scheme with a line of open balconies divided by square columns above. This was a house that blended Southwest adobe with Spanish features. The massing and proportions showed Goodhue at his best. There was no need for decoration because the forms, square walls contrasting with arched openings and flat roofs with a tiled hipped roof, were sufficient. As

FIG. 10-17. *La Cabaña—library with coffered ceiling and fireplace with tiled surround.*

with all of Goodhue's work, there would be refinement in the details and in the controlled use of wrought iron for balconies, door hardware, or interior fittings.

This would be Goodhue's dream house, his "castle in Spain," the culmination of his architectural development, an expression of all his efforts to free himself from historical repetition, from traditional guidelines, from the use of ornament to bring cohesion to a mixture of inspirations. There was no partner, no client, no clergy, no vestry, no committee to satisfy or hinder his personal inclinations and design expression. Here Goodhue was free of all obligations, except what would work for himself and his family, and what pleased him aesthetically. All his imaginary places, his unbuilt hilltop castles, and his basic adobe designs could be brought together to influence this personal statement. To his friends and colleagues, he expressed a fear that he would never have the money to build his Montecito retreat.

Chapter 11

GOODHUE'S NEW YORK STUDIO

1911–1924

After 31st of December this office, which you have never seen and which will paralyze you with its gorgeousness, will become the office of Bertram Grosvenor Goodhue.

—BERTRAM GROSVENOR GOODHUE[1]

The previous chapter provided a description of Goodhue's home life and of the houses that he took such pleasure in acquiring and creating for himself and his family. Now by visiting Goodhue's New York studio we can, like the *New York Times* reporter who was fascinated to find an unusual setting that was more residential than commercial, gain a glimpse into the working life of this eminent architect. We will also discover how the reception room provided an exhibit space for the various craftsmen that Goodhue used in his work, and how strong was his support of the Arts and Crafts Movement.

When Cram, Goodhue & Ferguson opened a branch in New York City in 1903, their office space was located at 170 Fifth Avenue. As their business grew, Goodhue felt a need for a larger and better space. In 1911 architects Maynicke & Franke designed a twelve-story mercantile building at 2 West 47th street, just off Fifth Avenue. An announcement in *Record and Guide* described the project: "Special attention has been given to the matter of fireproofing. All doors and windows will be of metal, with floors of concrete. The elevator and toilet accommodations have all been particularly featured in the plans. The façade will be of stone to the third story, and above this there will be terra cotta and brick."[2] During construction of this building, known as the Jackson Building, Goodhue persuaded his partners that it would be advantageous to ask Maynicke & Franke to add a penthouse to the top, which Goodhue could design as an office space suited to his needs and with the best possible light. It took a year to construct the new offices, but sometime before December 1912, Goodhue and his group moved in.

With a whole floor at his disposal, Goodhue was able to plan the space with the main offices, drafting rooms, and reception room having large windows, augmented by skylights over the north-facing drafting room and the lobby (fig. 11-1). Two small elevators opened into a brick-tiled lobby where a receptionist greeted and directed visitors. A central corridor led to the drafting rooms, toilets, and Goodhue's office and that of his secretary. The drafting rooms were spacious, with rows of large trestle tables at which the men stood or sat on high stools (fig. 11-2). A fireproof vault off of one drafting room housed all original ink-on-linen drawings.

As an article in the May 1913 issue of *Architecture* explained, "The offices are symbolic of that absence of commercialism which the firm expresses in all its work." This was especially evident in the grand reception room (fig. 11-3), "which both in size and richness, suggests the hall of some old English manor."[3] A *New York Times* reporter, who interviewed Goodhue in August 1913, was struck by such residential features as comfortable chairs around a massive table laden with magazines, richly bound books in an oaken cabinet, and a carved chest against a paneled wall.[4]

FIG. 11-1. *Floor plan of the New York offices of Cram, Goodhue & Ferguson. Goodhue designed the offices and had them built as a penthouse at 2 West 47th Street.*

The room was also designed to showcase the work of the artists and craftsmen with whom the firm collaborated. The window, which formed one wall, was especially important: "Facing the door is a great oriel window with a soft casement hanging through which streams the sunlight. Later the upper seven lights will be filled with stained glass showing the seven patron saints of architecture and the allied arts and crafts, done by the master glass workers of America and England."[5]

According to Albert Tannler in an article on the subject of stained glass and the Arts and Crafts Movement in the United States, a notable change in the art of stained glass took place at the beginning of the 1900s and was an important development in the Arts and Crafts Movement. The painterly approach and opalescent glass or "American Glass" of John La Farge and Louis C. Tiffany patented in the 1880s were superseded by a rediscovery of the art of mosaic stained glass as practiced in the Middle Ages. Four of Goodhue's favorite artists, Otto Heinigke, Harry Eldredge Goodhue, William Willet, and Nicola D'Ascenzo (1871–1954), were primarily responsible for the revival of the art of medieval stained glass. These and other artists who followed in their footsteps used colored glass to create a mosaiclike pattern, avoided obscuring the transparency of the glass by using paint only for shading and essential details, and followed the basic tenet of true craftsmanship that the designer must be involved in or at least

supervise every step of the fabrication of a window. Their aim was for the windows to become an integral part of the architecture. Harry Goodhue and others had traveled to Europe to study medieval glass methods—in particular, windows in French cathedrals. Harry's first success using antique glass was a chancel window for Cram, Goodhue & Ferguson's Emmanuel Church in Newport, Rhode Island.[6]

Goodhue wrote to his brother Harry about the latter's contribution to the stained-glass panels for his office: "As for St. Barbara, she is extremely satisfactory, I am glad to say, and now adorns the central one of the top lights in the reception room oriel."[7] In January 1915, Goodhue wrote another letter to Harry: "Willet has just set his little head of St. Dunstan in the reception room, and I am bound to admit that it is a corker; as things stand (and there is only one more to come) yours and Willet's produce the most emotion."[8] Unfortunately, there was confusion over St. Barbara. Goodhue had mistakenly assigned her both to his brother Harry and to James Powell & Sons, of London. Harry expressed his frustration and suggested that "if Powell's isn't as good as ours why can't you send it back and tell them so; get them to use St. James Allemanus, if they ever heard of him."[9]

From Goodhue's correspondence we understand that the panels were to be: St. Barbara, patron of architects (Harry Goodhue, Boston; and James Powell, London);

169

FIG. 11-2. *Goodhue's New York office— drafting room B with large windows facing west.*

FIG. 11-3. *Goodhue's office reception room, designed in the style of an English manor house.*

OPPOSITE
FIG. 11-4. *A gilded carving over the fire-place displays statues of famous church builders framing the partners' coats of arms.*

St. Joseph, patron of carpenters (Nicola D'Ascenzo, Philadelphia); St. Marinus, patron of masons (designed by Frederick Bartlett of Chicago and fabricated by Heinigke & Bowen, Brooklyn); St. Luke, patron of painters (Clayton & Bell); St. Dunstan, patron of metalsmiths (William Willet, Philadelphia); and St. James Allemanus, patron of glaziers (Harry Goodhue?).[10] This made a total of six. We are left to wonder if Goodhue was having difficulty finding a seventh saint, or a company to make another window. Regrettably, none of the panels have survived, probably because they were not permanently installed but made to hang in front of the existing glass. But during the time that Goodhue and later his Associates occupied the space, these panels must have provided first-class representations of Arts and Crafts stained-glass work.[11]

The arched ceiling, which was covered with an intricate plaster design executed by George Bankart (1866–1929) of Bridlington, England, provided another example of Goodhue's support of an important participant in the British Arts and Crafts Movement (fig. 11-5). Bankart had trained as an architect and taught at Leicester Municipal Technical and Art School before joining the Bromsgrove Guild in order to run his own plaster and lead works. Bromsgrove was an important Arts and Crafts center near Birmingham that manufactured objects in many media.

In 1907, Bankart moved to London.[12] As well as creating lead work and intricate plaster ceilings for many important buildings and country houses in England, Bankart wrote articles and books on the art of plasterwork. He despaired of modern methods of carved plaster, explaining that "by virtue of its nature, plaster was never intended to be carved, but to be modeled or cast."[13] Most of all, he advocated the return to the older methods of modeling plaster by hand, believing that the art of real plasterwork originated in the sixteenth and seventeenth centuries when the artists understood their material and its limitations. He wrote: "A true appreciation of the subtlety and beauty of plaster in decoration is best gained by working in wet plaster *in situ*."[14] Bankart also believed that the ornament should grow out of the groundwork. In 1916 the plaster artist considered coming to America, but Goodhue discouraged him because "the soft pleasant English plasterwork, of which you are the foremost exponent, is liked by only a few architects and by practically no clients. The ceiling you did for my reception room here remains as beautiful as ever."[15] Moreover, there would be considerable competition, and Bankart might find it difficult to comply with the regulations of the labor unions. In New York City, for example, the unions required that all plasterwork be modeled and executed by union labor. Goodhue admitted that he had managed to get around this requirement for his office ceiling.[16]

FIG. 11-6. *Goodhue's private office with windows looking onto a roof garden. The ceiling features sprinkler heads camouflaged as the four rivers of Paradise.*

In the same vein the wall paneling was superbly detailed. Johnson & Sherwin, a firm that Goodhue used on several projects, executed the work.[17] A telephone was embedded in a corner of the paneling, and a door to Goodhue's office was concealed on another wall. "On the entrance door is a beautiful Krasser lock, executed of finely finished hand-wrought Swedish steel. Beside the three coats of arms on the lock, the ring bears the seal of Solomon to keep out the evil spirits."[18]

In keeping with the ambience of an English manor house, the main focus of the room was a grand, Tudor-style fireplace with insignias of castles, the symbol for a builder, set in the plaster around the opening. Goodhue hoped that his use of rich colors painted on a background of burnished gold leaf for the mantel would encourage his clients to allow him to use color in their buildings. "And over the enormous fireplace was a mantel of singular interest, a mantel gay with gold, and the many colors that were the glory of ancient Gothic interiors. It bears the arms of the three members of the firm. The rich luster of the colors comes . . . from the burnished leaf gold background on which they are painted" (fig. 11-4).[19]

Cram's coat of arms had a German motto, STOLZ UND TREU (Proud and loyal). Ferguson's motto was in Latin, DULCIUS EX ASPERIS (The sweeter because obtained by hardships). Goodhue's motto, which he used in bookplates, and in insignias on cigarette cases and humidors, was also in

Latin: NEC INVEDIO NEC DESPICIO (I neither envy nor despise). However, *"invedio"* is a mistake for *invideo*.[20]

Bertram Goodhue held his ancestry in great respect and went to some trouble to select a coat of arms to which he thought he was entitled. His source was the *History and Genealogy of the Goodhue Family in England and America to the Year 1890*, compiled by the Reverend Jonathan E. Goodhue.[21] Rev. Goodhue described two coats of arms to which he felt the American branch of the Goodhue family had a claim. The first was referred to as "the 1738 Arms" granted to a Mary Goodhugh, widow of Richard Goodhugh in Seale, County of Kent, England. The second was identified as the "1790 Arms" which had been awarded to a William Goodhew of St. Paul's, Deptford, County of Kent.[22] For whatever reason, Bertram selected the 1738 Mary Goodhugh arms, described by Jonathan Goodhue as "Gules; a chevron vaire between three Talbots passant; argent; Crest of adoption, a Talbot as in the Arms; motto, Nec invedi[o], nec despicio."[23]

In niches on either side of the coats of arms were four statues representing history's great church builders identified on scroll-shaped plaques as: William of Sens, William of Wykeham, Prior Bolton, and Pugin Senior (fig. 11-4).[24]

An article in *Lutheran Church Art* grouped Cram and Goodhue with these men:

Never since the days of Prior Bolton, William of Sens, William of Wykeham and Pugin the Elder, have such men as Ralph Adams Cram and Bertram G. Goodhue been produced. . . . It was Cram and Goodhue who made the Gothic Restoration a reality. In their master hands Gothic ceased to be a fascinating study in archaeology. For the first time in four centuries it became a living thing,—vibrant with feeling. Future historians will record the names of not four, but six, great church builders: Cram and Goodhue among them.[25]

As there were three generations of Pugins involved in architecture, there could be some uncertainty about whether the Pugin Senior represented in the niche was Augustus Charles Pugin, who was the "elder (or senior)" Pugin with reference to his son, Augustus Welby Northmore Pugin, or was A. W. N. Pugin, who was the "elder (or senior)" Pugin with reference to *his* son, Edward Welby Pugin. Reference works use the terms "Pugin the Elder" and "Pugin Senior" in both these ways. But because A. W. N. Pugin was the preeminent English Gothic revivalist of the nineteenth century, whose work Cram and Goodhue looked to for inspiration and guidance, it is clear that it is he who is represented by the statue here in question.[26]

In contrast to the reception room, Goodhue's private office was quite small and unpretentious (figs. 11-6 and C-64). The room had three-quarter-height paneling on three sides, with concealed cabinets for storage and files. On the fourth side two casement windows opened onto a roof garden where Goodhue and his staff could enjoy green plants, colorful flowers, and a view of the New York skyline (fig. C-66). A Guastavino tile decorated the patio wall. The office ceiling, which was edged with a plaster decoration, had the requisite sprinkler heads, but they were far from ordinary, being camouflaged with bas-relief figures representing the four rivers of Paradise. The walls of a small private bathroom were covered from floor to ceiling in tiles with a Persian motif designed by Goodhue and manufactured by the Guastavino company (fig. C-65).

As well as being the birthplace of many exciting projects, these offices could be transformed into a setting for seasonal celebrations. During their years together in Boston, Cram and Goodhue had participated in a variety of theatrical events and had established an office party with entertainment to celebrate the Christmas season. Goodhue expanded on this practice after opening the New York office even though, as he wrote to Cecil Brewer, "I am not much of a Christian, as you know, so in a way feel a little 'out of it' when Christmas comes around, but I thoroughly approve of the sentiment behind the whole Christmas idea."[27] What began as a Christmas Eve party with an exchange of amusing gifts grew into more elaborate office revels with farcical skits

or plays put on by the staff, usually depicting some current project or event. An article in *Pencil Points* noted that one year "the play was 'The Thirteenth Floor, a Drafting Room Drama,' made up of incidents in the work of the office, which happens to be on the thirteenth floor."[28] An especially elaborate ceremony took place on Christmas Eve 1912, the year the new office space was opened (fig. 11-7): "The office had to be consecrated and bishops, prelates and acolytes, gorg[e]ous in brocaded robes, marched from room to room dedicating each by name: the lady chapel (the stenographer's room), the crypt (the vault), etc."[29] A few years later it was decided to move the celebration to January 5 to avoid conflict with other seasonal events, and so it became known as "Twelfth-Night."

In 1922, after a spoof on the activities of the office had been performed in the main drafting room, where the furniture had been rearranged to create a stage and seating for the audience, the staff and their guests gathered in the reception room. Here a Christmas tree, a log fire, soft lighting, and refreshments awaited the revelers. Lee Lawrie opened the proceedings by giving Mr. and Mrs. Goodhue a gold medal with Goodhue's likeness on one side and an outline of his greatest buildings on the other with the Latin motto PATRIAE AMOENITATEM EXTOLLIT (He elevates the pleasantness of his native land). Before refreshments could be served, there was an address from the master himself. As Goodhue introduced each member of his staff, he explained where they came from (there was an abundance of Britishers), described their special talent, and praised their contribution. To each he gave a bronze casting of Lawrie's medal.[30]

Goodhue expected and demanded high standards. He was a man who cared deeply for his staff, nurtured and trained promising young apprentices, and stayed in touch with the Britishers who left to fight for their country during World War I and with those men who moved on to become independent architects. He wrote warm letters to his personal secretary, Miss Marie Bachman, whom he described as "one of the closest-mouthed people in the world."[31] After many years of taking dictation and keeping his office in order, Miss Bachman had married one of her employer's best architects and renderers, Austin Whittlesey, in 1921. Two years later they moved to Los Angeles. Early in 1924, Goodhue had written to congratulate Mrs. Whittlesey on the birth of a son and to say that he expected to be coming out to California in April, adding that "I hope that you feel in shape to let me come and see you then, when I want to shake hands with young Mr. Whittlesey."[32]

In an appreciation published in September 1924 former employee John Moore wrote:

To be associated with Goodhue was to feel strongly his wonderful personality, his cheerfulness in the face of difficulties, and his charm. All members of his office staff were intensely loyal because of that personality which endeared them to him and to his ideals. It appeared that his one object in life was the creation of beautiful things, and he felt that the labour that should go towards their creation should in itself be carried out in happiness. To know that his men were happy in their work was of great importance to him because he knew that out of happiness would come the best they had to give.[33]

Goodhue's speech for the 1922 Twelfth-Night celebration clearly expressed this philosophy:

I can't begin to tell you how fond I am of every member of the office force,—how much I value them all, and their various abilities. Of this force I am but one, a man-in-a-blouse, so to speak, with this *difference*; that *I have the power of veto*. I believe it makes for happiness that men's work should be interesting and not always mere work, like that ruled by an "efficiency" fanatic,—therefore, it's perfectly well understood that anybody can look at books, smoke, talk and sing,—*especially* the latter. . . . And everybody is free to differ with me in my solution of any given problem (mind you, I always possess the veto power), so that, setting a man a job and then going away . . . I often come back to find my own solution drawn out, with another, and distinctly better one, alongside.[34]

This unusual studio, where most of Goodhue's great buildings were created, still exists. Fellow renters are no longer people like architect Harrie T. Lindeberg who occupied the tenth floor, or decorator Elsie De Wolfe who had a two-floor studio in Goodhue's time.[35] The building is now in the heart of the Diamond District. Goodhue's penthouse was divided into two office spaces, and until recently the medieval half, comprising the lobby, the reception room, Goodhue's office, and the roof garden, remained largely intact and unchanged.

After Goodhue's death the firm became the Bertram Grosvenor Goodhue Associates for a limited time until all of Goodhue's actual work was completed; then, by request of Lydia Goodhue ("I don't approve of having Bertram's name used after his own work is finished, and no amount of money would persuade me to give the office that privilege"),[36] the Goodhue name was dropped and the firm became Mayers, Murray & Phillip. They stayed at 2 West 47th Street until the partners disbanded in 1940 for the duration of World War II.[37] By the time the war ended, the three men had gone their separate ways. Phillip moved to California, and Murray to Rhinebeck, New York. Only Mayers remained in Goodhue's studio. After Mayers retired, a photographer leased the space. Then, from 1976 until 2003, R. O. Blechman, an illustrator and animated-film maker, lovingly restored and guarded the space until increased costs forced him to give it up (fig. C-63). Currently, Leon Megé, a jewelry designer, has taken part of the remaining office space. He is using the grand reception room as a workroom but has promised to retain the architectural features as a showplace of historic interest.

Chapter 12

THE SEARCH FOR STYLISTIC FREEDOM
1918–1924

I find some of my early architectural gods, notably among which was repetition, are disappearing, though what to substitute that shall be both beautiful and structural at the same time I haven't yet, and probably never will, hit upon.

—BERTRAM GROSVENOR GOODHUE[1]

The period of the early 1920s was an intensely busy and successful one for Goodhue. The projects on his drawing boards included churches, campuses, company towns, libraries, residences, competitions, a science academy, and a state capitol. Clients all across the country expected him to attend meetings, present designs and budgets, and oversee construction. The projects were both challenging and rewarding, and Goodhue was flattered to be in such demand. Fortunately, he had an excellent staff thoroughly schooled in his methods, but the master still needed to do the initial planning and design, and to set the tone for further development by his associates.

In order to show how Goodhue was striving to develop an architecture that would do away with allusions to particular styles and rely instead on the embodiment of sheer mass and volume,[2] some of his later secular projects will be described here. These projects show how Goodhue's experiments with a simpler architectural style that he was trying to "put over" on the Hawaiians, and was successfully implementing in his residential designs for the Daters and Henrys, became the foundation for new developments in his nonresidential work. Even his design for the chapel (1918–1928)—later named Rockefeller Memorial Chapel—at the University of Chicago, which Goodhue described as "a quite tremendous affair of a million and a half dollars paid for by Mr. Rockefeller,"[3] would break new ground in his interpretation of Gothic (fig. C-67). According to Oliver, the Rockefeller Chapel was "a stripped-down, austere, less scholarly version of his earlier ecclesiastical designs that revealed the direction but not the resolution of Goodhue's search for a new architectural expression."[4] In a thesis on his great-grandfather's work, John Rivers expressed the view that in simplifying the design for the Chicago chapel, Goodhue lost many of the essential elements of Gothic.[5] In spite of these comments, true though they may be, I find that the Rockefeller Chapel, with its wide, open nave, piers embedded in the aisle walls, minimal ornament, and windows of amber and blue-gray glass, has an atmosphere of elegance and sublimity highly appropriate for an academic institution. In fact, this project shows that the architect was testing the limits of Gothic before exploring new avenues of expression. In a letter to architect Paul Cret, Goodhue wrote: "I find its [i.e., Gothic's] forms attractive, . . . but I assure you I dream of something very much bigger and finer and more modern and more suited to our present-day civilization than any Gothic church could possibly be."[6]

Throughout his life, Goodhue had been critical of architectural schools that adhered to the Beaux-Arts style because they imposed too many rules and stymied freedom of expression. He believed that "principles are immutable but rules change. . . . In the beginning, in Greece that is, classical architecture was a matter of principles, but not of rules."[7] But, according to Goodhue, the

Romans changed this when Vitruvius devised the five orders of classical architecture, thereby imposing rules. He especially abhorred the Roman custom of using Greek elements such as columns for decoration when they had no structural purpose.

Goodhue and Cram had not been afraid, when the occasion merited it, to build in a classical style, but they did not follow all the rules. Their first neoclassical design was the Deborah Cook Sayles Library (1898–1902) in Pawtucket, Rhode Island, with bas-reliefs above the windows by Lee Lawrie. Goodhue's proposed design for a Memorial Arch at Chickamauga, Georgia (1899), incorporated classical motifs, as did his design for the Athens, Ohio, home of his cousin, General Charles Grosvenor. Waldron Gillespie's desire for a Roman villa in Montecito, California, provided Goodhue with the opportunity to explore a freer form of classicism, thus paving the way for later experiments in secular designs. In 1918, Goodhue explained to Peake Anderson: "Of course I'm not over-fond of classic work even at the best, though you will be amused to find that—due to the passage of years no doubt—I'm getting more and more classical myself."[8]

Goodhue's most novel interpretations of classicism are found in his designs for the National Academy of Sciences in Washington, D.C. (1918–1924), and the Nebraska State Capitol (1920–1932). It was George Ellery Hale, already familiar with Goodhue's work at the California Institute of Technology, and a close personal friend, who, in the spring of 1918, persuaded Goodhue to tackle the National Academy project.[9]

Hale, with his amazing energy, vision, and dedication, was the dynamic force responsible for seeing that the National Academy of Sciences and the National Research Council, formed by Hale in 1916 to provide scientific advice to the government, acquired a building of significance in place of leased space in the Smithsonian Institution. In 1915, Hale published an article in *Science* describing the proposed organization of the building and showing preliminary plans by Shepley, Rutan & Coolidge. Hale explained that "the design of an Academy building here reproduced is intended merely as a basis for discussion."[10] There were no further developments at that time because World War I interrupted Hale's fund-raising efforts.

Hale first approached Goodhue about a building for the National Academy in March 1918. By now he had the promise of funds from the Carnegie Corporation and had already discussed the project with the U.S. Commission of Fine Arts (CFA), which had requested that an architect be selected immediately.[11] In his "Notes on Proposed Building" Goodhue explained, "I worked with the idea of producing a modern and scientific building, built with modern and scientific materials, by modern and scientific methods for a modern and scientific set of clients."[12] However, numerous difficulties arose, causing the project to drag on for six years.

FIG. 12-1. *An undated sketch for an early design for the National Academy of Sciences. Goodhue probably drew this in April 1918 with a hilltop location in mind but before he had seen the Meridian site.*

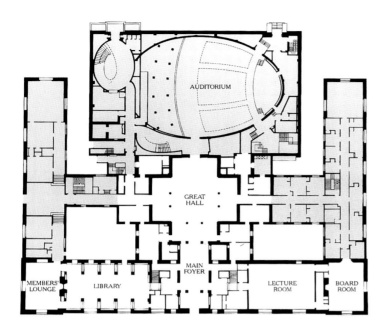

In April 1918, Goodhue visited Washington to review possible sites and reported to Hale that a site "snuggled in a depression" near the National Museum (now the Arts and Industries Building) was quite unsatisfactory and that other sites, including one on B Street, should be considered. He stated that he would begin sketch plans in accordance with Hale's requirements regardless of site.[13] On May 22, 1918, Hale wrote that "the plans you have prepared for us are amply sufficient for the present."[14] On June 11, 1918, Goodhue sent Hale a map of Washington with a site on Meridian Hill "at the end of the street that starts in front of the White House"[15] marked with a circle. He had mentioned this site in an earlier letter to Hale, but he himself had not seen it until now. Goodhue was especially enthusiastic because the site was "one of the highest points in Washington,"[16] for which he could design an impressive building at lower cost and uninhibited by the formality and styles of the classic buildings on the Mall. He wrote, "The picturesque possibilities of the place are limitless."[17] He did acknowledge that it was further away from the center of the city but noted that it was easily accessible by tram.

In the 1980s architectural historian Richard Guy Wilson discovered an undated pencil sketch by Goodhue in the Archives of the National Academy of Sciences. In his article entitled "Modernized Classicism and Washington, D.C.," Wilson suggested that this sketch was made specifically with the Meridian Hill site in mind.[18] After careful examination of the correspondence, I believe that this was Goodhue's first design for the academy, made in April 1918 *before* he had actually seen the Meridian Hill site, although he certainly had hopes

of finding a suitable hilltop. In a letter to Hale he writes of drawing this design "just as though I was working on an absolutely flat piece of paper with unlimited dimensions in all directions, making the building . . . the size it should be and seeing how it comes out."[19] Wilson described the design as a Byzantine-inspired domed building with low extending wings (fig. 12-1). In a letter to John Moore (February 1919), Goodhue wrote: "I have visualized a sort of loosely-knit and picturesquely grouped classical affair with big court yards and of very simple material. For myself I'd rather use rough stone, white-washed, than anything else but suppose this is too much to expect Washington to stomach."[20]

Although Hale appreciated the "superb architectural possibilities" of the Meridian Hill site, it was not suitable for several reasons: it had already been set aside as a park, the National Research Council (NRC) needed to be near the Army, Navy, and State departments, and in order to fulfill its promise as a museum the academy building should be easily accessible to the public.[21] In 1919, without consulting Goodhue, Hale and the academy officers purchased a much more significant location of approximately four acres on B Street between 21st and 22nd streets near the Pan American Union building.[22] Hale had already obtained an agreement from the Carnegie Corporation to give $5 million for a building and an operating endowment once a site had been found and purchased. Within a few months Hale had raised the $150,000 needed for the site through private donations; he then asked Goodhue to start work immediately on a new set of preliminary plans and elevations. He returned "the tentative plans you prepared last year for a much larger building than we can now afford to erect" with suggestions for reductions. He wrote: "The lofty dome should be omitted, but provision should be made for mounting a small coelostat telescope on the roof over the center of the hall."[23]

Not only was Goodhue devastated to have his hilltop site rejected, he was told that the budget, which he thought would be in the range of $4 million with at least $1.5 million available for the first phase of the design, had been reduced to $900,000, including architect's fees, but with future expansions still to be considered. Goodhue threatened to resign. He regarded the B Street site as flat and dull. Moreover, in the new location the academy would be adjacent to other government buildings, and would become one of the first buildings to form an appropriate background for the Lincoln Memorial, thus setting the tone for the rest of the avenue. This meant that the CFA would oversee the project to make sure that the design conformed to the 1901–1902 McMillan Plan's "Roman" city.[24]

Still resenting the loss of his hilltop site, Goodhue struggled with a new design. In early December 1919,

NATIONAL·ACADEMY·OF·SCIENCES
NATIONAL·RESEARCH·COVNCIL

FIG. 12-3. *National Academy of Sciences— south door with marble pediment. Owls guard the corners, and in the center the sun shines above a hand holding the figure of a man.*

Goodhue described the plan for the new site as "a hollow square tied across the middle by a link the center portion of which rose in the form of a Greek cross with dome ceiling."[28] Cross-axial loggias with courtyards in between would link the central building to wings forming the outer sides (fig. 12-2). Owing to the limited funds, the building would have to be constructed in phases, so Goodhue suggested delaying the front by building from the back forward. But the CFA and the academy committee wanted to see the important front façade built first.

Goodhue revised the design accordingly and was persuaded to make a presentation with some hurried perspectives. Charles Moore, chairman of the CFA, and the academy building committee voiced their approval, but much to Goodhue's shock the formal presentation to the CFA on March 26, 1920, was rejected. They requested that the façade be more classic and include a row of columns. Goodhue was outraged. In his project notes he wrote: "My attitude toward the Classic style—that is, the usual formal Classic—is very definite and very well known. The row of Corinthian columns was the last straw."[29] Again he threatened to resign, and when William Mitchell Kendall—a member of the subcommittee of the CFA that was to study the plans in more detail—confronted him at the Century Club in New York with the request that he be more classic, Goodhue replied, "I'm damned if I will."[30]

For the next eight months the project stalled. Goodhue asked for the criticisms in writing and remained obdurate. Moore appealed to Goodhue's patriotism to create a building appropriate for the architecture of the capital. Hale, fully aware of the sensitive nature of his architect and friend, worried that Goodhue

he presented two options, one design reminiscent of his original 1918 sketch described as a "treatment in the Persian style"[25] to be constructed of concrete at a cost of $1,500,000, and a design of reduced size to cost $900,000. It took a visit by Hale to Goodhue's office in New York to persuade the recalcitrant architect to develop the second scheme.[26] After reviewing the drawings, the council of the National Academy stipulated that "the building . . . for the Academy should conform more harmoniously to the style of architecture which has been adopted for other buildings of classical design now being erected in Washington."[27]

FIG. 12-6. *National Academy of Sciences, Washington, D.C., 1919–1924. This early photograph shows the reflecting pools before they were converted into flower beds.*

would withdraw. Free of the prejudices of the CFA, Hale was able to recognize the subtle classicism of Goodhue's design. He wrote: "It is thoroughly classic in feeling, and would not be out of harmony with the Lincoln Memorial, especially as the decorative treatment is purely Greek."[31]

Eventually, in November 1920, Goodhue realized that a personal and rather vague letter from Charles Moore, dated June 28, was supposed to have been an official letter "of authorization to begin work."[32] Taking into account the criticism of his architectural colleagues and aware that the earlier presentation had been done in a hurry, Goodhue now had professional renderings prepared. These included a perspective with landscaping as well as an aerial view showing the building in a parklike setting. Goodhue had made some changes to the windows in the corner pavilions and the attic, but he did not include any columns. In his previous experiments with "classic" he had progressed from freestanding Ionic columns supporting the pedimented entry porch of General Grosvenor's house in Athens, Ohio, to less obtrusive Ionic columns linked by bas-reliefs and integrated into the façade of Gillespie's villa in California. Now he was determined to move forward and design a simplified classical building without columns, especially when the columns would be purely ornamental.

Keeping in mind the restrained neoclassical architecture of Sir John Soane (1753–1837), who shocked his contemporaries by reducing "classical ornament to rudimentary grooved strips and diagrammatic mouldings,"[33]

Goodhue created the illusion of classic with a symmetrical façade divided in the center by an ornamented door (fig. 12-3). The classical theme was strengthened by a suggestion of pilasters framing the tall two-story windows and by an entablature with a rhythm of equally spaced windows topped by a copper cheneau composed of alternating owls and lynxes with coiled serpents guarding the corners (fig. 12-4). A quotation in Greek from Aristotle was incised into the marble below the cornice. The plainness of the façade was relieved by Lee Lawrie's exterior ornament, which consisted of a procession of the world's great scientists in bronze panels filling the spaces between the upper and lower windows (fig. 12-5). The landscaping included a hint of Persia in the form of three rectangular reflecting pools on axis with the main entry and lined with turquoise-colored tiles (fig. 12-6).[34]

Hale went to a great deal of trouble to find experts in the various scientific fields to help with the iconography. In contrast to the relatively simple exterior, the interior exploded with scientific symbolism that emphasized Greek and Egyptian themes. Everywhere, bas-reliefs, carvings, paintings, and tile work told the story of science. The Assembly Hall—the centerpiece of the building—had its ceiling and walls covered in Akoustolith tiles to create the best possible acoustics. These were coated with gesso so that Hildreth Meiere (1892–1961), a brilliant artist who specialized in murals and mosaics, could cover the dome, arches, and pendentives with symbolic paintings (fig. C-68). The principal scientific exhibits of the main hall consisted of a spectroscope, and a Foucault pendulum swinging over a base decorated with sun gods.

At the dedication of the building, Gano Dunn, chairman of the Building Committee, referred to the structure as a "Temple of Science."[35] When Goodhue was asked about the origins of the style, he referred to it as Alexandrian (300 B.C.–A.D. 400).[36] In a memorandum to the Carnegie Corporation, Gano Dunn wrote: "Little enough of Alexandrian civilization and practically nothing at all of its architectural style is known, so perhaps it is safe to class the National Academy–Research Council building as Alexandrian."[37] The idea of blending Egyptian elements with Greek may have originated in Hale's reference to modeling the National Academy on the most famous academies of the world, in particular the Museum of Alexandria. Such a theme also helped Goodhue to interpret history in his own way (fig. C-69).[38]

Finally, on May 12, 1921, Goodhue's design was approved. In April 1922, just as the construction contract was about to be let, Charles Walcott, a member of the Academy Building Committee, insisted, with the support of the CFA, that the specified facing material of Indiana limestone be changed to New York Dover marble. This required an additional expenditure of $150,000, which the Carnegie Corporation agreed could be taken out of the operating budget.[39] Goodhue added interest by laying the marble in an ashlar bond and following the Greek practice of "battering" the walls, making them slope inward as they rose and so giving the illusion of greater height.[40] Three factors contributed to the final success: a more realistic presentation; the appointment of Louis Ayres, a good friend of Goodhue and a fellow fisherman, as one of the replacements on the CFA for the ultraconservative members William Kendall and Charles Platt, whose terms had expired; and Goodhue's new stature as an architect following the award of the commission for the Nebraska State Capitol. In June 1923, Goodhue told Hale, who was traveling in Egypt and had been present at the opening of Tutankhamen's tomb, "The Classicists and my formalistic friends continue to say nice things about the building."[41]

In spite of this creative struggle, the National Academy project played an important role in Goodhue's search for a stylistic freedom. He had succeeded in abstracting and simplifying the formal historic classicism of Europe and imbuing the results with the kind of romantic and exotic qualities that appear in his other work. Wilson concluded that "the Academy demonstrates in its severe abstract classicism and the geometrical ornament . . . a native American source for modernized classicism, and what would be later called 'art moderne' or 'art deco.' The stylized and fanciful departures by Goodhue and his collaborators, Lawrie and Meiere, would be a source for many monumental designs in the next few years."[42]

Before completing his design for the academy, Goodhue had already begun work on the Nebraska State Capitol. In many ways the Washington project was the parent of the Nebraska structure, which has come to be regarded as Goodhue's greatest masterpiece. In desperate need of a new capitol building, the State of Nebraska, with the help of Thomas R. Kimball, a distinguished Nebraska architect, devised a competition. The program asked that submissions include the collaboration of "Architect, Sculptor, Painter, and Landscapist" and, surprisingly, set no boundaries regarding "plan, scope, style, type, or material."[43] The timing was perfect for Goodhue. The competition allowed him to move on from an interpretation of classicism restricted by Washington's requirements to "an opportunity of unparalleled freedom."[44]

The jury of three men had little difficulty in selecting Goodhue's design from the ten final submissions. Washington, D.C., architect Waddy Wood described the judges' reaction: "When we came into the room where the designs were displayed, we all ran over to the design with a tower. It took all of us, right off the bat! . . . We looked at each one for awhile, but always came back to that tower. It was the easiest judgment of my experience."[45] Lincoln is laid out in a grid street pattern, and the Capitol site is at the intersection of two main avenues surrounded by a level landscape. Goodhue devised a cross-axial plan, a more advanced version of the National Academy plan, to align with the avenues (fig. 12-7). A Greek cross intersected a square base 437 feet on each side. The base rises in stepped masses, two and a

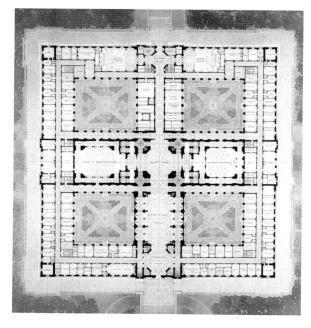

FIG. 12-7. *Nebraska State Capitol, Lincoln, Nebraska, 1920–1932—ground plan.*

FIG. 12-8. *Nebraska State Capitol—first stage of construction with old Capitol still in place.*

half stories in height, to support the central 400-foot domed tower that would dominate the building and the city around (fig. C-70). The tower would provide the most space for the least amount of money. Goodhue had succeeded in creating something different, a structure that was a radical departure from the traditional "veneered order and invariable Roman dome."[46] In his text accompanying the competition drawings, he explained: "So, while the architectural style employed may, roughly, be called 'Classic,' it makes no pretense of belonging to any period of the past. Its authors have striven to present . . . a State Capitol of the Here and Now, and naught else."[47]

Oliver found it ironic that Goodhue had finally managed to use one of his fantasy towers, like the one dominating his imaginary city of Traumburg, Bohemia, as the central feature of a building founded on classical precedents. Goodhue had incorporated a classical plan and used certain classical elements, such as columns supporting the dome, but with a freedom and abstraction that defied a true representation of the classical language.[48] The presence of a tower and the cruciform layout of the main floor with its navelike passage leading from an entry vestibule to a rotunda make the building seem like a secular cathedral and remind us that Goodhue was trained as a church architect.

The news of the competition's outcome was received at Goodhue's office on June 26, 1920. The office staff immediately telephoned their master, who was in Montreal at the time. Goodhue reported the incident to his brother Ned: "I was called up in my room from New York to hear the entire office giving three cheers over our having won the Nebraska Capitol competition. Let me tell you that this means 6% commission on $10,000,000. Add this amount to Yale, to the Academy of Sciences, and our other work, and we have close to $30,000,000. I know you will rejoice with me."[49]

The construction of the new Capitol was to be executed in five stages, making it possible to build around the old Capitol while it remained standing and occupied, a procedure that allowed the state to avoid renting temporary office space (fig. 12-8). Construction of the first stage began in November 1922. By February of the next year both the project and the architect were under investigation. Goodhue discovered that he had made a dangerous enemy in George E. Johnson, who was the State Engineer and Secretary of the five-member Capitol Commission. Johnson wanted to be put in charge of the construction, but Goodhue persuaded the other commission members "to award the work to a general contractor,"[50] someone with more experience in construction management. "From the date of this particular meeting he [Johnson] has been 'after me' with undying hatred."[51]

Johnson's trumped-up charges against Goodhue were preposterous: "dishonesty followed by gross negligence and gross incompetence."[52] The charges covered the full range of the project from alterations on the drawings to specifications being written in such a way that the work could not be bid competitively and would cost the state more than necessary.[53] To some extent this was true because Goodhue wanted the materials and the construction to be of the highest quality, and only certain craftsmen qualified. The sculptural program had been designed in collaboration with Lee Lawrie, and only Lawrie was capable of executing it. Goodhue had designed vaulted ceilings for the corridors of the first and second floors. For these he specified tiles that were both structural and sound-absorbent. Only one firm, the Guastavino company of New York, made such tiles and knew how to install them. Johnson also accused the architect of specifying inferior limestone, because it had too many variations. Goodhue had purposely selected three different grades—each one met the required structural specifications—in order to obtain subtle variations in color and in the amount of fossilized incrustation. Goodhue, who hated public speaking, "took the case in my own hands and made my own summing up. You will be amused to learn that I have developed into quite an impassioned and vigorous orator."[54] The committee appointed to investigate the charges found nothing wrong, though it faulted Goodhue for "not having the best interests of the state at heart."[55] Johnson, undeterred and determined to get his revenge, introduced a bill into the Legislature to have Goodhue dismissed. The bill was defeated by a vote of 49 to 40.

Goodhue related this dreadful experience in a long letter to Alderson B. Horne, an English friend, living in London: "Now I am completely exonerated, and of course, going on with the work. All the best people are saying, and all the best papers printing, very charming and flattering things about me; but the truth is the experience has been horrible. I feel years older than I did and am not sure the thing is over. Mr. Johnson is such a power that it is quite conceivable he may run for, and be elected, Governor."[56] In spite of this specter, Goodhue remained confident that the people of Nebraska would be satisfied: "I expect the first [section] . . . will impress the people and make them realize that I have done and am doing a good piece of work for them for a reasonable price and that the whole thing has been carried out with absolute honesty."[57]

The extensive iconography of the Capitol was outstanding. Goodhue assembled a brilliant team of artists and craftsmen sympathetic to his overall design to carry out a program that recorded the history of law and the geography of Nebraska, along with the life and lore of its people. Hartley Burr Alexander (1873–1939), professor of philosophy at the University of Nebraska, devised the iconographic scheme and composed the inscriptions, Lee Lawrie created the sculpture throughout, Hildreth Meiere designed the mosaic work (fig. C-71), and Augustus Vincent Tack (1870–1949) painted the murals of the Governor's Suite.

Several changes were made during the design development phase: the client changed the orientation from west to north; the size of the base was increased by 40 feet per

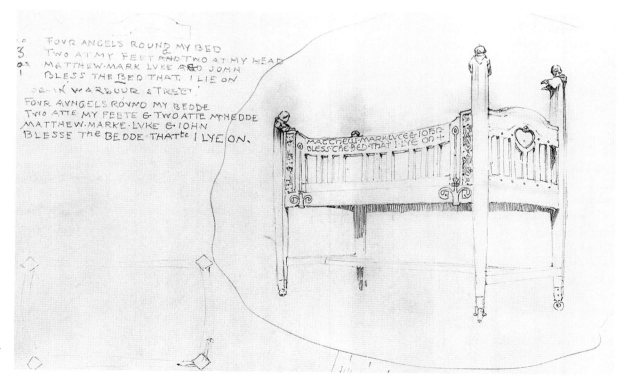

FIG. 12-9. *Goodhue's drawing of a child's crib with the four posts terminating in angels.*

side; the main entrance was changed from a flat front to a high arched recess between massive piers; the lines of the tower became simpler and bolder, with the main shaft terminating in four octagonal turrets in place of cupolas mirroring the main dome; and in keeping with the overall streamlining effect, Lawrie's sculptures, which were shown as three-dimensional in the competition drawings, became integrated with the substance of the structure. Goodhue had once drawn a child's crib with angels growing out of the four posts (fig. 12-9). In the Chapel of the Intercession, he had designed a carving of two angels growing out of the stone chancel parapet.[58] Now Lawrie created figures, like the statues of the lawgivers Solon, Solomon, Julius Caesar, and Justinian, that became extensions of the stone piers above the south entrance (fig. C-72). The only freestanding figure was the 19-foot-tall Sower with his sack of grain, standing on the pinnacle of the tower's dome (fig. 12-10).

Goodhue gave to each member of his artistic team the freedom of expression that had been awarded him in this project and had given him the opportunity to radically alter his architectural philosophy. This was also the first project for which Goodhue had given in to the recommendation of his engineers and forsaken the purity of masonry construction for a tower dependent on a skeleton frame of steel. In his revolutionary design for the Capitol, Goodhue had managed to create for America a building form that was both monumental and beautiful, and would affect the design of future tall buildings.[59] Renderings by Hugh Ferriss of Goodhue's proposed Convocation Tower in Madison Square, New York City, and the firm's submission for the Chicago Tribune Tower competition provided tantalizing images of Goodhue's future skyscraper designs. Had he lived, would he have overcome the problem of making a tall building both beautiful and profitable? By the time the Nebraska State Capitol was completed in 1932,[60] city skyscrapers were becoming the norm.

Among Goodhue's last and most important projects were two libraries. He was especially pleased to have won the commission to design the Sterling Memorial Library for Yale University, the alma mater of his famous ancestor, Colonel Thomas Grosvenor, and the university that Goodhue would have wished to attend if he had been given the opportunity. Goodhue reported on this new project to Sir Giles Gilbert Scott: "Of course, it has to be in the 'Gothic manner.' Anyhow, most of the other buildings at Yale are. . . . I've lost my taste for 'straight' Gothic, so I'm hoping to 'put over' something that won't be, although it will look like, Gothic. Burn a candle for me to St. Anthony!"[61] As with his scheme for Chicago's Rockefeller Memorial Chapel, Goodhue's design for the library was considerably simpler and more severe than Yale's existing Gothic buildings.

FIG. 12-10. *Nebraska State Capitol—the Sower ready to scatter his grain to the four corners of Nebraska*

In March 1924, Goodhue reported on the status of his architectural development to the British architect and writer William Lethaby, whom he held in great respect:

I regard myself as, in a sense, your disciple; at any rate, I try faithfully to have my work reflect the theories that, from reading your books, I think you hold. Next month I shall be 55, and for almost 35 of these years I have been working at architecture doing all sorts and kinds of dreadful things,—Classic, Gothic, and Goodness-Knows-What—and I still do. However, my Gothic is no longer anything like historically correct, and my Classic . . . is anything but book classic. . . . At Los Angeles, I have a Public Library in the same strange style, or lack of style, I have been telling you about.[62]

Goodhue's first design for the Los Angeles Public Library was done soon after the completion of the Panama-California Exposition in San Diego. Not surprisingly, the drawings showed a Spanish-style building with a tiled dome and arched openings. However, the necessary funds were unavailable until 1921 when the commission was revived. During this interim Goodhue's architectural ideas had changed. As he explained to Lethaby, he was moving away from historical forms of Gothic, Classic, and Spanish. The new design replaced the Spanish-style dome and rounded arches with more austere, cubistic forms that were similar to those he had used for the Nebraska State Capitol[63] and were a further evolution of the simple adobe cubes that were the basis of the Dater design and his own proposed residence in Montecito. In a letter to his former secretary, Goodhue commented that the design had changed radically from the first scheme but that he thought it much more dignified: "The more dignity that can be injected into Los Angeles the better"[64] (fig. 12-11).

The library was sited at the intersection of four streets, necessitating public entrances on all sides. In an article published in 1927, Goodhue's supervising architect, Carleton Winslow, now with his own practice in California, gave a concise description of the interior plan, which was laid out around a grand central rotunda, illuminated by four clerestory windows (fig. 12-12): "From the rotunda, passages lead to the main reading rooms, all of which have exterior exposure and form the outer perimeter of the building. Occupying, as it were, an inner ring between these reading rooms and the rotunda are the four divisions for the general bookstack . . . rising in seven tiers to the tower space and opening on the reading rooms they serve."[65]

The rotunda terminated in a tower, which, in turn, terminated in a tiled pyramidion with a finial in the form of a hand entwined with the serpent of knowledge and holding a golden torch (fig. C-74). Other spaces housed executive offices and more reading rooms. The plan was logical and simple, with the exterior form of the building reflecting the interior space. The construction was reinforced concrete in a simple post-and-beam system, and the exterior walls were finished in stucco and the interior painted.[66]

For the iconography, Goodhue brought together his favorite collaborators, Hartley Burr Alexander and Lee Lawrie. The "Light of Learning" theme was depicted in murals and inscriptions, with portraits of various literary and historical figures enlivening the scenes. The torch of knowledge balanced on the top of the pyramidion provided the finishing touch. As with the Nebraska Capitol, Lawrie's figures grew out of the architectural elements (fig. C-75). To show that the concrete surfaces were an integral part of the building, muralist Julian Ellsworth Garnsey (1887–1969) painted his scenes directly on the walls of the rotunda and the reading rooms. In the children's room, murals depicting the twelve episodes of Sir Walter Scott's

Ivanhoe recalled Goodhue's own fascination with the knight-errant. The landscaping included Goodhue's Persian signature, three terraced pools bordered by Italian cypresses on axis with the main entrance facing Flower Street.

Construction of the library was completed by the Goodhue Associates, with Carleton Winslow as principal architect. Goodhue's innovative design garnered criticism, both favorable and unfavorable. Some writers questioned the mixture of styles, or the fact that the decoration (in the form of the iconography) prevented the building from being truly modern. Oliver's summary caught the essence of the building: "Goodhue combined the calm discipline of a classical building, the romantic spirit of Persia, a pragmatic approach to construction, and a regional vernacular to create an Arcadian vision of civic order and monumentality."[67]

By the 1970s, the need for more space initiated a movement to destroy one of Los Angeles's rare urban gems.[68] After several years of indecision, the city came to its senses and decided to save, restore, and expand its central library. In 1983, Hardy Holzman Pfeiffer Associates were hired to design an addition and plan the restoration. Work was already under way when, on April 29, 1986, a disastrous fire, set by an arsonist on the fifth tier of the book stacks, destroyed over 375,000 books, the largest patent collection in the West, and other irreplaceable items.[69] Finally, in 1993, a fully restored library and its new wing were opened, and the public could once again enjoy access to an architectural landmark, which sits like a precious gem in a forest of glass skyscrapers (fig. C-73).

An important commission that Goodhue failed to win was the Chicago Tribune Tower (announced in 1922); his entry received only honorable mention, being considered too austere for a corporate headquarters. Another was the Liberty Memorial in Kansas City (announced in 1921): Goodhue was thrilled with the design and was certain it was a winner, but it was relegated to fourth place, probably because the solution did not adhere strictly to the program. Talbot Hamlin wrote about Goodhue's scheme for the memorial in glowing terms: "In its piled majesty there is no dictation of forms by a priori styles. Rather, the free classic details flow naturally from the mass. It is the mass composition that dominates; a mass conceived with a tremendous sense of climax, so that the whole has an austere and tragic emotionalism characteristic only of very great art."[70]

Though they were not the winning entries in every competition, it is clear that the projects described in this chapter, both built and unbuilt, marked an important change in Goodhue's career. Maintaining his respect for history, Goodhue had cast off the bonds of the past and was exploring an architecture of bold compositions free of any particular style.

FIG. 12-11. *Los Angeles Public Library, Central Building, 1921–1926.*

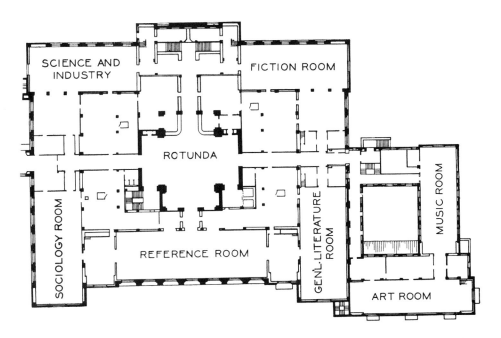

FIG. 12-12. *Los Angeles Public Library—second-floor plan.*

Chapter 13

A LIFE CUT SHORT

1869–1924

In the sudden death of Bertram Goodhue, the profession of Architecture has experienced a very great loss, and to his many friends his absence will seem incredible and irreparable. For upon the one side he was possessed of an unusual genius and upon the other of an equally unique and fascinating personality.

—C. HOWARD WALKER[1]

Goodhue did not have a robust constitution. As well as having a heart murmur, he was plagued increasingly by various health problems and was susceptible to stress and mood changes. Nevertheless, he threw himself into his work with great energy and passion. He described the intense pace of his life in a letter to Cecil Brewer:

> I am flying around every day—and this season of the year most of the night—like a chicken with its head cut off, answering letters, grinding out buildings . . . talking to clients, traveling all over the country, and as though this were not enough, dining out and dancing whenever my wife sees fit to so order.
>
> When I get home about seven o'clock, I am almost too tired to eat even at home, yet on the average . . . four nights out of the seven, I have to get into evening clothes and go out and talk to a lot of gibbering fools, usually finishing up by ripping up rugs immediately after coffee and dancing . . . like idiots until long after the time when respectable people have gone to bed. . . . Last night, we went to a Junior Cotillion. . . . It was not limited to juniors and there was nothing like a cotillion anywhere in sight; tangoes, on the other hand, and one steps and hesitation waltzes and God knows what not, were.[2]

Goodhue had projects under way from the East Coast, to the Midwest, to the Southwest, California, and Hawaii. He spent many hours on the train, often making use of the service of a train secretary to dictate let-

ters. He worried about being away from his office and missed the company of his colleagues and especially of his family. He smoked incessantly, and probably didn't eat or sleep well while traveling.

Goodhue's health began to deteriorate in August 1914 when a gallstone attack put him in the hospital for a week.[3] In January 1915 he started wearing glasses, and in December of that year sent a pen-and-ink drawing to a Mrs. Robert Ferguson in Tyrone, New Mexico, explaining that "it is probably my last pen and ink drawing for I find that my eyes grow less and less equal to working with the pen." Goodhue added, however, that he was exploring other mediums, sometimes using "charcoal, lithography, crayon, pencil, white chalk and last—but by no means least—a charcoal thumb and handkerchief."[4]

In February 1918 he wrote a concerned letter to his doctor about an attack of bronchitis: "Inside my chest I have a constant sensation of a small lame stone."[5] He was especially worried because of an imminent operation. In May 1918 he had surgery to repair a double hernia, probably caused by the incessant coughing. A letter to his brother Ned described the experience in detail:

> They laid me on a table. . . . The surgeon squirted some local anaesthetic into me with a hypodermic, picked up his carving knife and cut a nice little slit . . . in the middle on each side of my stomach. I watched while he fiddled around, picking up disgusting little tubes, clamping

Fig. 13-1. *Bertram Grosvenor Goodhue— a portrait taken not long before he died.*

up bleeding veins and the like. When he got through he sewed me up in what seemed to me a very careless manner. . . . The doctor said I might smoke through the operation but somehow I didn't care to. I think I must have feared that the smoke in his eyes might cause the knife to slip or something. Anyhow I had lunch and did smoke in the afternoon.[6]

Recuperation was slow and he had to give up a fishing trip with his son.[7]

During this period of ill health, Goodhue suffered two losses that affected him deeply. On December 11, 1918, at the age of forty-five, "my brother Harry who was closest to me of all in matters of taste and temperament died. . . . He died of cancer of the tonsils."[8] A month earlier one of his dearest friends, Cecil Brewer, had died. He wrote to Mrs. Brewer: "It will be an eternal regret of mine that I didn't realize as I should have the gravity of your husband's condition; the boyish cheerfulness of his letters deceived me."[9]

Despite poor health and too much work, Goodhue occasionally found time to draw and paint. In April 1919 he told his brother Ned that "I am hurrying like mad to try and finish up certain water colours for my one-man exhibition that begins, I believe, on the 10th of April. This means that I work from the time I get up . . . until I get ready to go to bed. Already I have four drawings finished and another almost so and have got to make about as many again."[10] Tragically, these watercol-

ors, along with a selection of paintings by Cecil Brewer that Goodhue had persuaded Mrs. Brewer to send over from England, were destroyed in a disastrous fire three days before the opening (scheduled for February 1920) of an exhibit organized by the Architectural League of New York.[11] This was not the first time that a fire had destroyed Goodhue's drawings. A fire at his home had seriously scorched some of his work. Then, several years later, a calamitous fire at the office of the publisher who was going to produce *A Book of Architectural and Decorative Drawings* destroyed some of the original sketches, back numbers of magazines, and even the zinc and copper plates themselves. As a result, the Boston publisher had to forgo the project. The remaining material was returned to New York, where it was cleaned and repaired as much as possible, and in 1914 another publisher produced the long-awaited book.[12]

By 1920 he was writing to friends and complaining of "getting old, fat and scant-o-breath"[13] (fig. 13-1). In January 1921, Goodhue was planning an expensive trip to Hawaii, Japan, China, and Korea with Lydia and his two children. He had already booked their passage and written enthusiastically to Hugh about the plans.[14] In late February he was suffering obscure pains, which a doctor thought might be related to his kidneys.[15] On April 16, 1921, he was operated on to remove a large stone from his left kidney, having successfully rid himself of one on the other side.[16]

FIG. 13-2. *Living room of Goodhue's apartment at 130 East 67th Street, New York City.*

OPPOSITE
FIG. 13-3. *Living room of Goodhue's New York apartment. Above the bookcase is a portrait of the Goodhues' daughter Frances painted by Albert Herter.*

Though the overseas trip had to be canceled, Goodhue was hoping to get in some fishing after his two-week stay in the hospital, and by August he was writing to his doctor to get permission to go moose hunting in Canada with Hugh: "I am getting pretty old and don't feel very energetic, even if I were perfectly sound in wind and limb which I am not, but I do want to get into the woods with Hugo before I give up entirely."[17] In early September, father and son did go to Canada "where Hugo got a fine pair of horns in true sportsmanlike fashion. I didn't shoot at all but had great fun watching him."[18] Two weeks later, Goodhue was in the hospital again to have another stone removed. He wrote: "I like hospitals; the whiteness of everything and the absence of any damned architecture or decoration is a distinct rest. Also there are pretty nurses to come in and soothe you at night by stroking your forehead."[19] In a letter to brother Ned, he explained: "Things are going well with me, lots of work coming in and I am feeling like a fighting cock even though the wound in my side still gapes."[20] The doctors had ordered several weeks of complete rest and encouraged a steamer trip. So Goodhue went to Europe for a month with his architect friend Donn Barber, where the two men rushed around visiting places of architectural interest, and Goodhue gave a talk to the Royal Institute of Architects in London.[21]

In early February 1922, Goodhue caught a bad cold during a rare snowstorm while visiting Arthur Fleming in Pasadena.[22] In April 1922, in one of his regular letters to Ned, Goodhue wrote: "As for myself, I am practically all right again. Indeed I suspect I would be absolutely all right if I could restrain my mad passion for cigarettes."[23] He told his cousin Constance that "it isn't very nice to be 53. . . . I think that I am actually at a disadvantage in not having a single grey hair in my head. . . . People expect so much more of me than they should."[24]

To make up for the canceled trip to the Orient, Goodhue took his family on a twelve-week tour of Europe from June 24 to September 17, 1922. He regarded the tour as his "Swan Song."[25] Moreover, it would help launch his daughter into adult life and prepare his son for Harvard. They traveled on the *Olympic* (George Ellery Hale and his wife were also passengers). The itinerary included Paris, where Goodhue hired a car to drive through France, Switzerland, and Italy, with stays in Milan, Venice, Perugia, Rome, and Florence. During their time in Italy, Goodhue visited marble centers to find appropriate marbles that could be used for the monolithic columns in the vestibule of the Nebraska State Capitol. On the way back they drove the length of the Corniche to Marseille, through Provence and the Midi to Paris, where they spent another week before ending the trip in London.[26]

With the children growing up and about to leave home, the Goodhues wanted to cut back on domestic help, so they decided to sell both the New York townhouse and the Briarcliff farm. The townhouse was sold in March 1923.[27] Several of the townhouses at the end of the block, including Goodhue's spectacular re-creation of a brownstone, were to be torn down and replaced with a new apartment building for which Goodhue was hoping to be the architect. He had already made drawings, but at least two other firms were bidding on the project.[28] The Goodhues moved to a large two-level apartment at 130 East 67th street (figs. 13-2 and 13-3). Cousin Con described the living room as "worthy of a palace" requiring huge pictures to fit it, one being a life-size portrait of the Goodhues' daughter Frances by Albert Herter.[29] The following year they sold the Briarcliff farm. In March 1924, Goodhue told Con:

> Although Lydia's hair is graying quite rapidly, her figure is as perfect as it always was, which is more than can be said of mine. I eat practically nothing for breakfast and drink lime water every night instead of whiskey, but . . . every time I order a pair of trousers I find my waist line two or three inches wider than before. I never claimed that romantic, personal beauty was my strongest point, but it is pathetic to feel so averse to any kind of physical effort, and to know that never again will the Canadian woods resound to the crack of my rifle.[30]

It seems clear that the pace of life, the stress of work complicated by the rigor of the Nebraska project, which Goodhue said had drawn him through a "knot hole,"[31] the constant travel, and the many illnesses, aggravated by an inability to cut down on smoking, were drawing the life relentlessly out of this great man just as he had reached the prime of his career.

On April 23, 1924, Goodhue and his wife had dinner with their friends the Everit Macys for the purpose of meeting Howard Carter, who had recently discovered the tomb of Tutankhamen in Egypt. The events of the evening were told in a letter from Frances (known as Franny) to her Uncle Ned (Commander Edward Goodhue).[32] After dinner they all went on to the theater. In the middle of the second act, Goodhue felt ill and left his seat. After a short time he came back to get his hat and coat and told Lydia that he was going home. He assured her that he was all right and she was not to come with him. Franny's letter gave the details:

> About ten minutes later when the curtain came down for a lapse of time, Mother and Mr. Carter left to telephone. He had to do it for her because it was in the men's washroom. He got Dad on the telephone, who said he had a doctor with him and was all right and for Mother not to come home. Of course she did at once. She had no money and no door key. When she got home she couldn't even

get into the apartment. . . . The doctor at that time was so busy with Dad that he couldn't leave to open the door. It took about fifteen minutes to get the pass-key. Poor Mother, can you imagine the agony of it?

> When she did get in Dad was unconscious and died very quietly soon afterwards, but he never knew that Mother had followed him home, and she keeps reproaching herself for not going at once with him, but you can understand how it happened.[33]

Later the family learned more details from Dr. Rollings, who had attended the dying architect in his last hour.

> He said that when he got here Dad was sitting in the big room, and he said he was all right [but] was uncomfortable and asked Dr. Rawlins [sic] to give him something. They went upstairs and Dad undressed himself and got into bed. Then he sat up in bed and said, "Let's have a cigarette" which they did. The doctor said he's never met a more entertaining man in his life. He told him all about meeting Mr. Carter etc. and in the middle of it he dropped back on his pillow unconscious, the way Mother found him. The doctor had given him an injection of morphine. Then he began to work on his heart. . . . But you can see that Dad hardly suffered at all compared to some of the attacks in the past. Dr. Connor came down and diagnosed it as angina-pectoris, not nervous indigestion. It seems a queer thing that none of the doctors have ever been able to warn us before! . . .

> . . . The one consolation is that Dad had such a peaceful death and he has always so dreaded horrible suffering, and angina-pectoris always necessitates that—if one recovers from the first attack. And Dad never could have stood the mental suffering of that, you know. He has never looked better in his life than he did just before he died.[34]

Goodhue's premature passing came as a great shock to his family, friends, and colleagues. The dedication of the National Academy of Sciences in Washington, D.C., was to have taken place five days later on Goodhue's fifty-fifth birthday. In a letter to Mrs. Whittlesey, his former secretary, Goodhue explained that it was to be "a very important affair in every way: Lawrie and I both in academic gowns, Mr. Coolidge on the steps."[35]

The family decided to hold the funeral service on April 26, 1924, in the Chapel of the Intercession. Though Cram was involved in the initial negotiations for the Chapel, the resulting design was entirely Goodhue's, and he regarded it as one of his best (figs. C-76 and C-77). Also, according to Franny, her father liked the vicar, Dr. Milo Hudson Gates. Franny's letter described the funeral:

> The funeral was this morning at 10.00 o'clock. Mother had Dad's casket completely covered with green and nothing but white flowers around it. The hundreds of other flowers

were back of it. Dr. Gates made the service just as short as possible and Mother didn't break down. . . . The men of the corner table at the Century Club and a few others of his intimate friends were chosen for Dad's pall-bearers. Mr. Lee Lawrie was so shocked by Dad's death that he was unable to serve and day before yesterday he sent two men from his studio down here (he couldn't do it himself) to make a death-mask of Dad and also one of his left hand.[36]

Immediately following the funeral, Goodhue's body was cremated at the Fresh Pond Crematory in New York City; his ashes were collected from there by his son Hugh two days later.[37] The family, together with Goodhue's friends and colleagues, felt that instead of having the remains buried at Pomfret, it was more appropriate to have them placed in the Chapel of the Intercession and have a suitable memorial tablet designed by his firm to mark his resting place.[38] Franny recounted their ideas to Ned:

> Dad said when we were abroad when we went to Westminster Abbey how nice it was to have all those memorial tablets there in remembrance of the different men. Of course he never suggested such a thing for himself but he naturally wouldn't.[39]

A Memorial Committee, composed of Goodhue's closest friends and colleagues, was formed to raise money for the proposed monument, which would cost $10,500. Its unveiling in the Chapel of the Intercession was planned for Palm Sunday, March 24, 1929. According to the committee's memorandum, many of the organizations with which Goodhue was associated were invited to send representatives to the ceremony: the American Institute of Architects, the Architectural League of New York, the Academy of Arts and Letters, the Royal Institute of British Architects, the Grolier Club, the Century Club, and the Society of the Cincinnati.[40]

Dr. Gates conducted the service and Frank Turner Harrat, organist and choirmaster, arranged the music, some of which was composed for the occasion. Milton B. Medary, former president of the AIA, and Royal Cortissoz, art critic of the *New York Herald Tribune*, gave brief addresses, and representatives of architectural and social organizations laid wreaths at the foot of the tomb, which contained the architect's ashes. It is not known where Goodhue's remains were stored in the five-year interim.[41]

The memorial took the form of a tomb made of Champville marble[42] recessed into the north wall of the transept near the baptismal font. Goodhue's firm, now the Bertram Grosvenor Goodhue Associates, designed the tomb, and Lee Lawrie, Goodhue's dear friend, executed the sculpture.[43]

Appropriately, the tomb and its sculptured figure recalled a medieval knight lying in state in a Gothic cathedral surrounded by symbolism depicting his life

(fig. C-78). In a booklet on the chapel, Dr. Gates described the tomb:

> The recumbent figure, beautifully rendered, is clad in his doctor's robes. At his feet is a figure of Pegasus, the winged horse, symbol of genius.
>
> The plain surfaces are adorned with castles, the symbol of builders, and the coat of arms of the Goodhue family, with its fine Latin motto: "NEC INVIDEO, NEC DESPICIO." The inscription under the motto is:

BERTRAM GROSVENOR GOODHUE MDCCCLXIX–MCMXXIV
THIS TOMB IS A TOKEN OF THE AFFECTION OF HIS FRIENDS
HIS GREAT ARCHITECTURAL CREATIONS THAT BEAUTIFY
THE LAND AND ENRICH CIVILIZATION ARE HIS MONUMENTS[44]

The arch above the tomb is adorned with bas-reliefs of the architect's greatest designs. From right to left, they are: St. Bartholomew's Church, Church of St. Vincent Ferrer, California Building in San Diego, St. Thomas Church, Los Angeles Public Library, Yale Library (not built), Nebraska State Capitol, Rockefeller Memorial Chapel at the University of Chicago, El Fureidis, Convocation Tower (not built), Chapel of the Intercession, California Institute of Technology, Baltimore Cathedral (not built), National Academy of Sciences, and West Point Cadet Chapel.

Above the arch is a Latin inscription, NIHIL TETIGIT QUOD NON ORNAVIT—"He touched nothing which he did not adorn,"[45] a fitting tribute to an architect of exceptional vision.

Following Goodhue's sudden death, there was an outpouring of grief over the tragedy of a leading architect snatched from his life's work at the moment of his greatest success, and a profusion of tributes for his past achievements.

FIG. 13-4. *Detail of Lee Lawrie's portrait of Goodhue for his tomb in the Chapel of the Intercession.*

Chapter 14

GOODHUE'S DEVELOPMENT FROM GOTHIC REVIVALIST TO MODERNIST PIONEER

Bertram Grosvenor Goodhue was an architect of victorious vision, an artist luminous
with imagination and sensitive of conscience, a workman zealous of perfection,
giving to his generation better than they knew. On his works is impressed the seal of nobility,
and men of the future, beholding them, will at once know for what ends genius is born godlike.

—HARTLEY BURR ALEXANDER[1]

Although residential commissions were only a small part of Goodhue's complete portfolio, they played a significant role, providing a parallel picture of the evolution that took place in his nonresidential work. Unlike Frank Lloyd Wright, whose association with Louis Sullivan had brought him into contact with a clientele receptive to new ideas, Goodhue, through his ecclesiastical work, had attracted clients who expected and wanted traditional designs, the Aldred residence being a prime example. However, each new domestic project gave the architect, always striving for greater simplicity, an opportunity to experiment with a different historical vocabulary.

Goodhue was called a "Gothicist" because much of his early work was derived from medieval sources, but he didn't like labels and he soon proved that he was capable of designing in any style. To all historical styles Goodhue brought his own interpretation, using only those elements that were appropriate. He captured the spirit of Gothic without copying actual images, giving his buildings a new vitality. As his ideas on architecture evolved, his use of historical forms changed, with less connection to the original source of influence. The same philosophy was applied to his residential work, where designs were based on a modern interpretation of classical, Tudor, or Spanish architecture.

Because of America's great variations in atmospheric, geographic, and cultural conditions, Goodhue concluded that it was wiser to create buildings that would fit the climate, landscape, and history of a particular region than seek to develop a uniform architectural style. In the dry, desert climate of California and the West he found the perfect opportunity to use Spanish-inspired architecture. As a result of his design for the Panama-California Exposition, Goodhue found himself in high demand. Commissions included the Coppell residence in Pasadena, where the simple adobe forms that Goodhue was developing for the mining town of Tyrone and the campus of the California Institute of Technology were combined with a touch of the elaborate Churrigueresque ornamentation of the main exposition building. But the Coppell residence and the Caltech buildings were the last ones to have elaborate decoration. Goodhue was determined to create architecture devoid of "spinach."[2]

Between 1915 and 1918, at the same time that he was attempting to persuade the people of Hawaii to agree to the introduction of an architecture combining indigenous materials with Spanish and Southwest features, Goodhue had the opportunity to explore his new ideas in the residential design for Henry Dater in Montecito. This in turn led to the Philip Henry house in Scarborough and the projected residence for himself in

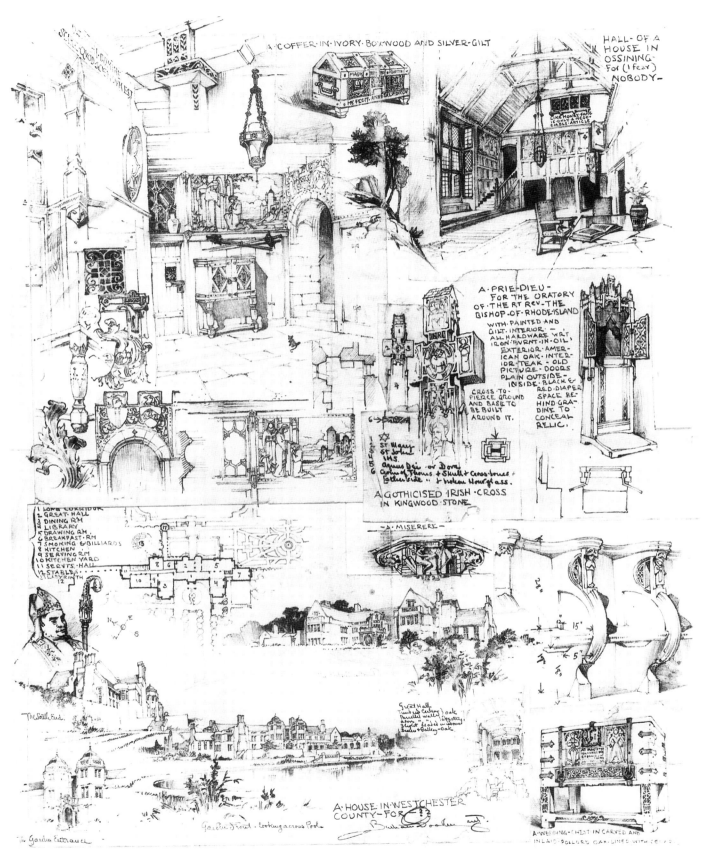

A·COFFER·IN·IVORY·BOXWOOD·AND·SILVER-GILT

HALL·OF·A
HOUSE·IN
OSSINING·
For (I fear)
NOBODY—

A·PRIE·DIEU·
FOR THE ORATORY
OF·THE RT REV·THE
BISHOP·OF·RHODE·ISLAND

WITH·PAINTED·AND
GILT·INTERIOR·—
ALL HARDWARE·WRT·
IRON·BURNT·IN·OIL·
EXTERIOR·AMER-
ICAN·OAK·INTER-
IOR·TEAK·OLD
PICTURE·DOORS
PLAIN·OUTSIDE·
INSIDE·BLACK &
RED·DIAPER
SPACE·BE-
HIND·GRA-
DINE·TO
CONCEAL
RELIC.

CROSS·TO·
PIERCE·GROUND
AND·BASE·TO
BE·BUILT
AROUND·IT.

1 ST Mary
2 ST John
3 IHS.
4 Agnus Dei · or Dove
5 Crown of Thorns + Skull + Cross·bones +
6 Other·side " + broken Hourglass·

A·GOTHICISED·IRISH·CROSS
IN·KINGWOOD·STONE

1 LONG CORRIDOR
2 GREAT HALL
3 DINING RM
4 LIBRARY
5 DRAWING RM
6 BREAKFAST·RM
7 SMOKING & BILLIARDS
8 KITCHEN
9 SERVING RM
10 KITCHEN YARD
11 SERVTS·HALL
12 STABLES·
13 LABYRINTH

N E W S

—A·MISERERE—

The South End

Great Hall
Timber Ceiling) oak
Panelled walls)
apron " " tapestry
Floor · leaded in wound
Screen + Gallery · Oak

The Garden Entrance

Garden Front · Looking across Pool

A·HOUSE·IN·WESTCHESTER
COUNTY—FOR—

A WEDDING·CHEST·IN·CARVED·AND
INLAID·POLLARD·OAK·LINED·WITH·CEDAR

195

Montecito, which would have been the crowning glory of his residential work, "without one particle of ornament beyond a little semi-Spanish wrought iron work."[3] These last three houses were especially significant, for they marked a radical change in Goodhue's philosophy: a determination to free himself from the yoke of historical inspirations and develop his own architectural language, a language of bold forms, simple lines, and plain surfaces. This new stage was evident in the last civic works of his life, the Nebraska State Capitol and the Los Angeles Public Library.

Throughout his life Goodhue practiced the principles of the Arts and Crafts Movement, believing that the industrial age was destroying beauty and that it was important to encourage individual expression and utilize handicrafts whenever possible. Goodhue told his Canadian friend Percy Nobbs that he dreamt of a craft-focused architectural practice in which his designs would be built by ten of the best men, all experts in their different fields, with the architect acting as "a humble director of the others." Perhaps, like the Aztecs of old, the architect would smooth a place in the ground and draw with his cane each section to be built. But he knew that this was impossible because "real craftsmanship today is, except in very rare cases, entirely missing and therefore a concrete block perfectly cast without any pretense of tooling is better to my mind than a 'six or eight cut' block of stone surfaced by a machine."[4] During the construction of St. Thomas Church in New York City, Goodhue experienced resistance to his requirement that the "surfacing was to be done by hand, as many different hands as possible . . . and that no two blocks should be made consciously alike."[5] Nevertheless, Goodhue was cognizant of the problem of economics. The use of traditional materials and methods, such as stone carving, was labor-intensive and expensive. When necessary, Goodhue was ready to replace a historically correct material with a modern substitute. In his own office, the "stonework" of the oriel window and fireplace was a cast-concrete imitation made by the Economy Concrete Company to show clients that this could be aesthetically satisfying.

Provided the budget was sufficient, Goodhue used the best craftsmen for the interior design of his clients' houses. There are numerous examples of finely detailed paneling, intricately modeled plaster or beamed-and-coffered ceilings, fireplaces with handmade tile surrounds and carved mantels, staircases with wrought-iron or hand-carved railings and newel posts, specially designed light fixtures, and, in his own townhouse and studio, examples of the revived art of medieval stained glass.

For all his buildings, Goodhue demanded the highest standards of materials and workmanship. To this end he gathered around him the best architects, engineers, draftsmen, illustrators, sculptors, muralists, painters, and craftsmen. All those who contributed to his creations became part of a team and were respected for their role in the resulting work.

Goodhue's greatest contribution to the Arts and Crafts Movement was renewing the art of book design following the example of William Morris in England. Goodhue was as much at home designing intricate borders or initials as he was drawing the bold lines of an architectural composition (fig. 14-1).

His versatility in all things was amazing. The inscription above his tomb—"He touched nothing which he did not adorn"—summarized his ability to make everything beautiful. However "modern" his future work might have become, Goodhue would have always demonstrated his search for beauty. Christine Smith explained: "Art was the vehicle that Goodhue used to express the ideal that he perceived and longed to realize." He drew on the past to create illusionary settings and to stimulate people's imagination in the hope that they would experience a spiritual awakening through art (fig. 14-2).6 Goodhue's love affair with the past, exemplified particularly in his *voyages imaginaires*, contributed to his romanticism and was an essential component of his architectural philosophy.

Goodhue also wrote prose and poetry, and contributed clearly thought out discussions on architecture to magazines. He loved music, and played the piano and the guitar by ear. He threw himself passionately into his work, but he loved to socialize, to spend time with his family, to travel for pleasure, and to hunt and fish in the backwoods of Pennsylvania or the wilds of Canada.

He could draw and paint in any medium (see fig. C-79), and his renderings were considered the best that the profession of architecture had witnessed. Oliver wrote: "A symbiotic relationship could be observed between Goodhue's drawings and his architecture. His drawings are pictorial, disciplined, and yet intensely dramatic and even rhapsodic—and so was his architecture."[7] As a tribute to Goodhue's greatness following his death, his drawings were exhibited in America and England, and the American Institute of Architects posthumously awarded him their Gold Medal for his contributions to architecture.

When opening an exhibit of Goodhue's drawings in London, Sir Giles Gilbert Scott pointed out that the artist's last architectural work coincided with the waning of the Beaux-Arts movement: "It was just then, when he might have been the governing force in a new movement, that death took him away. In that respect his death was a great tragedy for architecture in America."[8]

Sir Giles's image of Goodhue provides a glimpse of what might have been and raises the question: What role did Goodhue play in America's transition to modernism? In a 1998 publication, Carter Wiseman expressed his

Fig. 14-2. *Pen-and-ink drawing of Xanadu. Goodhue made this for his friend Elmer Grey.*

belief that Goodhue would have had the talent and flexibility to compete with Ludwig Mies van der Rohe (1886–1969) and Walter Gropius (1883–1969).[9] Goodhue's entry into modernism may have lagged behind that of others, but his last secular projects not only promised a resolution in his own search for a new architectural language but foreshadowed a style that would have equaled the styles of the leading European architects. Goodhue, consistently the individualist, would have firmly rejected any suggestion that he become a member of a new movement or follow its rules, but he would have mingled with the leaders and held his own in any discussion or argument. The direction of Goodhue's architecture suggested the development of a creative solution that would be different both from the stark simplicity of the Miesian school and from the work of those architects whose embellishments of the "neoclassic cube has . . . led to the fragmentation of its mass into a nervously linear pattern of precast concrete components."[10]

Putting aside these suppositions, it is difficult to gauge Goodhue's contribution to modernism, because even with his discovery of a stylistic freedom his buildings continued to reflect the traditions of the past. Oliver spoke of the difficulty of evaluating his work because he was "too advanced to be a 'traditionalist' and too conservative to be a 'modernist.'"[11] In 1927, only three years after Goodhue's death, Fiske Kimball, while acknowledging his architectural skill and artistry, faulted him on "the question of leadership," even though his contemporaries regarded him as a leader and renowned teacher. Kimball claimed that Goodhue's late work represented "not a transition but a tardy compromise" between traditional forms and modernism, and that his ideas for a new form of architecture were vague and undeveloped.[12] Most assessments of Goodhue's place in twentieth-century architectural history suggest that in the rush to establish a universal modernism stripped of historical references before and after World War II, Goodhue was largely ignored and that it was not until the postmodern period that his work was appreciated again. Christine Smith, for example, in her 1999 essay on Goodhue in *American National Biography*, wrote that "Kimball is right: Goodhue was not a pioneer in modern architecture. Only in the postmodern period have scholars reevaluated his contribution in terms not only of their intrinsic quality, but also of their cultural significance."[13] In his introduction to the 1976 reprint of the Whitaker volume, Paul Goldberger wrote, "His skills were missed by most observers on the vanguard of the developing modern movement." But those observers were architects and critics who disavowed any dependence on history, however free of visionary theorizing. Nevertheless, Goldberger felt certain that Goodhue's reputation would be renewed "as the values of composition and the respectability of history come once again into the fore."[14]

With these comments in mind it is interesting to note that, in contrast with Kimball's view, the most recent editions of Sir Banister Fletcher's survey of architectural history accord Goodhue an important leadership role in the history of modernism:

> The assimilation of Modernism into the architectural mainstream during the 1920s and 1930s was led not by Wright or younger advocates of the avant-garde, however significant their work, but by architects schooled in the academic tradition who now believed that new avenues of exploration must be pursued if design was to retain its vitality. As in Europe, so in America efforts were made to create an architecture that broke away from the past in its modelling of form and simplification of effect, yet retained some obvious references to familiar traditions.
>
> Among the earliest and most respected works of this genre is Bertram Goodhue's State Capitol, Lincoln, Nebraska. . . .
>
> Widespread application of the approach to Modernism represented by Goodhue's work occurred in the commercial sphere, notably in skyscraper design, in which American architects continued their unrivalled leadership. Much of their inspiration came from American work, including that of Louis Sullivan, [Cass] Gilbert, and Goodhue. . . .[15]

Keeping in mind these reevaluations, it seems surprising that awareness of Goodhue's work appears to be limited to architectural enthusiasts. One reason may be that, except for churches in New York City,

Goodhue designed relatively few landmark buildings in major cities. Those that he did design are scattered across the continent from Washington, D.C., to Southern California and as far away as Hawaii. Moreover, some of those buildings, such as the National Academy of Sciences, are only accessible to an elite group of people. Goodhue's highly acclaimed exposition complex would have been better known if he had won the commission for the 1915 Panama-Pacific International Exposition in San Francisco instead of the Panama-California Exposition in remote San Diego. The Nebraska State Capitol is regarded as Goodhue's greatest achievement. Lincoln, the building's home, used to be on the main train line but is now a flyover city in the Midwest. The Los Angeles Public Library is a gem, but library visitors tend to be unaware of their architectural surroundings, and the innovative design is now overshadowed by a mass of high-rise towers. Only a few know that Goodhue designed residences because most of them are privately owned and not accessible to the general public.

Wiseman wrote that Goodhue, having been born "in the heyday of American architectural eclecticism," died "just as European Modernism was about to sweep architectural history from the collective memory. But what Goodhue accomplished in the interim!"[16] His contribution to modernism may lack wide recognition, but his churches, colleges, libraries, public buildings, and private homes stand as tributes to the greatness of his work (fig. 14-3). All his structures were incredibly well built and have stood the ravages of time. The present owners of his residences attest enthusiastically to the soundness of the construction and the quality of the exterior and interior details.

A careful examination of Goodhue's correspondence and family scrapbooks has shed more light on his character and the details of his personal life. Donn Barber, a close friend, recalled the importance of his upbringing: "He took great pride in and never forgot the fact that he was descended from old Connecticut stock, and boasted that he had had no foreign training. He gloried in the fact that he was self-taught, and got his education in the office and on the work and not in the schools."[17] His lack of a formal education was both his strength and his weakness. It gave him an inner freedom, a chance to develop his individuality unhampered by the structure of a university or the rules of an architectural school. Though he boasted of not being a college man, he suffered from feelings of inferiority and longed for academic recognition, at least in the form of an honorary degree or two. He admitted that "egotism is a serious fault of mine . . . but please allow that it's a little bit like whistling to keep up one's courage."[18]

Barber's eulogy continued with a summation of Goodhue's personality:

Fig. 14-3. A Fantasy—*this drawing by Goodhue is a collage of some of his many buildings.*

He had so many lovable and endearing traits and to a high degree he possessed temperament, that indispensable attribute of genius. He was also blessed with a sense of humor and played at his work with a sort of contagious gaiety and exhilaration which radiated to all those with whom he came in contact. He was, *first of all* and *always*, an *architect*, and took infinite pleasure and pride in so being. . . .

He was high-minded, proud and impulsive, with an inability to comprehend baseness of any character in others. He had a sort of defensive sharpness in his manner and speech, his abruptness was often misconstrued, but underneath his seeming severity he was sensitive, gentle and simple and he loved sheer beauty more than anything in all the world.[19]

Physician and author Sir Thomas Browne (1605–1682) wrote, "Life itself is but the shadow of death, and souls departed but the shadows of the living."[20] Chapter 1 of this book opened with an image of the artist Bertram Goodhue, in 1891, the shadow from a large sombrero shielding his face from the Mexican sun. A mere thirty-three years later, the shadow of death stole away this artist, now a renowned architect, in the prime of his career. At the moment of his passing, Goodhue was on the verge of achieving a stylistic freedom, leaving us to wonder about the form of his future buildings. Alas, we can only dream of what might have been, and enjoy the legacy that he left behind.

NOTES

KEY TO PRIMARY SOURCES

Goodhue Papers   Avery Architectural and Fine Arts Library: Drawings and
                          Archives. Columbia University, New York, New York.
BPL   Boston Public Library: Cram, Goodhue & Ferguson Papers.
                          Boston, Massachusetts.
Hale Papers   Institute Archives, California Institute of Technology,
                          Pasadena, California.
NAS   Archives, National Academy of Sciences, Washington, D.C.
Nebraska Capitol Archives Nebraska Capitol Collections, Lincoln, Nebraska.
Family Archives   In the possession of Nicholas Goodhue, Los Angeles, California.
Danenhower Archives   In the possession of Sylvia Danenhower, Pomfret, Connecticut.
John Rivers Collection   Photographs of Goodhue's original pen-and-ink drawings are in
                          the possession of John Rivers, Boston, Massachusetts.
                          The original drawings are on loan to the Boston Public Library.

ABBREVIATIONS OF PERSONAL NAMES

BGG   Bertram Grosvenor Goodhue
CCB   Cecil Claude Brewer
CGA   Constance (Con) Grosvenor Alexander (Bertram's cousin)
EEG   Commander Edward (Ned) Eldredge Goodhue
EGT   Elaine Grosvenor Thompson (Sylvia Danenhower's sister)
FLO   Frederick Law Olmsted, Jr.
FWF   Frank William Ferguson
GEH   George Ellery Hale
HDB   Hoyle, Doran & Berry
HEG   Harry Eldredge Goodhue
JDM   John D. Moore
JWG   James Waldron Gillespie
NAS   National Academy of Sciences

Preface

1. Bertram Grosvenor Goodhue, *A Book of Architectural and Decorative Drawings* (New York: Architectural Book Publishing Co., 1914; second printing, 1924) (hereafter *A Book of Drawings*).
2. Richard Oliver, *Bertram Grosvenor Goodhue* (New York: Architectural History Foundation; Cambridge, Mass.: MIT Press, 1983) (hereafter Oliver, *Goodhue*).
3. Richard Oliver, in *Architectural Design* 47 (June 1977): 445.
4. *Bertram Grosvenor Goodhue: Architect and Master of Many Arts*, ed. Charles Harris Whitaker (New York: American Institute of Architects Press, 1925) (this volume cited hereafter as Whitaker, *BGG*, except in citations of Whitaker's introductory essay, cited as Whitaker, essay in *BGG*). This work was reprinted in 1976 by Da Capo Press, New York, with a new introduction by Paul Goldberger (the five watercolors reproduced in color in the original edition are reproduced in black and white in the reprint edition).
5. Romy Wyllie, *Caltech's Architectural Heritage: From Spanish Tile to Modern Stone* (Los Angeles: Balcony Press, 2000).
6. The thirty-three years span Goodhue's career from 1891, when he had completed his apprenticeship, to his death in 1924.
7. BGG to William A. Boring, January 1920, Goodhue Papers. Quoted in Oliver, *Goodhue*, p. 5, and in Whitaker, essay in *BGG*, p. 14.
8. Ralph Adams Cram, *My Life in Architecture* (Boston: Little, Brown & Co., 1936), p. 77 (hereafter Cram, *My Life*).
9. Frances (Franny) Goodhue to EEG, April 26, 1924, Danenhower Archives.
10. Sir Giles Gilbert Scott, opening remarks for "Exhibition of the Work of the Late Bertram Grosvenor Goodhue," *Architectural Association Journal* 41, no. 470 (April 1926): 205.

Chapter 1
AN ARCHITECT IS BORN *1869–1891*

1. BGG to W. Frazer Gibson, January 2, 1913, Goodhue Papers.
2. Bertram Grosvenor Goodhue, *Mexican Memories: The Record of a Slight Sojourn Below the Yellow Rio Grande, with Illustrations by the Author* (New York: Geo. M. Allen Co., 1892), p. 162 (hereafter *Mexican Memories*).
3. *The New England Historical and Genealogical Register* 72 (April 1918): 139–140.
4. BGG to Miss Gertrude Vinton, July 18, 1919, Goodhue Papers. Responding to her suggestion that Bertram or a family member buy the house, Goodhue wrote, "Ned feels just as I do. . . . We'd like nothing better than to have it in the family again [but] the fact that it has been in other hands for 30 years takes away most of the sentiment from the fact that we had it for two hundred years before." However, the reference to the house as being "in other hands" was not altogether accurate. According to Ned's records (Danenhower Archives), the first four owners were Grosvenors; in 1847, Emily Grosvenor inherited the house from her father, Benjamin Hutchins Grosvenor. Emily married Horace Sabin, so the name of the owner until Emily's death was Sabin. This must have been the thirty-year gap to which Bertram referred. Ned purchased the Sabin property in 1933. He spent his retirement years restoring the house and furnishing it with family furniture and heirlooms. Having no heirs, he left it to his nephew, William, who chose not to live there. It stood empty for thirty years before Sylvia Danenhower (Mrs. G. W. Danenhower III), a Grosvenor descendant, and her husband purchased it in 1973.

5. Whitaker, essay in *BGG*, p. 12.
6. Goodhue's résumé written for his children, Family Archives.
7. *Trinity College (Hartford, Conn.) Bulletin, 1924–1925*, listing the death of Bertram Grosvenor Goodhue, Class of 1911 (honorary): "Son of Charles Wells Goodhue—He was a manufacturer of sacking and kindred materials and later a farmer."
8. Elaine Grosvenor Thompson (Sylvia Danenhower's sister), telephone conversation with author, June 16, 2004 (hereafter EGT memories). Elaine told me about her mother's memories of Bertram and his family. Her mother was a Grosvenor cousin.
9. Albert M. Tannler, "Harry Eldredge Goodhue," *Stained Glass* 99, no. 1 (Spring 2004): 54, 61 n. 7. Tannler explains that Harry Goodhue was listed as "Henry" in Rev. Jonathan E. Goodhue's *History and Genealogy of the Goodhue Family in England and America to the Year 1890* (Rochester, N.Y.: E. R. Andrews, Printer & Bookbinder, 1891) but that in a copy owned by Harry's youngest son, William, "Henry" has been crossed out and rewritten as "Harry."
10. Oliver, *Goodhue*, p. 1. Oliver obtained family information from Rev. Jonathan E. Goodhue's book cited in n. 9.
11. Oliver, *Goodhue*, pp. 2, 239 n. 7.
12. Note in Family Archives.
13. Oliver, *Goodhue*, p. 2.
14. Autograph Book of Helen Grosvenor Goodhue, Family Archives.
15. Oliver, *Goodhue*, p. 2.
16. Whitaker, essay in *BGG*, p. 15. Whitaker wrote that Bertram did the lettering, but in a handwritten note in a family copy of the Whitaker volume, Hugh Goodhue stated that "his mother lettered it, according to his brother Edward Eldredge Goodhue."
17. BGG to CGA, January 30, 1919, Goodhue Papers.
18. BGG to W. Frazer Gibson, January 2, 1913, Goodhue Papers.
19. Ibid. The entry under "Grosvenor" in Patrick Hanks, ed., *Dictionary of American Family Names* (New York: Oxford University Press, 2003), is as follows: "status name for a person who was in charge of the arrangements for hunting on a lord's estate, from Anglo-Norman French *gros* 'great', 'chief' + *veneo(u)r* 'hunter'."
20. BGG to Thomas W. Drummond, October 13, 1915, Goodhue Papers.
21. BGG to Gibson (above, n. 18).
22. Whitaker, essay in *BGG*, p. 12.
23. The playbills and reports were found in a scrapbook that Bertram's cousin, Constance Grosvenor Alexander (CGA), kept on her cousin's life (Danenhower Archives) (hereafter Con's Scrapbook). Cousin Con was the daughter of Helen's sister.
24. Reverdy Whitlock, "William Huntington Russell and the Collegiate and Commercial Institute," *Journal of the New Haven Colony Historical Society* 18, no. 4 (December 1969): 83–89 (hereafter Whitlock, "C.C.I."). Whitlock explained that after Russell became the institute's sole proprietor in 1848, it became more commonly known as "The Russell School."
25. Ibid., p. 86.
26. Henry S. Washington to C. H. Whitaker, February 15, 1925, Family Archives.
27. Ibid.
28. Jorge Bird y Arias to BGG, March 16, 1907, Goodhue Papers.
29. David E. Small to BGG, February 3, 1913, Goodhue Papers.
30. David E. Small to BGG, February 28, 1913, Goodhue Papers.
31. BGG to Harry C. Crosby, April 17, 1916, Goodhue Papers.
32. Goodhue Papers. Janet Parks informed me that she had found this drawing in Harry Crosby's autograph book, which she had acquired for the Avery collection (Janet Parks, e-mail to author, September 9, 2005).

33. Whitlock, "C.C.I.," p. 86.

34. Whitaker, essay in *BGG*, p. 13.

35. Ibid., p. 14.

36. BGG to Gibson, January 2, 1913, Goodhue Papers.

37. Agreement between Charles Goodhue and Renwick, Aspinwall & Russell, September 1884, Family Archives.

38. BGG, "The Late James Renwick" (Boston, June 28, 1863), Family Archives.

39. W. H. [i.e., William Hamilton] Russell to "My dear Billie," April 17, 1885, Family Archives. Oliver surmises that "Billie" was "very likely General W. H. Russell of New Haven" (Oliver, *Goodhue*, p. 6), i.e., William Huntington Russell, head of the school that Goodhue had attended. However, he does not explain his basis for this identification, which is almost certainly incorrect. Reverdy Whitlock, whose wife is the great-granddaughter of William Huntington Russell, told me (telephone conversation, September 22, 2005) that no one would have dared address the formidable General Russell as "Billie" and added that there is no record of any family connection or other relationship between the two Russells that might have given rise to such familiarity (Whitlock explained that he and his wife have done extensive research on her great-grandfather and the Russell family and have not found any relative by the name of William Hamilton Russell). Oliver characterized the letter to "Billie" as a reply to "a letter of introduction," but this seems inconsistent with the fact that the letter was written some seven months after Goodhue began working for the firm. "Billie" was probably a family friend.

40. Oliver, *Goodhue*, pp. 6–7.

41. Ibid., p. 5.

42. See preface, n. 7.

43. EGT and SD memories.

44. Whitaker, essay in *BGG*, p. 16.

45. Unattributed quotation in Whitaker, essay in *BGG*, p. 17.

46. Illustrated in Oliver, *Goodhue*, p. 7.

47. Oliver, *Goodhue*, p. 12.

48. Cited above, n. 2.

49. *Mexican Memories*, p. 16.

50. Ibid., pp. 27–28.

51. Ibid., p. 62.

52. Ibid., p. 92.

53. John Fleming, Hugh Honour, and Nikolaus Pevsner, *The Penguin Dictionary of Architecture*, 3d ed. (Harmondsworth: Penguin Books, 1980), pp. 74–75, s.vv. "Churriguera, Jose Benito de," and "Churrigueresque Style."

54. *Mexican Memories*, pp. 156–158. Goodhue wrote, "You needn't look up this name, it isn't on any map." In the previous paragraph he had remarked that the village "is not in any part of Mexico you will be likely to pass through."

55. Ibid., p. 166.

Chapter 2

THE BOSTON YEARS *1891–1903*

1. Cram, *My Life*, p. 77.

2. Albert M. Tannler, "Harry Eldredge Goodhue," *Stained Glass* 99, no. 1 (Spring 2004): 54–67. Membership in BASA was open to "persons who are practicing or studying Art, or are following a profession or industry allied to Art" (see ibid., p. 55).

3. Ibid., p. 54.

4. The Grosvenor home still stands. In 1925 it was acquired by the Rectory School, founded in 1920 by Rev. Frank H. Bigelow, rector of Christ Church, Pomfret. The building is now the Main House of this elite junior boarding school that has always focused on helping children with learning differences.

5. Douglass Shand-Tucci, *Ralph Adams Cram: Life and Architecture*, vol. 1, *Boston Bohemia, 1881–1900* (Amherst: University of Massachusetts Press, 1995), p. 479 n. 3 (hereafter Shand-Tucci, *Boston Bohemia*).

6. CGA to BGG, December 19, 1914, Goodhue Papers.

7. In 1894, Harry married Mary Louise Wright and presumably left his mother's house. Constance has photographs of Harry and Mary Louise at 83 Brattle Street (Danenhower Archives).

8. Con's Scrapbook, Danenhower Archives.

9. Unidentified newspaper article, March 1892, in Con's Scrapbook, Danenhower Archives.

10. Notes in Con's Scrapbook, Danenhower Archives.

11. Christine Smith, *St. Bartholomew's Church in the City of New York* (New York: Oxford University Press, 1988), p. 36 (hereafter Smith, *St. Bartholomew's*).

12. Shand-Tucci, *Boston Bohemia*, p. 21.

13. Ibid.

14. Oliver, *Goodhue*, p. 12.

15. RAC to BGG, June 24, 1891, BPL.

16. Ibid., P.S.

17. "Architect," 1916, Goodhue Papers. This was a curriculum vitae written by Goodhue. In a letter quoted by Whitaker, essay in *BGG*, p. 14, Goodhue wrote that he "went to Boston and became head draughtsman for the firm of Cram & Wentworth." In his essay "Partnership" in Whitaker, *BGG*, p. 29, Cram refers to Goodhue's initial position in the firm as "draughtsman." In *My Life*, p. 76, Cram wrote: "He was promptly taken on as one of our first draughtsmen."

18. Printed announcement, Con's Scrapbook, Danenhower Archives.

19. Ethan Anthony of HDB/Cram & Ferguson, Boston, telephone conversation with author, January 14, 2004.

20. RAC to Gen. H. V. Boynton, April 5, 1899, BPL.

21. Cram, *My Life*, p. 69.

22. Ibid., p. 76.

23. BGG to CCB, April 18, 1912, Goodhue Papers. Goodhue's relationship with Brewer is explained in chap. 5.

24. BGG to H. G. Gennert, May 19, 1913, Goodhue Papers.

25. See chap. 1; Oliver, *Goodhue*, p. 242 n. 41.

26. Cram, *My Life*, p. 71.

27. Shand-Tucci, *Boston Bohemia*, pp. 85–96.

28. RAC to Benjamin D. Hyde, February 20, 1899, BPL.

29. The firm's correspondence from the establishment of Cram & Wentworth in 1889 until the establishment of two offices in 1903 is in bound "Letter Books" at the Boston Public Library. The library also has the firm's Ledger Books, which recorded accounting transactions. Regrettably, all but one of the firm's Job Books, which were retained at the HDB offices and listed all jobs alphabetically by city, were destroyed a few years ago by a partner of Hoyle, Doran & Berry, who inherited Cram & Ferguson's practice and their office records. The remaining book, for the last few letters of the alphabet, was of no help in verifying whether the early residential designs that I have mentioned were built. My best resource has been Ann Miner Daniel's thesis, "The Early Architecture of Ralph Adams Cram, 1889–1902" (University of North Carolina at Chapel Hill, 1978).

30. Cram, *My Life*, p. 77.

31. Arthur S. Link, foreword to Phyllis B. Dodge, *Tales of the Phelps-Dodge Family* (New York: New-York Historical Society, 1987).

32. John E. Ellsworth, *Simsbury: Being a Brief Historical Sketch of Ancient and Modern Simsbury, 1642–1935* (Simsbury, Conn.:

Simsbury Committee for the Tercentenary, 1935). According to this publication, the properties of the father and uncle were purchased in 1917 by the Ethel Walker School (a prestigious girls' boarding school), which had outgrown its six-year-old home in Lakewood, New Jersey. Two years later Mr. and Mrs. George Alfred Cluett purchased the Walter Dodge property and gave it to the school in memory of their daughter, who had died during the influenza epidemic of 1919. In this same year Bertram Goodhue's daughter, Frances, was working hard to improve her grades at the elite boarding school (BGG to Miss Ethel Walker, April 17, 1919, Goodhue Papers).

33. Albert M. Tannler, "Seeking Pittsburgh at the Longfellow House and Finding Japan," *PHLF News*, January 2005, p. 17. Tannler's article explains that Americans became interested in Japanese design following the 1876 Centennial Exhibition in Philadelphia. After a visit to Japan in 1877, Edwin S. Morse, director of the Peabody Museum in Salem, Massachusetts, published *Japanese Homes and Their Surroundings* (1885).

34. Margaret Henderson Floyd, *Henry Hobson Richardson: A Genius for Architecture* (New York: Monacelli Press, 1997), pp. 275, 280.

35. Shand-Tucci, *Boston Bohemia*, pp. 402–410.

36. RAC to Horace Slingluff, December 29, 1898, BPL.

37. Shand-Tucci, *Boston Bohemia*, p. 320, fig. 82a, b.

38. Cram, *My Life*, p. 101.

39. BGG to Dr. Reusch, January 16, 1899, BPL.

40. Sylvester Baxter, *Spanish-Colonial Architecture in Mexico*, with photographic plates by Henry Greenwood Peabody and plans by Bertram Grosvenor Goodhue, 10 vols. (Boston: J. B. Millet, 1901) (hereafter Baxter, *Architecture in Mexico*). There was also a "grand de luxe edition" published in 12 vols.

41. Bertram Grosvenor Goodhue, "Our Picturesque Neighbor, Mexico (Illustrated from the Author's Photographs)," *The Churchman*, February 16, 1901, and March 9, 1901.

42. FWF to Mr. Horton, February 6, 1899, BPL.

43. General Charles Grosvenor's father, Peter, was a son of Colonel Thomas Grosvenor (Bertram's great-grandfather). Peter and his family had moved to Ohio in 1838.

44. Champ Clark, *My Quarter Century of American Politics* (1920), 2:320, quoted in *Dictionary of American Biography*, s.v. "Grosvenor, Charles Henry."

45. *Dictionary of American Biography*, s.v. "Grosvenor, Charles Henry."

46. Jane Hamilton (Mrs. Daniel H. Hamilton, Jr., Gen. Grosvenor's great-granddaughter), letter to author, November 4, 2002.

47. Ibid.

48. Description based on photographs provided by Jane Hamilton.

49. BGG to Gen. Charles Grosvenor, October 22, 1901, Ohio University Archives. I am indebted to George W. Bain, head of the Robert E. and Jean R. Mahn Center for Archives and Special Collections, Ohio University Libraries, for sending me copies of Goodhue's letters concerning General Grosvenor's house and of his renderings and floor plans for it.

50. BGG to Gen. Charles Grosvenor, November 13, 1901, Ohio University Archives.

51. "Homecoming: OU Dedicates Alumni Center," *The Messenger* (Athens, Ohio), October 9, 1981. Information on the history of General Grosvenor's house is also found in a brochure for the Konneker Alumni Center, 52 University Terrace, Ohio University (2004).

52. Information on the Huff mansion was supplied by Albert M. Tannler, Historical Collections Director, Pittsburgh History & Landmarks Foundation, who shared with me the research material for his article "Historic Huff House" in the *Pittsburgh Tribune-Review Focus*, July 11, 2004, pp. 8–11 (hereafter Tannler, "Huff House").

53. RAC to William Augustus Huff, September 5, 1899, BPL. In his article "Huff House," Tannler says that the architect may have been Beezer Brothers of Altoona, who had designed other Colonial Revival houses in Greensburg for the Huff family.

54. RAC to W. A. Huff (n.53). William Huff's brother George and General Charles Grosvenor were Republican colleagues in Congress.

55. RAC to William Augustus Huff, September 11, 1899, BPL.

56. Rose Huff, daughter of William A. Huff, letter to her nephew, Pittsburgh architect William S. Huff, about 1970, cited by Tannler, "Huff House." Rose Huff was telling her nephew about the design of his grandfather's house and the family's visit to Boston. A photocopy of a fragment of this letter is in Westmoreland County File III, James D. Van Trump Library, Pittsburgh History & Landmarks Foundation.

57. Tannler, "Huff House." In 1968 Katharine Huff Horn, daughter of William Huff, donated the house to Christ Church, and two years later the church sold the building to the YWCA of Westmoreland County.

58. Ralph Adams Cram, *Church Building* (Boston: Small, Maynard & Co., 1901).

59. Ralph Adams Cram, "Partnership," in Whitaker, *BGG*, p. 30 (hereafter Cram, "Partnership").

60. Cram, *My Life*, p. 78.

61. Ibid.

62. Banister Fletcher, *A History of Architecture*, 17th ed., rev. R. A. Cordingley (New York: Charles Scribner's Sons, 1963), p. 988.

63. Oliver, *Goodhue*, p. 28.

64. Ingalls Kimball, "Bertram Grosvenor Goodhue, Artist, MDC-CCLXIX–MCMXXIIII [i.e., 1869–1924]" (published as an insert in the *American Printer*, 1924).

65. James F. O'Gorman, "'Either in Books or [in] Architecture': Bertram Grosvenor Goodhue in the Nineties," *Harvard Library Bulletin* 35 (1987): 165–183.

66. Cram, *My Life*, p. 84.

67. Cram, "Partnership," p. 31.

68. Louise Imogen Guiney, quoted in Shand-Tucci, *Boston Bohemia*, p. 340.

69. Quoted in Oliver, *Goodhue*, p. 27.

70. Oliver, *Goodhue*, pp. 27–28.

71. Ibid., p. 27.

72. *Encyclopaedia Britannica*, 15th ed. (1974), *Micropaedia*, s.v. "Grolier de Servières, Jean."

73. Cram married Elizabeth Carrington Read in 1900; Goodhue was best man. Goodhue married Lydia Thompson Bryant in 1902; Cram was an usher.

74. Cram, *My Life*, p. 79.

Chapter 3
FROM PERSIA TO MONTECITO 1901–1906

1. Bertram Grosvenor Goodhue, "Of Persian Gardens," in *A Book of Drawings*, p. 89 (hereafter BGG, "Of Persian Gardens").

2. Oliver, *Goodhue*, p. 248 n. 50.

3. BGG to Ruth Baldwin, August 30, 1916, Goodhue Papers. Ruth Ann Baldwin joined Universal as a screenwriter in 1913. She also tried her hand at directing and married actor and director Leo Pierson.

4. BGG to Gen. Charles Grosvenor, October 22, 1901, Ohio University Archives.

5. Hugh Goodhue, note, Family Archives. Oliver (*Goodhue*, p. 41) understates the distance as "over four hundred miles."

6. Benjamin Burges Moore, *From Moscow to the Persian Gulf* (New York: G. P. Putnam's Sons, 1915). The route taken by Gillespie and Goodhue was penciled in on the map in Goodhue's copy of the book. Oliver (*Goodhue*, p. 41) mistakenly mentioned Samarkand as one of the cities that they visited. As Hugh Goodhue noted in a letter to the Architectural History Foundation dated June 1, 1985, "they never went to Samarkand, which was almost 900 miles away [from Teheran] in the then Russian Turkestan." That letter also contained corrections of several other errors in Oliver's book. Unfortunately, there was no second edition to incorporate those corrections.

7. BGG, "Of Persian Gardens," pp. 89–97.

8. Ibid., p. 90.

9. "Of Persian Gardens," typescript version, Family Archives.

10. BGG, "Of Persian Gardens," p. 90.

11. Ibid., p. 97.

12. *Dictionary of American Biography*, s.v. "Gillespie, William Mitchell."

13. David F. Myrick, *Montecito and Santa Barbara*, 2 vols. (Pasadena, Calif.: Pentrex Media Group, 1988–1991; second printing, 2001), 2:243 (hereafter Myrick, *Montecito*).

14. Ibid.

15. Quoted in John R. Southworth, F.R.G.S., *Santa Barbara and Montecito* (Santa Barbara: Oreña Studios, 1920), p. 19.

16. George R. Stewart, *American Place-Names* (New York: Oxford University Press, 1970), p. 305. Stewart notes that "in the usage of the Spanish-Americans who settled the Southwest, *monte* meant 'wood, forest, thicket,' and never 'mountain'" (ibid., pp. 304–305).

17. David Gebhard, introduction to *Santa Barbara Architecture: From Spanish Colonial to Modern*, by Herb Andree et al., 3rd ed., ed. Bob Easton and Wayne McCall (Santa Barbara: Capra Press, 1995; reprinted with corrections, Santa Monica: Hennessey & Ingalls, 2005), p. 7.

18. Oliver, *Goodhue*, p. 42, refers to El Fureidis as having been completed in 1903. Hugh Goodhue corrected this to 1906 in his letter to the Architectural History Foundation (above, n. 6).

19. Bertram Grosvenor Goodhue, "The Villa Fosca and Its Garden," in *A Book of Drawings*, p. 36.

20. Hugh Goodhue, note, Family Archives.

21. BGG to Ruth Baldwin, August 30, 1916, Goodhue Papers.

22. BGG to CCB, August 18, 1915, Goodhue Papers.

23. Una Nixson Hopkins (Mrs. George J. Hopkins), "El Fureides: 'The Little Paradise,'" *The Craftsman* 29, no. 1 (October 1915): 34.

24. Ibid., p. 39.

25. Ibid.

26. Henry H. Saylor, "The Best Twelve Country Houses in America, VI, El Fureidis, the Home of J. Waldron Gillespie, Esq., at Montecito, Cal.," *Country Life in America* 28, no. 6 (October 1915): 29 (hereafter Saylor, "Country Houses").

27. Translation provided by Amir Nour, Professor of Art, Truman College, Chicago.

28. Hugh Goodhue, note on back of a photograph, Family Archives.

29. Myrick, *Montecito*, 2:249.

30. Yates Satterlee, conversation with author, January 28, 2004.

31. Saylor, "Country Houses," pp. 28–31.

32. Oliver, *Goodhue*, p. 42.

33. Elizabeth de Forest, "Old Santa Barbara Gardens: How They Came to Be," *Pacific Horticulture* 38, no. 4 (Winter 1977–78): 31–36.

34. The dome of St. Bartholomew's was modeled on the Panama-California dome and built after Goodhue's death.

Chapter 4

A DIVISION OF LABOR *1902–1911*

1. Cram, *My Life*, p. 79.

2. BGG to Wells Goodhue, October 29, 1915, Goodhue Papers.

3. Boston newspaper (no name), April 8, 1902, Danenhower Archives.

4. Boston newspaper (no name), April 8, 1902, Family Archives.

5. Oliver, *Goodhue*, p. 44.

6. BGG to Rev. Marcus H. Carroll, November 21, 1913, Goodhue Papers.

7. BGG to Verulam (no first name or initials), August 30, 1902, Family Archives.

8. Boston newspaper (no name or date), Family Archives.

9. BGG to Montgomery Schuyler, October 24, 1910, Goodhue Papers.

10. Montgomery Schuyler, "The Works of Cram, Goodhue & Ferguson, 1892–1910," *Architectural Record* 29 (January 1911): 106–109 (hereafter Schuyler, "Works of CG&F").

11. Oliver, *Goodhue*, p. 248 n. 46.

12. BGG to Mrs. John Nicholas Brown, February 2, 1914, Goodhue Papers.

13. *An American Landmark: The Newport Estate of John Nicholas Brown* (New York: Sotheby's International Realty, 1986) (advertising brochure on file at Newport Historical Society).

14. Ibid.

15. Ibid.

16. "John Nicholas Brown" (obituary), *Newport Daily News*, October 10, 1979.

17. Ronald M. Potvin, Historic Site Administrator, John Nicholas Brown Center, Brown University, e-mail message to author, October 6, 2003. Mr. Potvin generously provided plans, photographs, and other research material on Harbour Court.

18. T. Curtis Forbes, "Harbour Court Destined to Be Yacht Club," *Newport Daily News*, June 4, 1987.

19. *American National Biography* (New York: Oxford University Press, 1999), s.v. "Harriman, Edward Henry."

20. Arden Conference Center, http://www.ardenhouse.com/ (accessed October 5, 2004; site now discontinued).

21. Oliver, *Goodhue*, pp. 30–31.

22. Ibid., p. 101.

23. BGG to CCB, January 21, 1915, Goodhue Papers.

24. Bill Blanck, "The Story of the Dobbs Ferry Library from 1899 to 2003," *The Ferryman* (Dobbs Ferry Historical Society), April, September, and December 2003. I am indebted to Bruce Richards for bringing this article to my notice and for providing copies of old photographs.

25. Bruce Richards, e-mail message to author, July 6, 2004. By chance, I met Richards and learned about his project when visiting the office of Hoyle, Doran & Berry in Boston.

26. "Helen Chase, Park House Donor, Dies," *Waterbury Republican*, July 2, 1953. I am indebted to Sheila A. Lafferty, University Librarian, E. H. Kirschbaum Library, University of Connecticut, Waterbury Campus, for sending this article and other material about the Chase family.

27. *History of New Haven County, Connecticut*, vol. 3 (Chicago and Boston: Pioneer Historical Publishing Co., 1930), brought to my attention by Sheila A. Lafferty.

28. *Encyclopedia of Connecticut Biography* (New York: American Historical Society, 1917), s.v. "Chase, Augustus."

29. Diaries of Helen Chase, Mattatuck Museum.

30. "Helen Chase, Park House Donor, Dies" (see n. 26).

31. Historic Resources Inventory, State of Connecticut, Mattatuck Museum.

32. BGG to William Rutherford Mead, December 5, 1910, Goodhue Papers.

33. Arthur N. Starin, *Growing Up and I Find a Frontier* (Royal Oak, Md.: Mary Elizabeth Starin, 1973) (hereafter Starin, *Growing Up*).

34. Oliver, *Goodhue*, p. 95.

35. BGG to E. S. Wheeler, June 15, 1910, Goodhue Papers.

36. BGG to Percy E. Nobbs, McGill University, Montreal, June 28, 1910, Goodhue Papers.

37. BGG to HEG, June 20, 1911, Goodhue Papers.

38. BGG to Rev. F. S. Luther, June 30, 1911, Goodhue Papers.

39. This sentence is presented as it appears in a typewritten transcription in the Family Archives. The Trinity College motto, however, is PRO ECCLESIA ET PATRIA (included in the college seal, which can be seen, for example, in each issue of the *Trinity Reporter*). Possibly, the word order of the motto was inadvertently altered in the transcription.

40. BGG to EEG, June 30, 1911, Goodhue Papers.

41. BGG to Sr. Don Jorge Bird y Arias, June 23, 1920, Goodhue Papers.

Chapter 5
ANGLOPHILIA *1913–1916*

1. BGG to CCB, May 6, 1918, Goodhue Papers.

2. "Smith and Brewer: An Inventory of Their Drawings," Alexander Architectural Archive, University of Texas at Austin, http://www.lib.utexas.edu/taro/utaaa/00046/aaa-00046.html (accessed August 31, 2005).

3. BGG to Mrs. Cecil Brewer, February 6, 1919, Goodhue Papers.

4. Helen Worden, "Where Are the Rich?" *New York World-Telegram*, October 20, 1942 (hereafter Worden, "Where Are the Rich?"). Aldred's companies included the Shawinigan Water & Power Company in Canada and, in the United States, the Baltimore Consolidated Gas, Electric Light & Power Company, and the Pennsylvania Water & Power Company. He was also a major stockholder in the Gillette Safety Razor Company. I am indebted to Fr. Januario of St. Josaphat's for supplying a wealth of information on the Aldred Estate and for allowing me to visit.

5. Terry Winters, Researcher, National Register of Historic Places Inventory—Nomination Form, March 11, 1977, St. Josaphat's Archives.

6. Monica Randall, *The Mansions of Long Island's Gold Coast* (New York: Rizzoli, 1987), p. 11.

7. Quoted in Worden, "Where Are the Rich?"

8. Worden, "Where Are the Rich?"

9. BGG to CCB, September 24, 1917, Goodhue Papers.

10. Oliver, *Goodhue*, pp. 103-104.

11. BGG to CCB, May 6, 1918, Goodhue Papers.

12. Ibid.

13. *New York Times*, December 7, 1940, p. 15.

14. "Old Tapestries Sold," *New York Times*, December 8, 1940, p. 60.

15. "Ukrainian Church Buys Estate on Long Island," *New York Times*, May 23, 1944, p. 32.

16. Quoted in Worden, "Where Are the Rich?"

17. Orin F. Finkle, "The Estate of Mr. and Mrs. John E. Aldred," *North Shore Nostalgia* (Locust Valley, N.Y.), June–July 1983.

18. BGG to George P. Bankart, January 8, 1916, Goodhue Papers.

19. Henry Wadsworth Longfellow (1807–1882), *The Song of Hiawatha* (1855), pt. III.

20. Arthur N. Starin, "Recollections Regarding the Kitchi Gammi Club Building and Its Architect, Bertram Grosvenor Goodhue," Report to the Kitchi Gammi Club, January 1969. Anne Paine Williams kindly provided a copy of this report.

21. Ibid.

22. Oliver, *Goodhue*, p. 97.

23. Ibid., p. 98.

24. BGG to Mrs. F. W. Paine, December 26, 1913, Goodhue Papers.

25. Lawrence J. Sommer, "Landmark Structures of Duluth: Their History and Architecture" (M.A. thesis, University of Minnesota, 1971), p. 64 (hereafter Sommer, "Duluth").

26. "The Life & Times of Guilford Graham Hartley, 1853–1922" (unpublished essay written 1919–1920; the main author is an unnamed female employee of the *Duluth News-Tribune*), Northeast Minnesota Historical Center, University of Minnesota-Duluth. This material and the Sommer thesis were provided by Patricia Maus, Curator of Manuscripts.

27. *Duluth News-Tribune*, April 25, 1954, quoted in Sommer, "Duluth," p. 61.

28. "Cavour Hartley, Son of Duluth Pioneers" (obituary), *Duluth News-Tribune*, January 22, 1986.

29. BGG to FLO, December 31, 1913, Goodhue Papers.

30. Ibid.

31. BGG to G. G. Hartley, December 31, 1913, Goodhue Papers.

32. Fiona McKee, telephone conversation with author, May 26, 2004.

33. BGG to FLO, December 31, 1913, Goodhue Papers.

34. Goodhue's correspondence with Hartley (n. 31) and Olmsted (n. 29) gives no first name for Mr. Merrill. He could be Joseph Merrill, for whom Goodhue made a sketch for a house at Little Boar's Head, New Hampshire, in 1895 (chap. 2). There is no record of either house being built.

35. BGG to FLO, December 31, 1913, Goodhue Papers.

36. Ibid.

37. Lawrence Sommer, letter to author, August 13, 2004. Sommer kindly shared his knowledge of Duluth architecture and provided photographs of the Paine farm cottage and barn.

38. I am indebted to Anne Paine Williams, granddaughter of Frederic William Paine, who provided information about and photographs of the family farm, as well as copies of letters from F. Rodney Paine to his father, Frederic W. Paine, March 21 and March 22, 1924, which discuss the construction of the barn.

39. BGG to Dr. Samuel W. Lambert, January 11, 1913, Goodhue Papers.

40. Dr. Samuel W. Lambert to BGG, January 14, 1913, Goodhue Papers.

41. BGG to H. G. Gennert, May 19, 1913, Goodhue Papers.

Chapter 6
FROM A CITY-IN-MINIATURE TO A COMPANY TOWN *1911–1918*

1. Bertram Grosvenor Goodhue, introduction to *The Architecture and the Gardens of the San Diego Exposition*, described by Carleton Monroe Winslow (San Francisco: Paul Elder & Co., 1916), p. 6 (this volume cited hereafter as *San Diego Exposition*).

2. Bertram Grosvenor Goodhue, "The Home of the Future: A Study of America in Relation to the Architect" (the first of a series of articles by various architects), *The Craftsman* 29, no. 5 (February 1916): 544 (hereafter BGG, "Home of the Future").

3. BGG to JWG, March 31, 1911, Goodhue Papers.

4. BGG to FLO, December 19, 1910, Goodhue Papers.

5. BGG to FLO, December 28, 1910, Goodhue Papers.

6. Aaron Betsky, "American Monographs," *Progressive Architecture*, February 1985, pp. 171–172 (hereafter Betsky, "American Monographs").

7. Elmer Grey to BGG, January 4, 1911, Goodhue Papers.

8. Bruce Kamerling, *Irving J. Gill. Architect* (San Diego: San Diego Historical Society, 1993), pp. 86–87.

9. Ibid., p. 88.

10. Thomas S. Hines, *Irving Gill and the Architecture of Reform* (New York: Monacelli Press, 2000), pp. 180–183.

11. FLO to BGG, September 27, 1911, Goodhue Papers.

12. Oliver, *Goodhue*, p. 109.

13. Clarence S. Stein, "A Triumph of the Spanish-Colonial Style," in *San Diego Exposition*, p. 12 (hereafter Stein, "Triumph").

14. Ibid., pp. 12–13.

15. Baxter, *Architecture in Mexico*, 1:10–12 (see chap. 2, n. 40).

16. Stein, "Triumph," p. 14.

17. BGG, introduction to *San Diego Exposition*, pp. 7–8.

18. Oliver, *Goodhue*, p. 112.

19. Carleton Monroe Winslow, "Descriptive Notes of the Architecture and Gardens of the San Diego Exposition," in *San Diego Exposition*, p. 36. Winslow quotes the King James translation of Deut. 8:8, but I have given the Douay translation since it is closer to Jerome's Latin.

20. Ibid., p. 20.

21. Kevin Starr, *Americans and the California Dream* (New York: Oxford University Press, 1973), p. 409.

22. Douglass Shand-Tucci, *Ralph Adams Cram: Life and Architecture*, vol. 2, *An Architect's Four Quests: Medieval, Modernist, American, Ecumenical* (Amherst and Boston: University of Massachusetts Press, 2005), p. 83 (hereafter Shand-Tucci, *Four Quests*).

23. Ibid., p. 68.

24. Both Cram and Goodhue had participated, without success, in the original 1889 competition for the design of this cathedral. When the winner, Thomas Heins, died, the cathedral trustees decided not to work with his successor, Grant LaFarge. After a brief attempt at another competition, they appointed Cram as consultant architect. It was not unusual for Cram and Goodhue to work independently, but Goodhue felt that this particular appointment might adversely affect his own reputation at the very moment when he was applying for membership in the renowned Century Club.

25. Cram, *My Life*, p. 79.

26. Shand-Tucci, *Four Quests*, p. 100.

27. BGG to RAC and FWF, April 25, 1907, HDB Archives.

28. Lee Lawrie, "Sculpture," in Whitaker, *BGG*, p. 34. According to Lawrie's account, "when Goodhue was given a gold medal by the American Institute of Architects for the reredos, he returned it with the request that my name be engraved on it with his."

29. Quoted in Oliver, *Goodhue*, p. 64.

30. RAC to Rev. Ernest M. Stires, April 14, 1916, St. Thomas Archives.

31. Quoted in Oliver, *Goodhue*, p. 122.

32. BGG to CCB, February 5, 1914, Goodhue Papers.

33. BGG to Rev. Maurice W. Britton, August 28, 1913, Goodhue Papers.

34. Rev. Maurice W. Britton to BGG, September 8, 1913, Goodhue Papers.

35. BGG to EEG, August 20, 1913, Goodhue Papers.

36. BGG to Colonel J. M. Carson, November 25, 1913, Goodhue Papers.

37. Shand-Tucci, *Four Quests*, p. 95.

38. BGG to Henry G. Gennert, September 22, 1913, Goodhue Papers.

39. BGG to RAC, December 31, 1914, Goodhue Papers.

40. Shand-Tucci, *Four Quests*, p. 95.

41. Lydia Goodhue to RAC, July 2, 1929(?), Cram Papers, BPL. Except for one typed letter, all the letters are in Lydia's handwriting, which is extremely difficult to read. Moreover, the letters had only the day and month but no year identification. With the help of Yates Satterlee, the family member most familiar with his grandmother's writing, I sorted and deciphered the letters and assigned approximate year dates based on known family events. The archive does not contain Cram's replies.

42. Oliver, *Goodhue*, p. 124.

43. BGG to Henry Chase, August 17, 1915, Goodhue Papers. This project never went beyond the discussion phase.

44. BGG to Elmer Grey, December 29, 1914, Goodhue Papers.

45. BGG to George Wilberforce Horsefield, February 6, 1919, Goodhue Papers.

46. Ibid.

47. Margaret Crawford, "Bertram Goodhue, Walter Douglas and Tyrone, New Mexico," *Journal of Architectural Education* 42, no. 4 (Summer 1989): 25–33 (hereafter Crawford, "Tyrone").

48. BGG to FLO, December 31, 1913, Goodhue Papers.

49. Robert B. Riley, "Gone Forever: Goodhue's Beaux Arts Ghost Town," *AIA Journal* 50 (August 1968): 67–70 (hereafter Riley, "Ghost Town").

50. BGG to Miss Mary Rockwell, December 2, 1915, Goodhue Papers.

51. Riley, "Ghost Town," p. 69.

52. Oliver, *Goodhue*, p. 152.

53. BGG, "Home of the Future," p. 543.

54. Ibid., pp. 449–451.

55. BGG to Walter Douglas, October 1, 1917, Goodhue Papers.

56. Crawford, "Tyrone," p. 25.

57. Ibid.

58. Ibid., p. 31.

59. Ibid.

60. Riley, "Ghost Town," p. 70.

Chapter 7

GOODHUE'S SPANISH MANNER *1915–1924*

1. BGG, "Home of the Future," p. 544.

2. Romy Wyllie, *Caltech's Architectural Heritage: From Spanish Tile to Modern Stone* (Los Angeles: Balcony Press, 2000), p. 22 (hereafter Wyllie, *Caltech's Architectural Heritage*).

3. George Ellery Hale, "The National Academy of Sciences," in Whitaker, *BGG*, p. 45.

4. Wyllie, *Caltech's Architectural Heritage*, pp. 35–37.

5. Quoted in Tim Gregory, "The Herbert Coppell House: A History" (Pasadena, May 2000) (hereafter Gregory, "History"). I am most grateful to Gary Cowles for sharing with me many articles and photographs pertaining to the Coppell estate, including Gregory's history, which Mr. and Mrs. Cowles commissioned.

6. Samuel S. Vaughan, *The Little Church: One Hundred Years at the Church of the Atonement, 1868–1968, Tenafly, New Jersey* (Tenafly, N.J.: Church of the Atonement, 1969).

7. "Herbert Coppell" (obituary), *New York Times*, October 30, 1931.

8. BGG to Mrs. Bertram G. Goodhue, September 5, 1916, Goodhue Papers.

9. *Artesonado* means a ceiling decorated with carved panels. See Basilio Pavón Maldonado, "Artesonado," in *The Dictionary of Art*, ed. Jane Turner (New York: Grove, 1996), 2:528–530.

10. BGG to CCB, September 24, 1917, Goodhue Papers.

11. "Old Mansion Becomes Two Complete Homes," *Pasadena Star-News*, October 22, 1950.

12. "'Mi Sueno'—Estate of Herbert Coppell, Esq., Pasadena, California," *Arts and Decoration* 112 (March 1920): 314–316.

13. Ellen Leech, "The Setting for a Film," *California Southland*, May 1921, p. 10; "Wealth (1921)," Internet Movie Database, http://www.imdb.com/title/tt0012822 (accessed November 8, 2005).

14. Gregory, "History"; *National Cyclopaedia of American Biography* 35 (1949): 138–139, s.v. "Church, George Myers."

15. BGG to Dr. Frederick Peterson, April 18, 1916, Goodhue Papers.

16. Deborah Nevins and Robert A. M. Stern, *The Architect's Eye: American Architectural Drawings from 1799–1978* (New York: Pantheon Books, 1979).

17. Richard Oliver, in *Architectural Design* 47 (June 1977): 445.

18. BGG to Eugene Klapp, June 14, 1916, Goodhue Papers.

19. BGG to EEG, June 7, 1917, Goodhue Papers.

20. "Will Rival Greatest Houses," *Pasadena Star-News*, July 29, 1916.

21. Ibid.

22. BGG to Mrs. William Miller Graham, April 17, 1916, Goodhue Papers.

23. BGG to C. Peake Anderson, April 23, 1917, Goodhue Papers.

24. BGG to CCB, August 14, 1917, Goodhue Papers.

25. BGG, "Home of the Future," p. 544.

26. BGG to CCB, August 14, 1917, Goodhue Papers.

27. BGG to CCB, November 23, 1917, Goodhue Papers.

28. Ibid.

29. Ibid.

30. BGG to Mrs. Leo Pierson (Ruth Baldwin), August 13, 1917, Goodhue Papers.

31. Ibid.

32. BGG to T. A. Jaggar, Jr., November 20, 1917, Goodhue Papers.

33. BGG to Mrs. Leo Pierson (Ruth Baldwin), May 3, 1918, Goodhue Papers.

34. BGG to CCB, May 6, 1918, Goodhue Papers.

35. Ibid.

36. BGG to JWG, March 20, 1918, Goodhue Papers.

37. *The Honolulu Academy of Arts: Its Origin and Founder* (Honolulu: Honolulu Academy of Arts, 1984), p. 18. This is a condensation of a history by Sister Grace Marian, M.M. I am indebted to Ron Chapman, Head Librarian, Honolulu Academy of Arts, for sending me this brochure and other materials on the academy.

38. Goodhue died before the family members reached New York. Hardie Phillip completed the design.

39. "New Honolulu Museum Building Opened," *Museum News* (American Association of Museums) 5, no. 2 (May 15, 1927).

40. "Residence of Harold Castle and Family," State of Hawaii, State Historic Preservation Division, Significant Buildings Inventory.

41. Carter was the second governor of the Territory of Hawaii and a director of C. Brewer & Co. The Carters lived in the house from 1928 until Mrs. Carter's death in 1945.

42. National Register of Historical Places Inventory (U.S. Department of the Interior, 1980).

Chapter 8
A SIMPLER ARCHITECTURE *1916–1918*

1. BGG, "Home of the Future," p. 449.

2. Michael Redmon, "History 101," *Santa Barbara Independent*, February 5, 1998. See also Myrick, *Montecito*, 1:157–158 (see chap. 3, n. 13).

3. BGG to JWG, March 10, 1917, Goodhue Papers.

4. Myrick, *Montecito*, 2:450.

5. BGG to Henry Dater, February 10, 1915, Goodhue Papers.

6. BGG to Lt. Col. John D. Moore, December 29, 1915, Goodhue Papers.

7. BGG to Lt. Col. John D. Moore, February 11, 1916, Goodhue Papers.

8. Oliver, *Goodhue*, p. 165.

9. I am indebted to Gail Jansen and Kellam de Forest (son of Lockwood de Forest) of the Austin Val Verde Foundation for giving me a private tour of the house and gardens, and for providing additional information.

10. BGG to JWG, April 11, 1917, Goodhue Papers.

11. BGG to JWG, March 20, 1918, Goodhue Papers.

12. Janet Parks and Alan G. Neuman, *The Old World Builds the New: The Guastavino Company and the Technology of the Catalan Vault, 1885–1962* (New York: Avery Architectural and Fine Arts Library and the Miriam and Ira D. Wallach Art Gallery, Columbia University, 1996). The quoted words appear on p. 11.

13. BGG to JWG, May 3, 1918, Goodhue Papers.

14. Ibid.

15. T. A. Jaggar, Jr., to BGG, October 31, 1917, Goodhue Papers.

16. Marilyn McMahon, "Val Verde History," *Santa Barbara News-Press*, May 25, 1997, D8.

17. Myrick, *Montecito*, 1:179.

18. Elane Griscom, "Val Verde's Dr. Warren Austin," *Montecito Magazine* 14, no. 1 (Spring 1994): 34–35. Dr. Austin came to Santa Barbara after World War II, with the unusual credentials of having been personal physician to the Duke and Duchess of Windsor while he was stationed in the Bahamas. The royal couple had introduced him to Montecito society through the famous flyer Beryl Markham.

19. Jim Buckley, "Austin's Val Verde OK'd," *Montecito Journal*, December 31, 1998.

20. Ben Hellwarth, "Neighbors Appeal Val Verde Permit," *Santa Barbara News-Press*, January 5, 1999.

21. Susan Chamberlin, letter to the editor, *Santa Barbara News-Press*, December 30, 1999.

22. BGG to CCB, September 24, 1917, Goodhue Papers.

23. *Dictionary of American Biography*, Supplement 2, s.v. "Vanderlip, Frank Arthur."

24. Mary Cheever, *The Changing Landscape: A History of Briarcliff Manor–Scarborough* (West Kennebunk, Me.: published for the Briarcliff Manor–Scarborough Historical Society by Phoenix Publishing, 1990), pp. 90–91, 102.

25. "Noteworthy Houses by Well-Known Architects – IV. Bertram Grosvenor Goodhue, Architect: The Home of Philip W. Henry Overlooks, Almost Overhangs, the Hudson River at Scarboro, N.Y.," *House Beautiful* 47, no. 2 (February 1920): 77–80. I found this article in Con's Scrapbook at the home of Sylvia Danenhower.

26. Ibid., p. 77.

27. Ibid.

28. Ibid., p. 80.

29. Ibid., p. 128.

30. Ibid.

31. Ibid.

32. John Cheever, "The Housebreaker of Shady Hill," in *The Stories of John Cheever* (New York: Vintage International, 2000), p. 257. I am grateful to Sol Stein for bringing this story to my attention.

33. BGG to the Council of the Grolier Club, January 24, 1917, Goodhue Papers.

34. Eileen Weber, the Briarcliff village historian, who has lived in the area all her life, identified the lot from Goodhue's sketches as No. 50 Revolutionary Road. My thanks to Carl and Mimi Boe for helping with this research.

35. BGG to Lt. Col. John D. Moore, February 6, 1919, Goodhue Papers.

36. The two drawings, which were published in Whitaker, *BGG*, plate I, were there labeled "Sketches for a House in Westchester, New York." The actual drawings each have a handwritten note in the lower right-hand corner reading "House for Frederick Peterson, near Brewster, N.Y." However, the drawings clearly illustrate Goodhue's letter to John Moore describing the Walter Douglas house in Scarborough (Westchester County, N.Y.). I asked John Rivers for clarification. He recalled that his mother (Goodhue's granddaughter) had complained that several drawings were mislabeled when they were assembled for a show.

37. BGG, "Home of the Future," pp. 454–455.

Chapter 9

PITTSBURGH PICTURESQUE AND LONG ISLAND TUDOR *1919–1924*

1. BGG, "Home of the Future," p. 544.

2. I am grateful to Albert M. Tannler for bringing this house to my attention and for providing much of the research material. I am also indebted to Laura Colhouer, who was one of the owners of the larger part of the house (1331 Bennington) during the period that I was researching this book. She provided historical information as well as architectural drawings of the original house and its alterations.

3. G. H. Edgell, *The American Architecture of To-day* (New York: Charles Scribner's Sons, 1928), p. 205.

4. James D. Van Trump, *Life and Architecture in Pittsburgh* (Pittsburgh: Pittsburgh History & Landmarks Foundation, 1983), p. 204.

5. Ibid., p. 11.

6. Ibid., p. 16.

7. The two parcels of land were deeded to Mrs. Myler in April and October 1919. Two other parcels were deeded subsequently.

8. In 1929 the American Radiator Company merged with Standard Sanitary Manufacturing Company. In 1967 the name was changed to American Standard. See http://www .americanstandard-us.com/ (accessed September 25, 2004).

9. John W. Jordan, *Encyclopedia of Pennsylvania Biography* (New York: Lewis Historical Publishing Co., 1919).

10. "Building Permits," in *Builders' Bulletin* 4, no. 19 (January 10, 1920): 8.

11. "Contracts Awarded," in *Builders' Bulletin* 4, no. 10 (November 8, 1919): 6.

12. The third parcel of land for the addition to 1333 Bennington was purchased June 1, 1923, and the construction contract was awarded June 30, 1923, with Goodhue listed as architect. See *Builders' Bulletin* 7, no. 44 (June 30, 1923): 9.

13. "Post-Medieval Houses," *Old House Journal*, March–April 2001. Laura Colhouer drew my attention to this article and sent me a copy of it.

14. *The Charette: A Little Journal of Rejuvenation Published Every Month by the Pittsburgh Architectural Club Incorporated* 2, no. 4 (April 1921): 4.

15. Whitaker, *BGG*, plate CLXXII.

16. BGG to CCB, September 24, 1917, Goodhue Papers.

17. BGG, "Home of the Future," pp. 543–544.

18. Walter C. Kidney, "Two Granules on the Mountain of Knowledge," *PHLF News*, July 1994.

19. BGG to Mrs. Wilton Lloyd-Smith, April 21, 1924, SPLIA Archives. I am grateful to Robert MacKay, Director of the Society for the Preservation of Long Island Antiquities (SPLIA), for giving me access to the society's archives. I discov- ered that they had inherited two boxes containing all the cor- respondence between the Lloyd-Smiths and the Goodhue Associates, and others involved in the building project. In September 2005, Mr. MacKay kindly gave all the Lloyd-Smith material to the Avery Library.

20. Ibid.

21. Ibid.

22. BGG to Wilton Lloyd-Smith, April 22, 1924, SPLIA Archives.

23. Jenny Lawrence provided a copy of a video that she made when she interviewed her grandmother, Marjorie Fleming, for her ninetieth birthday in 1984. I am also indebted to Ms. Lawrence for providing a copy of "The Lloyd-Smith Women," a family history, which she organized and designed. It consists of transcripts of recorded conversations with Marjorie Fleming Lloyd-Smith Woolley, her daughters, and some of her grand- daughters. The interviewees provided memories of their lives, and of their time spent at Kenjockety. Unless otherwise noted, all information on the Fleming and Lloyd-Smith families and their property at Lloyd's Neck is taken from this document.

24. Wilton's father, Walter, was a twin who decided that he and his brother should hyphenate their middle names to their last name. So, by court order, Walter became Lloyd-Smith and his brother, Wilton, became Merle-Smith.

25. *National Cyclopaedia of American Biography* 30 (1943): 401–402, s.v. "Lloyd-Smith, Wilton."

26. Wilton Lloyd-Smith, memorandum re Taxes, July 20, 1925, SPLIA Archives. Lloyd-Smith bought 67 acres from Mrs. Howard Barney and a total of 34 acres from two tracts owned by the Norman Smith heirs and W. J. Matheson, respectively.

27. "Buys 67 Acre Tract at Huntington, L.I.," *The Sun and the Globe* (New York), July 25, 1923.

28. Laura Lee Rogers to Mrs. Wilton Lloyd-Smith, February 23, 1925, SPLIA Archives. Rogers' letterhead read: Laura Lee Rogers, Nomenclator, Boudinot Place, Elizabeth, N.J. It is not clear from the correspondence that Ms. Rogers suggested the name Kenjockety.

29. "The Lloyd-Smith Women." There were originally five daugh- ters: Marne, Josephine (who died of polio at age four), Clara, Virginia, and Diane. Jenny Lawrence, the family historian, is the daughter of Marne Lloyd-Smith Hornblower.

30. Diane Lloyd-Smith Hewat's memories, in "The Lloyd-Smith Women."

31. Marjorie Lloyd-Smith to BGG, April 10, 1923, with enclo- sure, "Thoughts About House," SPLIA Archives.

32. Marjorie Lloyd-Smith Woolley, in "The Lloyd-Smith Women."

33. Diane's memories, in "The Lloyd-Smith Women."

34. Warren H. Manning, "Report on Visit to the Estate of Wilton Lloyd-Smith, Huntington, Long Island," September 7, 1928, SPLIA Archives.

35. Warren H. Manning to Mrs. Wilton Lloyd-Smith, November 7, 1929, SPLIA Archives.

36. Ibid.

37. Marjorie Lloyd-Smith Woolley, in "The Lloyd-Smith Women."

38. Paula Rice kindly provided the information on subsequent owners. I am grateful to Paula and Bruce Rice for allowing me to visit their home and study drawings and photographs of the original Lloyd-Smith estate.

39. *Club House for the Rensselaer Society of Engineers, Troy, New York* (pamphlet). Amy Rupert, Assistant Institute Archivist, Institute Archives and Special Collections, Folsom Library, Rensselaer Polytechnic Institute, kindly sent me this pamphlet as well as photographs of the completed building.

40. Rob Steere, e-mail re: Bertram Goodhue posted to Design Community discussion list, April 6, 2004, http://www

.designcommunity.com/discussion/34890.html (accessed September 5, 2005).

Chapter 10
GOODHUE'S OWN ABODES 1908–1924

1. Robert Craighead, "Homes of Well-Known Architects: The Home of Mr. Bertram Grosvenor Goodhue, New York City," *House Beautiful* 39, no. 3 (February 1916): xxv (hereafter Craighead, "Homes").
2. A note in Con's Scrapbook, Danenhower Archives.
3. BGG to Mrs. Charles R. Swords, November 24, 1915, Goodhue Papers.
4. New York City Department of Buildings Alteration Application No. 1885 (1905). Christopher Gray, founder of the Office for Metropolitan History, an organization that researches the architectural history of New York City, kindly researched the purchase of the townhouse at the New York City Department of Buildings. See also Christopher Gray, "A Renowned Architect's Home of His Own," Streetscapes, *New York Times*, sec. 11, January 22, 2006.
5. BGG to Messrs. Douglas Robinson, Chas. S. Brown Co., July 14, 1913, Goodhue Papers.
6. New York City Directory for 1905–1906. Information provided by Christopher Gray.
7. Craighead, "Homes," p. 65.
8. Ibid.
9. Ibid.
10. Ibid.
11. The Bucks County Historical Society, "Henry Chapman Mercer," http://www.mercermuseum.org/bchs/bchs_hcm.html (accessed August 26, 2005).
12. BGG to Mrs. F. B. Mason, March 15, 1910, Goodhue Papers.
13. Craighead, "Homes," p. 66.
14. The Latin text given here has been taken from a photograph of the piano in the Family Archives. The translation given is a corrected version of the rendering provided by Craighead, who does not quote the original Latin. The date at the end of the inscription is not legible in the photograph but has been presented here as MCMVII on the basis of Craighead's translation.
15. Craighead, "Homes," p. 66.
16. BGG to Percy E. Nobbs, October 13, 1910, Goodhue Papers.
17. In 1838 the clock traveled by road and canal to Ohio, where Thomas Grosvenor's son, Peter, moved. It stayed in Ohio until the late 1800s, when the Athens Grosvenors decided to return the clock to Helen Grosvenor Goodhue (Bertram's mother and granddaughter of Thomas Grosvenor) so that it could reside in its original home in Pomfret. "The story is told that when the box containing the clock arrived at the depot, a little boy ran to the Goodhue house to tell the family that the body had arrived" (Jane Hamilton, letter to author, January 4, 2003). Helen Grosvenor left the clock to her eldest son, Bertram. When his widow decided to move permanently to California, she sent the clock back to brother Ned, who was now living in Grosvenor Place, Pomfret. It was Lydia's understanding that Ned would keep it for one of Bertram's children. Ned wrote: "I shall be particularly glad to keep the old clock <u>for the family</u>. Storage would do it no good. I wound it each Sunday morning for so many years it seems part of my youth" (EEG to Lydia Goodhue, January 31, 1934, Family Archives; underlining in original). Ned, who never married, died in 1943 and left his Pomfret home and its contents to brother Harry's son, William. Unfortunately, there was a disagreement between William and Lydia Goodhue as to the disposition of the clock.

When William sold the Pomfret house to Sylvia Danenhower, he took the clock to his home in Belmont, Massachusetts. In 1973 he gave the clock to Jane Hamilton's mother, Constance Stewart Grosvenor, the granddaughter of General Grosvenor, who had inherited the clock when it resided in Ohio. And so it traveled again, ending up in the home of Thomas Heyward Motte Hamilton, Jane Hamilton's son, in South Carolina. Information for this account of the clock came from Jane Hamilton (letters to author, January 4, 2003, and February 24, 2005) and from a collection of papers in the Danenhower Archives entitled "Facts About a Clock," consisting of an anonymous typewritten history of the clock and copies of correspondence exchanged between William Goodhue, Lydia Goodhue Kimball, Hugh Goodhue, and Frances Goodhue Satterlee, July 10, 1944–August 8, 1944.
18. Craighead, "Homes," p. 68.
19. Ibid.
20. Ibid.
21. Ibid.
22. Ibid.
23. BGG to HEG, November 3, 1916, Goodhue Papers.
24. Smith, *St. Bartholomew's*, p. 36 (see chap. 2, n. 11).
25. Goodhue maintained that he did not object to Hugh attending confirmation classes provided that "the class gives impartially all information on all sides of the subject . . . and the views of other great religious beliefs as well as the Christian" (BGG to Rev. Samuel S. Drury, February 14, 1922, Goodhue Papers).
26. BGG to Rev. Samuel S. Drury, February 8, 1922, Goodhue Papers.
27. Quoted in Hartley Burr Alexander, "The Nebraska Capitol," in Whitaker, *BGG*, p. 45.
28. Theodore H. Price to BGG, March 27, 1922, Family Archives.
29. BGG to Theodore H. Price, April 11, 1922 (not sent), Family Archives.
30. *Mexican Memories*, pp. 61–82 (see chap. 1, n. 2).
31. Craighead, "Homes," p. xxv. Christopher T. Apostle, Director of the Old Master Paintings Department of Sotheby's, has concluded that the painting in question, still in the possession of the Goodhue family, is most likely not Sienese but Florentine, perhaps the work of the Master of San Jacopo a Mucciana, who worked in the third quarter of the fourteenth century (Christopher T. Apostle, letter to Charles Credaroli, September 24, 2002). A note on the back in Goodhue's handwriting states that he bought it in 1909 and that it came from the collection of Arthur Ray, Glasgow (Family Archives).
32. Craighead, "Homes," p. xxv.
33. Goodhue's great-grandfather, Colonel Thomas Grosvenor (1744–1825), had been an original member of the society.
34. *Encyclopaedia Britannica*, 15th ed., *Micropaedia*, s.v. "Cincinnati, Society of the." The city of Cincinnati, Ohio, was named in honor of the society in 1790 (ibid., s.v. "Cincinnati").
35. BGG to Bryce Metcalf, December 20, 1911, Goodhue Papers.
36. In the process Goodhue rediscovered lost relatives, turning up some black sheep and, to his dismay, a cousin who asked to be paid for signing the waiver.
37. Bryce Metcalf to BGG, July 10, 1916, Goodhue Papers.
38. BGG to CCB, February 2, 1917, Goodhue Papers.
39. Ibid.
40. BGG to HEG, December 19, 1911, Goodhue Papers.
41. The front of the house was in Briarcliff and the back in Ossining.
42. Henry G. Gennert to BGG, September 20, 1913, Goodhue Papers. In this letter Goodhue's lawyer explained the complications of the title. Thirty acres of the property had been owned by Philip Acker, the grandfather of Mary Collyer. On his death

in 1847 the property was left to his children, one of whom had disappeared from home prior to 1847 and had not been located since, hence the missing heir. In 1853, Mary's father, Jesse Acker, obtained a deed to the property from all his siblings except the missing brother, William Acker. When Jesse Acker died in 1881, he left the property to his daughter Mary Collyer. Gennert suggested that Goodhue either ask for a reduction in the price because Mrs. Collyer owned only seven-eighths of the property, or bring suit against Mary Collyer to establish clear title. There was no correspondence explaining the outcome.

43. BGG to CCB, May 28, 1913, Goodhue Papers.
44. Dale Vargas, "A Court at Pinner," Eton Fives Association, http://www.etonfives.co.uk/articles/pinner.court.html (accessed August 31, 2005).
45. Lederle & Provost to BGG, June 3, 1913, Goodhue Papers.
46. BGG to CCB, February 5, 1914, Goodhue Papers.
47. BGG to CCB, March 3, 1914, Goodhue Papers.
48. BGG to CGA, November 1, 1916, Goodhue Papers.
49. BGG to Miss Alice Eldredge, May 9, 1916, Goodhue Papers.
50. BGG to CCB, November 1, 1916, Goodhue Papers.
51. BGG to CCB, January 13, 1915, Goodhue Papers.
52. BGG to Henry Chase, August 17, 1915. The projects under discussion were an opera house, an agricultural college, and the Union railway station. Funds were simply not available.
53. BGG to Carleton Winslow, February 18, 1914, Goodhue Papers. Bishop Johnson was a good friend, who was enthusiastic about the cathedral design, but the outspoken architect thought he had upset the Building Committee: "They seemed to resent a statement made in one of my letters that to obtain everything they wanted would probably necessitate a 'jerry-built' structure, to which of course I could not bring myself" (ibid.).
54. BGG to CCB, August 20, 1918, Goodhue Papers.
55. Ibid.
56. Ibid.
57. BGG to Wells Goodhue, January 28, 1921, Goodhue Papers.
58. BGG to JWG, December 15, 1920, Goodhue Papers.
59. BGG to Lt. Clarence S. Stein, November 11, 1918, Goodhue Papers.
60. BGG to Mrs. Leo Pierson (Ruth Baldwin), November 17, 1919, Goodhue Papers.
61. BGG to C. Peake Anderson, November 12, 1918, Goodhue Papers.
62. BGG to Lt. Clarence S. Stein, November 11, 1918, Goodhue Papers.
63. Oliver was in error when he identified the drawing reproduced in his fig. 117 as "Study sketches for the Bertram Goodhue House, Montecito, California, 1918" (Oliver, Goodhue, p. 167). This error was among the corrigenda sent by Hugh Goodhue to the publisher of Oliver's book to be taken account of in a second edition of the book, which, however, never appeared (see chap. 3, n. 6). All efforts to identify this particular sketch have been unsuccessful. It is possible that Goodhue made the drawing in response to one of several tentative requests for Montecito estates that he received.
64. The night scene is at the Avery and the day scene is still in the family.

Chapter 11
GOODHUE'S NEW YORK STUDIO *1911–1924*

1. BGG to Col. J. M. Carson, August 20, 1913, Goodhue Papers.
2. *Record and Guide*, October 21, 1911, p. 595.
3. "The New Offices of Cram, Goodhue & Ferguson, New York," *Architecture* 27 (May 1913): 95 (hereafter "New Offices").

4. "Offices of Bertram Grosvenor Goodhue in New York," *New York Times*, August 24, 1913 (hereafter "Offices of BGG").
5. "New Offices," p. 95.
6. Albert M. Tannler, "'We Only Have One Window': Stained Glass and the Arts & Crafts Movement in the United States," *Journal of Stained Glass* 28 (2004): 61–78.
7. BGG to HEG, October 28, 1913, Goodhue Papers. Albert M. Tannler provided all the references to the office's stained-glass panels from the Goodhue Papers at the Avery Library. Tannler has published several articles on the life and work of Harry and Wright Goodhue, in particular "Harry Eldredge Goodhue: Pioneer of American Stained Glass," *Stained Glass* 99, no. 1 (Spring 2004): 54–67, and "Harry Wright Goodhue: Stained Glass of Unsurpassed Distinction and Rare Beauty," *Stained Glass* 99, no. 2 (Summer 2004): 134–147.
8. BGG to HEG, January 26, 1915, Goodhue Papers.
9. HEG to BGG, February 2, 1915, Goodhue Papers.
10. Albert Tannler and Peter Cormack provided this information. As Tannler and Cormack note, St. James Allemanus was also referred to as Blessed James of Ulm and was really James Grissinger, or Griesinger, who was born in 1407 in Ulm, Germany, and died in 1491.
11. Albert Tannler, e-mail to author, August 5, 2003. An illustration of the Willet panel appears in William Willet, "The Art of Stained Glass," *Architecture* 37, no. 4 (April 1918): 85.
12. Quintin Watt, ed., *The Bromsgrove Guild: An Illustrated History* ([Great Britain]: Bromsgrove Society, 1999), pp. 13, 27, 55. I am grateful to Pamela Kingsbury for sending me information on George Bankart.
13. George P. Bankart, "Modern British Plasterwork, I: An Architect and Craftsman's Views," *Architectural Review* 23 (1908): 226–232.
14. Ibid., p. 227.
15. BGG to George P. Bankart, January 8, 1916, Goodhue Papers.
16. Ibid.
17. BGG to John T. Comes, May 5, 1914, Goodhue Papers.
18. "New Offices," p. 115.
19. "Offices of BGG."
20. See below, n. 23.
21. Rev. Jonathan E. Goodhue, *History and Genealogy of the Goodhue Family in England and America to the Year 1890* (Rochester, N.Y.: E. R. Andrews, Printer & Bookbinder, 1891) (hereafter J. Goodhue, *History*).
22. Ibid., pp. 4–5, and illustrations at front of volume. After careful examination of Rev. Goodhue's rather muddled history, Nicholas Goodhue and I have concluded it is unlikely that the American Goodhues can claim a coat of arms. Correspondence between Nicholas Goodhue and Timothy Duke, the Chester Herald, College of Arms, London, England (the letters are dated May 2002 to March 2004), was the basis for our findings. Duke explained that as Mary Goodhugh (1738 Arms) was a widow, her arms could only be passed on if she married someone who also had the right to bear arms. Her arms would then be quartered with her new husband's. The "1790 Arms" were to be borne by all male-line descendants of William Goodhew of St. Paul's, Deptford, and all other descendants of his paternal grandfather, William Goodhew of Sutton at Hone, Kent (arms were commonly extended to a grantee's grandfather so that the grantee's brother(s) or first cousin(s) could also bear them). Bertram's first American ancestor was William Goodhue of Ipswich, Massachusetts, who emigrated from England around 1635. He was born about 1612 in Deptford, Kent; so it is impossible that he could be identified with the 1790 grantee or with the grantee's grandfather, who could not have been born before 1670 at the earliest.

23. J. Goodhue, *History*, p. 5. Jonathan's text actually has "invedis," though that is certainly a typographical error, since the accompanying drawing of the arms shows "invedio." But that is a mistake for *invideo*. Unfortunately, when adapting the drawing for his own use, Bertram failed to recognize and correct the error. Only where the motto appears on his tomb does the correct spelling occur (see chap. 13).

24. A photograph of the fireplace before the statues disappeared is in the collection of Goodhue papers at the Avery Library. William of Sens (1174–1179) was a master mason who became famous for his design of a new choir for Canterbury Cathedral after the Norman choir burned in 1174. William of Wykeham (1324–1404) was one of the first architects to use the Perpendicular style; his work included the rebuilding of a large part of Windsor Castle (1360–1369), colleges at Oxford and Winchester, and the Cathedral at Winchester. Prior Bolton (died 1532) was referred to by Henry VII as "Maister of the Works" and is thought to have been responsible for the chapel of Henry VII at Westminster. Pugin Senior was Augustus Welby Northmore Pugin (1812–1852), best known for the British Houses of Parliament (1836). See *Macmillan Encyclopedia of Architects*, ed. Adolf K. Placzek, 4 vols. (New York: Free Press, 1982), s.vv. "William of Sens and William the Englishman," "William of Wykeham," and "Pugin, Augustus Welby Northmore"; Russell Sturgis, *A Dictionary of Architecture and Building*, 3 vols. (New York: Macmillan, 1901–1902), s.v. "Bolton, William."

25. "Bertram Grosvenor Goodhue," *Lutheran Church Art* 2, no. 6 (May 1924).

26. I am grateful to Peter Cormack, Albert Tannler, and Nicholas Goodhue for helping me sort out the Pugins.

27. BGG to CCB, December 15, 1916, Goodhue Papers.

28. "Twelfth-Night in Mr. Goodhue's Office," *Pencil Points* 3, no. 2 (February 1922): 26 (hereafter "Twelfth-Night").

29. "New Offices," p. 115.

30. "Twelfth-Night," p. 22.

31. Ibid., pp. 25–26.

32. BGG to Mrs. Whittlesey, February 14, 1924, Goodhue Papers.

33. John D. Moore, "Bertram Grosvenor Goodhue: An Appreciation," *Architecture* (Sydney), September 1924, pp. 8–11.

34. "Twelfth-Night," p. 22.

35. Christopher Gray, "One Artist Preserves the 1912 Studio of Another," Streetscapes, *New York Times*, sec. 11, April 16, 2000.

36. Lydia Goodhue to RAC, October 23, 1924 or 1925 (no year date was given), BPL Archives.

37. "I closed my office about 18 months ago for the duration and all of my records, drawings, etc. are in storage. . . . I am now working for the Army Air Corps" (Hardie Phillip to CGA, August 18, 1943, Danenhower Archives).

Chapter 12
THE SEARCH FOR STYLISTIC FREEDOM *1918–1924*

1. BGG to C. Peake Anderson, November 12, 1918, Goodhue Papers.

2. Oliver, *Goodhue*, p. 193.

3. BGG to John D. Moore, February 6, 1919, Goodhue Papers.

4. Oliver, *Goodhue*, p. 142.

5. John R. Rivers, "The Architectural Development of Bertram Grosvenor Goodhue (1869–1924)" (B.A. thesis, Wesleyan University, Middletown, Conn., 1972), pp. 92–93 (hereafter Rivers, "BGG").

6. Quoted in Whitaker, essay in *BGG*, p. 27.

7. Address by Bertram Grosvenor Goodhue quoted in "Twelfth-Night in Mr. Goodhue's Office," *Pencil Points* 3, no. 2 (February 1922): 24.

8. BGG to C. Peake Anderson, November 12, 1918, Goodhue Papers.

9. I am indebted to Janice Goldblum, Archivist of the National Academy of Sciences, for bringing to my attention a thesis by Sarah Morrissa Dreller, "Bertram G. Goodhue's 'Alexandrian' Style: The National Academy of Sciences Building, Washington D.C., 1919–1924" (Master of Architectural History thesis, University of Virginia, 1999) (hereafter Dreller, "BGG's 'Alexandrian' Style"). This in turn led me to an article on the National Academy by Richard Guy Wilson (see below, n. 18) and to the Hale Papers, the originals of which I discovered were in the Archives at the California Institute of Technology.

10. George E. Hale, "National Academies and the Progress of Research," *Science*, January 1, 1915, pp. 13–17.

11. GEH to BGG, March 5, 1918, Hale Papers. Hale told Goodhue that he and Clipston Sturgis were the two architects being considered. He felt obligated to consider both men but much preferred Goodhue.

12. BGG, "Notes on Proposed Building for National Academy of Sciences in Washington, D.C.," sent to GEH, April 8, 1920, Hale Papers (hereafter BGG, "Notes for NAS").

13. BGG to GEH, April 11, 1918, Hale Papers.

14. GEH to BGG, May 22, 1918, Hale Papers.

15. BGG to GEH, April 17, 1918, Hale Papers.

16. BGG to GEH, June 11, 1918, Hale Papers.

17. Ibid.

18. Richard Guy Wilson, "Modernized Classicism and Washington, D.C.," in *American Public Architecture: European Roots and Native Expressions*, ed. Craig Zabel and Susan Scott Munshower, Papers in Art History from the Pennsylvania State University, vol. 5 (University Park, Pa.: Pennsylvania State University, 1989), 284 n. 19 (hereafter Wilson, "Modernized Classicism").

19. BGG to GEH, April 11, 1918, Hale Papers.

20. BGG to John D. Moore, February 6, 1919, Goodhue Papers.

21. GEH to BGG, June 20, 1918, Hale Papers.

22. In 1931, B Street was widened and renamed Constitution Avenue.

23. GEH to BGG, September 29, 1919, Hale Papers.

24. The McMillan Plan, named for Senator James McMillan of Michigan, was the 1901–1902 Senate Parks Commission Plan for Washington, D.C. Daniel Burnham, Charles F. McKim, and Augustus Saint-Gaudens prepared the plan. The principal buildings—the White House, the Capitol, the Washington Monument, and the Lincoln Memorial—would be laid out in a geometrical composition. Buildings along B Street would be part of the plan. As the National Academy of Sciences was to be the first of these buildings, it would set a precedent for future buildings along the street. In 1910, Congress created the Commission of Fine Arts to execute the plan.

25. NAS Council Meeting Minutes, December 19, 1919, Hale Papers. On January 22, 1920, Hale sent Brockett a correction to the minutes: "I do not think the style of the building designed by Mr. Goodhue can be called 'Persian,' though the design has some points of resemblance to Persian buildings. I should therefore omit the clause 'one of these buildings being a building with treatment in the Persian style.'"

26. BGG to GEH, November 25, 1919, Hale Papers.

27. NAS Council Meeting Minutes, December 19, 1919, Hale Papers.

28. BGG, "Notes for NAS."

29. Ibid.

30. Ibid.
31. GEH to Charles D. Walcott, June 25, 1920, Hale Papers.
32. BGG to John Russell Pope, November 9, 1920, Hale Papers.
33. John Fleming, Hugh Honour, and Nikolaus Pevsner, *The Penguin Dictionary of Architecture*, 3rd ed. (Harmondsworth: Penguin Books, 1980), pp. 300–301, s.v. "Soane, Sir John." In a letter to Hale (October 25, 1919, Hale Papers), Goodhue wrote that he thought they would be forced to build in concrete but that because "weather doesn't suit it, [it will be] necessary to devise some form of architecture consisting mainly of great paneled walls, the nearest precedent for which we have being the so-called Soanean style, . . . devised by Sir John Soane."
34. The U.S. Bureau of Fisheries stocked these pools with successive generations of exotic fish. In 1951, when repair costs became prohibitive, the tile was removed and the pools were turned into planters. See Peregrine S. White, *National Academy of Sciences, National Research Council: A Temple of Science*, rev. and ed. Fredrica W. Wechsler (Washington, D.C.: National Academy Press, 1984), p. 11 (hereafter White, *NAS*).
35. Gano Dunn, Chairman of the Building Committee, address delivered at the dedication of the National Academy of Sciences, April 28, 1924, Hale Papers.
36. White, *NAS*, p. 12.
37. Gano Dunn, "Memorandum to the Carnegie Corporation of New York on the Building Designed by Bertram G. Goodhue for the National Academy of Sciences and the National Research Council and the Progress of Its Construction," May 31, 1923, Hale Papers.
38. Dreller, "BGG's 'Alexandrian' Style," pp. 31–45.
39. Gano Dunn to GEH, April 8, 1922, Hale Papers.
40. Rivers, "BGG," p. 109.
41. BGG to GEH, June 5, 1923, Hale Papers.
42. Wilson, "Modernized Classicism," p. 279.
43. Quoted in Oliver, *Goodhue*, p. 186.
44. Oliver, *Goodhue*, p. 186.
45. Quoted in Oliver, *Goodhue*, p. 187.
46. From the descriptive text submitted by Goodhue, reprinted in "Nebraska Capitol Competition," *American Institute of Architects' Journal* 8 (1920): 299–306, as quoted in Oliver, *Goodhue*, p. 187.
47. Ibid.
48. Oliver, *Goodhue*, p. 190.
49. BGG to EEG, July 15, 1920, Goodhue Papers.
50. BGG to Alderson B. Horne, June 28, 1923, Goodhue Papers. Goodhue told Horne that "Mr. Johnson's record was not good" and that "he was known as a grafter."
51. Ibid.
52. Ibid.
53. "Investigation of Bertram Goodhue," 42nd Session of the Legislature, 1923, Nebraska Capitol Collections.
54. BGG to EEG, April 16, 1923, Goodhue Papers.
55. BGG to Alderson B. Horne, June 28, 1923, Goodhue Papers.
56. Ibid.
57. Ibid.
58. Oliver, *Goodhue*, p. 199.
59. Ibid., p. 206.
60. The Capitol was paid for entirely by tax revenues, which was one reason why the construction was spread over a ten-year period.
61. BGG to Sir Giles Gilbert Scott and Lady Scott, January 7, 1924, Goodhue Papers.
62. BGG to William Lethaby, March 7, 1924, Goodhue Papers.
63. Oliver, *Goodhue*, p. 226.
64. BGG to Mrs. Whittlesey, January 10, 1924, Goodhue Papers.
65. Carleton Monroe Winslow, "The Los Angeles Public Library," *Western Architect* 36, no. 2 (February 1927): 21–22.
66. Oliver, *Goodhue*, p. 226.
67. Ibid., p. 232.
68. Paul Goldberger, "A Landmark Manages to Cheat the Wrecking Ball," *New York Times*, October 10, 1993. The west garden with its reflecting pools had already been torn up to make space for a parking lot. As part of the Hardy Holzman Pfeiffer restoration, the parking lot was changed back into a garden, which includes terraced pools, fountains, and tile work telling the story of language.
69. John Morris, "Los Angeles Library Fire—Learning the Hard Way," *Canadian Library Journal*, August 1987. The fire was concentrated in the book stacks, making it necessary to aim gallons of water into the stacks, which ran down the building and damaged another 700,000 books.
70. Talbot Faulkner Hamlin, "Bertram Grosvenor Goodhue," *The Nation*, June 10, 1925, p. 661. The plan and the south elevation of Goodhue's design for the Liberty Memorial are shown in Oliver, *Goodhue*, p. 217, figs. 148 and 149.

Chapter 13
A LIFE CUT SHORT *1869–1924*

1. C. Howard Walker, "Bertram Grosvenor Goodhue" (eulogy read at the Annual Meeting of the Tavern Club, May 5, 1924), Family Archives.
2. BGG to CCB, February 5, 1914, Goodhue Papers.
3. BGG to EEG, August 31, 1914, Goodhue Papers.
4. BGG to Mrs. Robert Ferguson, December 4, 1915, Goodhue Papers.
5. BGG to Dr. G. M. Goodwin, February 19, 1918, Goodhue Papers.
6. BGG to EEG, May 17, 1918, Goodhue Papers.
7. BGG to CCB, August 20, 1918, Goodhue Papers.
8. BGG to Mrs. Cecil Brewer, February 6, 1919, Goodhue Papers.
9. Ibid.
10. BGG to EEG, April 7, 1919, Goodhue Papers.
11. Miss Bachman (Goodhue's secretary) to Mrs. Cecil Brewer, February 17, 1920, Goodhue Papers.
12. E. Donald Robb, "An Explanation and Acknowledgment," in *A Book of Drawings*.
13. BGG to Mrs. Arthur Molesworth, June 22, 1920, Goodhue Papers.
14. BGG to Hugh Goodhue, January 25, 1921, Family Archives.
15. BGG to Dr. Nellis B. Foster, February 28, 1921, Goodhue Papers.
16. BGG to EEG, April 7, 1921, Goodhue Papers.
17. BGG to Dr. Nellis B. Foster, August 2, 1921, Goodhue Papers.
18. BGG to Wells Goodhue, January 9, 1922, Goodhue Papers.
19. Ibid.
20. BGG to EEG, April 24, 1922, Goodhue Papers.
21. BGG to Wells Goodhue, January 9, 1922, Goodhue Papers.
22. BGG to Mrs. Ellen B. Van Kleek (Cousin Ellen), March 1, 1922, Goodhue Papers.
23. BGG to EEG, April 24, 1922, Goodhue Papers.
24. BGG to CGA, May 12, 1922, Goodhue Papers.
25. BGG to CGA, November 24, 1922, Goodhue Papers.
26. Ibid.
27. BGG to EEG, March 17, 1923, Goodhue Papers.
28. BGG to EEG, May 12, 1922, Goodhue Papers.
29. Con's Scrapbook, Danenhower Archives.
30. BGG to CGA, March 19, 1924, Goodhue Papers. It should be

noted that in this letter Goodhue spoke of replacing his evening whisky with lime water. In his youth Goodhue was known as a beer drinker. Like most gentlemen of his era, he enjoyed fine wines and prided himself in maintaining a good cellar even during Prohibition. Owing to his many illnesses, he had tried unsuccessfully to give up smoking, but he did manage to reduce his alcohol intake. It should be noted that his enjoyment of liquor did not amount to alcoholism as suggested by Aaron Betsky in his review of Oliver, *Goodhue*, in *Progressive Architecture*, February 1985, p. 171.

31. BGG to GEH, June 5, 1923, Goodhue Papers.

32. Frances (Franny) Goodhue to EEG, April 26, 1924, Danenhower Archives (hereafter FG to EEG, April 26, 1924). Oliver (*Goodhue*, p. 284 n. 56) gave the details of the architect's last night as remembered many years later by Hugh and Frances. I discovered this letter among Sylvia Danenhower's family papers and have included the quotations to shed more light on the events of that tragic evening.

33. FG to EEG, April 26, 1924.

34. Ibid. (the death certificate was signed by R.W.H. Rollings, M.D.). In view of Douglass Shand-Tucci's reference to unnamed "rumormongers" suggesting that "Goodhue's death was by his own hand" (Shand-Tucci, *Four Quests*, p. 96), it is useful to have this detailed account of the actual circumstances of his death.

35. BGG to Mrs. Whittlesey, February 14, 1924, Goodhue Papers.

36. FG to EEG, April 26, 1924.

37. James M. Wetterer of Fresh Pond Crematory, telephone conversation with Nicholas Goodhue, March 4, 2006.

38. A gravestone bearing Goodhue's dates and the words "Buried in the Chapel of the Intercession" was placed in the family plot in Pomfret.

39. FG to EEG, April 26, 1924.

40. Memorandum of meeting of the Goodhue Memorial Committee, February 18, 1929, Family Archives.

41. Oliver (*Goodhue*, p. 235) wrote that the ashes "were buried at Fresh Pond Cemetery," presumably having misread "Crematory" as "Cemetery" in the death certificate. According to James M. Wetterer of the crematory, their records show that Goodhue's body was cremated on April 26, 1924, and his remains picked up by Hugh Goodhue on April 28, 1924.

42. Champville marble is a beige-colored marble quarried in France.

43. Milo Hudson Gates, *A Description of the Chapel of the Intercession, Trinity Parish, New York* (1931), pp. 13–15.

44. Ibid. Concerning the coat of arms and the motto, see chap. 11.

45. Ibid., p. 15. "Tetigit" is misspelled as "tetiget" in the carving above the tomb but appears correctly in Gates's booklet. The inscription is a variation of a line of the epitaph composed by Dr. Samuel Johnson for Oliver Goldsmith.

Chapter 14
GOODHUE'S DEVELOPMENT FROM GOTHIC REVIVALIST
TO MODERNIST PIONEER

1. Hartley Burr Alexander, "The Nebraska Capitol," in Whitaker, *BGG*, p. 45.

2. BGG to Mrs. Leo Pierson (Ruth Baldwin), August 13, 1917, Goodhue Papers.

3. BGG to C. Peake Anderson, November 12, 1918, Goodhue Papers.

4. BGG to Percy E. Nobbs, March 10, 1910, Goodhue Papers.

5. Ibid.

6. Smith, *St. Bartholomew's*, p. 37 (see chap. 2, n. 11).

7. Richard Oliver, in *Architectural Design* 47 (June 1977): 445.

8. Sir Giles Gilbert Scott, opening remarks for "Exhibition of the Work of the Late Bertram Grosvenor Goodhue," *Architectural Association Journal* 41, no. 470 (April 1926): 206.

9. Carter Wiseman, "Most Underrated Architect," *American Heritage* 49, no. 3 (May–June 1998): 46 (hereafter Wiseman, "Most Underrated").

10. Vincent Scully, *Modern Architecture* (New York: George Braziller, 1967), p. 36.

11. Oliver, *Goodhue*, p. 234.

12. Fiske Kimball, "Goodhue's Architecture: A Critical Estimate," *Architectural Record* 62 (December 1927): 539.

13. Christine Smith, "Goodhue, Bertram Grosvenor," *American National Biography* (New York: Oxford University Press, 1999), 9:242.

14. Paul Goldberger, introduction to the 1976 reprint of Whitaker, *BGG* (see preface, n. 4).

15. *Sir Banister Fletcher's "A History of Architecture,"* 20th ed., ed. Dan Cruickshank (Oxford: Architectural Press, 1996), pp. 1496, 1499. This passage first appeared (with minor differences) in the 19th ed., ed. John Musgrove (London: Butterworths, 1987), p. 1411.

16. Wiseman, "Most Underrated," p. 46.

17. Donn Barber, "Bertram Grosvenor Goodhue (1869–1924)," *Architectural Record* 55 (May 1922): 469–470 (hereafter Barber, "BGG").

18. BGG to Mrs. Leo Pierson (Ruth Baldwin), November 17, 1919, Goodhue Papers.

19. Barber, "BGG," p. 469.

20. Sir Thomas Browne, "The Garden of Cyrus" (1658), chap. 2.

SELECTED BIBLIOGRAPHY

BOOKS AND ARTICLES BY GOODHUE

Baxter, Sylvester. *Spanish Colonial Architecture in Mexico*, with photographic plates by Henry Greenwood Peabody and plans by Bertram Grosvenor Goodhue. 10 vols. Boston: J. B. Millet, 1901. There is also a "grand de luxe edition" in 12 vols.

Goodhue, Bertram Grosvenor. Introduction to *The Architecture and the Gardens of the San Diego Exposition*, described by Carleton Monroe Winslow. San Francisco: Paul Elder & Co., 1916.

————. *Book Decorations*. New York: Grolier Club, 1931.

————. *A Book of Architectural and Decorative Drawings*. New York: Architectural Book Publishing Co., 1914; second printing, 1924.

————. "The Home of the Future: A Study of America in Relation to the Architect." *The Craftsman* 29, no. 5 (February 1916): 449–455, 543–544.

————. *Mexican Memories: The Record of a Slight Sojourn Below the Yellow Rio Grande, with Illustrations by the Author*. New York: Geo. M. Allen Co., 1892.

BOOKS ABOUT GOODHUE AND HIS BUILDINGS

Luebke, Frederick C., ed. *A Harmony of the Arts: The Nebraska State Capitol*. Lincoln: University of Nebraska Press, 1990.

Oliver, Richard. *Bertram Grosvenor Goodhue*. New York: Architectural History Foundation; Cambridge, Mass.: MIT Press, 1983.

Smith, Christine. *St. Bartholomew's Church in the City of New York*. New York: Oxford University Press, 1988.

Whitaker, Charles Harris, ed. *Bertram Grosvenor Goodhue: Architect and Master of Many Arts*. New York: American Institute of Architects Press, 1925. Reprinted with introduction by Paul Goldberger. New York: Da Capo Press, 1976.

Wyllie, Romy. *Caltech's Architectural Heritage: From Spanish Tile to Modern Stone*. Los Angeles: Balcony Press, 2000.

GENERAL BOOKS

Andree, Herb; Noel Young; and Patricia Halloran. *Santa Barbara Architecture: From Spanish Colonial to Modern*. Photography by Wayne McCall. 3rd ed. Edited by Bob Easton and Wayne McCall. Santa Barbara: Capra Press, 1995. Reprinted with corrections, Santa Monica: Hennessey & Ingalls, 2005.

Cheever, Mary. *The Changing Landscape: A History of Briarcliff Manor–Scarborough*. West Kennebunk, Me.: Published for the Briarcliff Manor–Scarborough Historical Society by Phoenix Publishing, 1990.

Cram, Ralph Adams. *My Life in Architecture*. Boston: Little, Brown & Co., 1936.

Day, Frank Miles. *American Country Houses of Today*. New York: Architectural Book Publishing Co., 1912.

Edgell, G. H. *The American Architecture of To-day*. New York: Charles Scribner's Sons, 1928.

Fleming, John; Hugh Honour; and Nikolaus Pevsner. *The Penguin Dictionary of Architecture*. 3rd ed. Harmondsworth: Penguin Books, 1980.

Fletcher, Banister. *Sir Banister Fletcher's "A History of Architecture."* 20th ed. Edited by Dan Cruickshank. Oxford: Architectural Press, 1996.

Hines, Thomas S. *Irving Gill and the Architecture of Reform*. New York: Monacelli Press, 2000.

Inskip, Peter. *Edwin Lutyens*. New York: Rizzoli, 1979.

Kamerling, Bruce. *Irving J. Gill, Architect*. San Diego: San Diego Historical Society, 1993.

Kaplan, Wendy. *"The Art That Is Life": The Arts & Crafts Movement in America, 1875–1920*. Boston: Little, Brown & Co., 1987.

Lethaby, William R. *Architecture, Mysticism and Myth*. London, 1891. Reprint, New York: George Braziller, 1975.

Mackay, Robert B.; Anthony K. Baker; and Carol A. Traynor, eds. *Long Island Country Houses and Their Architects, 1860–1940*. New York: W. W. Norton & Co., 1997.

Myrick, David F. *Montecito and Santa Barbara*. 2 vols. Pasadena, Calif.: Pentrex Media Group, 1988–1991; second printing, 2001.

Randall, Monica. *The Mansions of Long Island's Gold Coast*. New York: Rizzoli, 1987.

Scully, Vincent. *Modern Architecture*. New York: George Braziller, 1967.

Shand-Tucci, Douglass. *Ralph Adams Cram: Life and Architecture*. Vol. 1, *Boston Bohemia, 1881–1900*. Amherst: University of Massachusetts Press, 1995.

————. *Ralph Adams Cram: Life and Architecture*. Vol. 2, *An Architect's Four Quests: Medieval, Modernist, American, Ecumenical*. Amherst: University of Massachusetts Press, 2005.

Stamp, Gavin. *Edwin Lutyens: Country Houses: From the Archives of "Country Life."* London: Aurum Press, 2001.

List of Buildings and Projects

A revised version of the list in Richard Oliver, *Bertram Grosvenor Goodhue* (New York: Architectural History Foundation; Cambridge, Mass.: MIT Press, 1983), pp. 285–288.

This is primarily a list of works in which Goodhue was involved. However, a few works that were mainly Cram's responsibility have been included. They are marked "CGF/RAC."

Residential projects are in **bold italics**.

Abbreviations

CWG   Cram, Wentworth & Goodhue
CGF   Cram, Goodhue & Ferguson
BGG   Bertram Grosvenor Goodhue
RAC   Ralph Adams Cram
MMP   Bertram Grosvenor Goodhue Associates; later evolved to Mayers, Murray & Phillip

Key to Residential Projects

**   Indicates built and extant.
*   Indicates built but since demolished.
No asterisk   Indicates the project was never built.

1889	Competitive design for Cathedral of St. John the Divine, New York City (BGG)
1890	Winning competitive design for Cathedral of St. Matthew, Dallas, Texas (BGG)
1891–1892	Proposed Cathedral of St. Matthew, Dallas Texas (CWG)
1891–1895	All Saints' Church, Ashmont, Massachusetts (CWG); reredos, 1899 (CGF)
1892	Church of St. John the Evangelist, St. Paul, Minnesota (CWG)
1892–1893	St. Paul's Church, Brockton, Massachusetts (CWG)
1893	Competitive design for City Hall, New York City (CWG)
1893	***Competitive design for Walter Phelps Dodge house, Simsbury, Connecticut (CWG)***
1893–1894	Christ Church, Hyde Park, Massachusetts (CWG)

1893–1894	Church of the Open Word, Newtonville, Massachusetts (CWG)
1894	***Arthur May Knapp house, Fall River, Massachusetts** * (CWG/RAC)*
1895	***Proposed house for Joseph Merrill, Little Boar's Head, New Hampshire (CWG)***
1894	First Congregational Church, Plymouth, Massachusetts (CWG)
1894	Proposed Unitarian Church, Somerville, Massachusetts (CWG)
1894–1899	All Saints' Church, Brookline, Massachusetts (CWG)
1894–1904	St. Andrew's Church, Detroit, Michigan (CWG & CGF)
1895–1896	Second Congregational Church, Exeter, New Hampshire (CWG)
1895–1898	Newton Corner Methodist Episcopal Church, Newton Corner, Massachusetts (CWG)
1895–1900	Church of SS. Peter and Paul, Fall River, Massachusetts (CWG & CGF)
1896	Proposed St. Paul's Church, Rochester, New York (CWG)
1896	Christ Church, Waltham, Massachusetts (CWG)
1896	The Phillips Church, Exeter, New Hampshire (CWG)
1896–1899	Public Library, Fall River, Massachusetts (CWG & CGF)
1897–1898	Church of Our Saviour, Middleborough, Massachusetts (CGF)
1897–1910	St. Stephen's Church, Fall River, Massachusetts (CWG & CGF)
1898	Proposed First Parish Meeting House, Cambridge, Massachusetts (CGF)
1898	***Hammond House Apartments, Charlestown, Massachusetts** * (CGF)*
1898	***Baldwin house, Brookline, Massachusetts** * (CGF/RAC)*
1898	***John A. Logan house, Bala Cynwyd, Pennsylvania** * (CGF)*
1898–1902	Deborah Cook Sayles Public Library, Pawtucket, Rhode Island (CGF)
1899	Competitive design for a memorial monument, Dorchester Heights, Massachusetts (CGF)
1899	Proposed Carnegie Library, Atlanta, Georgia (CGF)
1899	Proposed Chickamauga Memorial Arch, Georgia (CGF)

1899	*Ruth A. Benson house, Cambridge, Massachusetts*** *(CGF)*
1899	*Richmond Court Apartments, Brookline, Massachusetts*** *(CGF)*
1899	*William A. Huff house, Greensburg, Pennsylvania*** *(CGF/RAC) {now YMCA of Westmoreland County}*
1899	*General Charles Grosvenor house, Athens, Ohio*** *(CGF) {now Konneker Alumni Center, Ohio University}*
1899	St. Luke's Hospital (altar and reredos), Roxbury, Massachusestts (CGF)
1899–1906	St. Stephen's Church, Cohasset, Massachusetts (CGF)
1900–1902	Emmanuel Church, Newport, Rhode Island (CGF)
1901	Public Library, Nashua, New Hampshire (CGF)
1902	St. Mary's Church, Walkerville, Ontario, Canada (CGF)
1902	Mortuary Chapel for Lewis Day, Norwood, Massachusetts (CGF)
1902–1906	*James Waldron Gillespie house, El Fureidis, Montecito, California*** *(CGF)*
1902	Campus plan for Sweet Briar Institute, Sweet Briar, Virginia (CGF)
1903–1910	Campus plan and additions to the United States Military Academy, West Point, New York, including the Cadet Chapel (Goodhue), post headquarters (Cram and Goodhue), gymnasium (Cram), and many lesser buildings, including stables, cadet barracks, and officer housing (CGF)
1904	Competitive design for Cathedral of St. John in the Wilderness, Denver, Colorado (CGF)
1904–1905	*Mrs. J. N. Brown house, Harbour Court, Newport, Rhode Island*** *(CGF/RAC) {now New York Yacht Club}*
1904–1906	Hibbard Memorial Chapel, Grace Church, Chicago, Illinois (CGF/NY)
1905	*Competitive design for E. H. Harriman house, Arden, New York (CGF)*
1905	La Santísima Trinidad, procathedral of Havana, Cuba (CGF/NY)
1905	St. James's Church, South Pasadena, California (CGF/NY); chancel, 1914 (BGG); tower, 1924 (BGG)
1905–1906	*Renovation of Goodhue's townhouse, New York City* (CGF/NY)*
1905–1913	St. Thomas Church, New York City (CGF); reredos, 1914–1920 (BGG)
1907	Proposed St. Thomas's College, Washington, D.C. (CGF/NY)
1907	Proposed Church of Los Todos Santos, Guantánamo, Cuba (CGF/NY)
1907	All Saints' Cathedral, Halifax, Nova Scotia, Canada (CGF/NY)
1907	Proposed "House of Studies," Washington, D.C. (CGF/NY)
1907	Proposed "Community House for the Paulist Fathers," New York City (CGF/NY)
1907–1909	St. John's Church, West Hartford, Connecticut (CGF/NY); parish house, 1914 (BGG)
1908	Christ Church, West Haven, Connecticut (CGF/NY)
1908–1913	Taft School, Watertown, Connecticut (CGF/NY)
1909	St. Mark's Church, Mt. Kisco, New York (CGF/NY); tower, 1920 (BGG)
1909	Russell Sage Memorial Presbyterian Church, Far Rockaway, New York (CGF/NY)
1909	*Village Hall, Dobbs Ferry, New York (BGG) Sketch for alteration to 1842 building, finalized in 2004***
1909	*Miss Helen Chase house, Middlecross, Waterbury, Connecticut*** *(CGF/NY) {now a multifamily house}*
1909–1910	Dutch Reformed Church ("South Church"), New York City (CGF/NY)
1909	Campus plan for the Rice Institute, Houston, Texas (CGF); individual buildings by Cram & Ferguson
1909–1912	First Baptist Church, Pittsburgh, Pennsylvania (CGF/NY); pulpit and war memorial, 1919–1924 (BGG)
1910	Christ Church, Bay Ridge, Brooklyn, New York (CGF/NY); parish house, 1917 (BGG)
1910	St. Paul's Church, New Haven, Connecticut (CGF/NY)
1910	Proposed cathedral and hospital, Los Angeles, California (CGF/NY)
1910	St. John's Church, Newport, Rhode Island (CGF/NY)
1910	Second Presbyterian Church, Lexington, Kentucky (CGF/NY)
1910–1913	Kitchi Gammi Club, Duluth, Minnesota (CGF/NY)
1910–1915	St. Paul's Church, Duluth, Minnesota (CGF/NY)
1910	G. G. Hartley office building, Duluth, Minnesota (CGF/NY)
1910–1914	Chapel of the Intercession, New York City (CGF/NY)
1911	Office building for the Economy Concrete Company, New Haven, Connecticut (CGF/NY)
1911	Competitive design for Northwestern University, Evanston, Illinois (CGF/NY)
1911	Washington Hotel, Colón, Panama Canal Zone (CGF/NY)
1911–1915	Panama-California Exposition, San Diego, California: Consulting Architect (BGG); individual buildings (CGF/NY)
1911–1924	Proposed Cathedral of the Incarnation, Baltimore, Maryland (CGF/NY & BGG)
1913	Trinity Episcopal Church, Asheville, North Carolina (CGF/NY)
1913	Ford Dormitory, Rutgers College, New Brunswick, New Jersey (CGF/NY)
1913	Competitive design for a city hall, Waterbury, Connecticut (CGF/NY)
1913	New York office of Cram, Goodhue & Ferguson (CGF/NY)
1913–1915	Alterations to Christ Chapel, Trinity Episcopal Church, Buffalo, New York (CGF/NY & BGG)
1913–1915	Parish House of St. Peter's Church, Morristown, New Jersey (CGF/NY & BGG)
1913–1916	Campus plan and buildings for the Virginia Military Institute, Lexington, Virginia (CGF/NY & BGG)
1913–1918	*J. E. Aldred house, Ormston, Locust Valley, New York*** *(CGF/NY & BGG) {now St. Josaphat's Monastery}*
1913–1914	*Cavour Hartley house, Duluth, Minnesota*** *(CGF/NY & BGG)*
1913–1914	*Alteration to an existing farmhouse, Briarcliff, New York* (CGF/NY & BGG)*
1913–1914	*Proposed house for Bertram Goodhue, Briarcliff, New York (CGF/NY & BGG)*

1914   *FIRM SPLIT*

1914   St. Andrew's Chapel, St. James's Church, Chicago, Illinois (BGG)

1914   New York City building, Panama-Pacific International Exposition, San Francisco, California (BGG)

1914–1916 Congregational Church, Montclair, New Jersey (BGG)

1914–1918 Church of St. Vincent Ferrer, New York City (BGG)

1914–1918 *Company town plan and individual buildings, including housing, Tyrone, New Mexico (BGG)*

1914–1919 St. Bartholomew's Church, New York City (BGG); dome and community house, 1930 (MMP)

1915   *Proposed house for Dr. Frederick Peterson, Westchester County, New York (BGG)*

1915–1916 *Herbert Coppell house, Mi Sueño, Pasadena, California** (BGG) {In 1950, the main house was split into two private residences and the garage was converted to a single residence.}*

1915–1917 Campus plan for the California Institute of Technology (BGG)
         Gates Laboratory of Chemistry, 1917 (BGG); Gates Annex, 1927 (MMP)
         Culbertson Hall, 1921 (BGG)
         Bridge Laboratories of Physics: East Bridge, 1922 (BGG); Bridge Annex, 1924 (BGG); West Bridge, 1925 (BGG & MMP)
         High Voltage Research Laboratory, 1923 (BGG)
         Guggenheim Aeronautical Laboratory, 1928 (MMP)
         Dabney Hall of the Humanities, 1928 (MMP)
         Kerckhoff Laboratories of the Biological Sciences: West Kerckhoff, 1928 (MMP); East Kerckhoff, 1939 (MMP)
         Robinson Laboratory of Astrophysics, 1932 (MMP)
         Crellin Laboratory of Chemistry, 1937 (MMP)
         Arms Laboratory of the Geological Sciences, 1938 (MMP)
         Mudd Laboratory of the Geological Sciences, 1938 (MMP)

1915–1918 *Henry Dater house, Días Felices, Montecito, California** (BGG) {now Austin Val Verde Foundation}*

1916–1917 Grolier Club, New York City (BGG)

1916–1917 Montecito Country Club, Santa Barbara, California (BGG)

1917   Campus plans for Oahu College and Kamehameha School, Honolulu, Hawaii (BGG)

1918   United States Marine Corps base, San Diego, California (BGG)

1918   United States Naval Air Station, San Diego, California (BGG)

1918   *Philip Henry house, La Paz, Scarborough, New York** (BGG)*

1918   *Proposed house for Walter Douglas, Scarborough, New York (BGG)*

1918   *Proposed house for Bertram Goodhue, Montecito, California (BGG)*

1918–1924 National Academy of Sciences Building, Washington, D.C. (BGG)

1918–1928 Rockefeller Memorial Chapel, University of Chicago, Chicago, Illinois (BGG & MMP)

1919   Cloister for St. Paul's Church, Concord, New Hampshire (BGG)

1919–1922 *Mrs. William Myler house, Pittsburgh, Pennsylvania** (BGG) {now two private residences}*

1920   *House, La Cabaña, for Bertram Goodhue, Montecito, California** (BGG)*

1920–1924 Proposed Sterling Memorial Library, Yale University, New Haven, Connecticut (BGG)

1920–1932 Nebraska State Capitol, Lincoln, Nebraska (BGG & MMP)

1921   Pulpit in Holy Trinity Church, Pittsburgh, Pennsylvania (BGG)

1921   Proposed Convocation Tower, New York City (BGG)

1921   Competitive design for the Liberty Memorial, Kansas City, Missouri (BGG)

1921   Proposed church in Watertown, Connecticut (BGG)

1921–1926 Los Angeles Public Library, Central Building, Los Angeles, California (BGG, MMP; Carleton Winslow, associated architect)

1922   Parish house for All Saints' Church, Johnson City, New York (BGG)

1922   Memorial Battle Chapel, American Church of the Holy Trinity, Paris, France (BGG)

1922   Memorials in St. Mary's Church, Tuxedo, New York (BGG)

1922   Competitive design for the Tribune Building, Chicago, Illinois (BGG)

1922–1927 Honolulu Academy of Arts, Hawaii (BGG & MMP)

1923–1924 Reredos for St. Martin's Church, Providence, Rhode Island (BGG)

1923–1924 *Rensselaer Society of Engineers Club House, Troy, New York** (BGG)*

1923–1924 Wolf's Head Society (Phelps Association) Building, Yale University, New Haven, Connecticut (BGG & MMP)

1924–1926 *Wilton Lloyd-Smith house, Kenjockety, Lloyd Harbor, New York** (BGG & MMP)*

1924–1926 Christ Church, Bronxville, New York (BGG & MMP)

1924–1926 Trinity Lutheran Church, Fort Wayne, Indiana (BGG & MMP)

1924–1927 *Harold Castle house, Kailua, Oahu, Hawaii** (BGG & MMP) {now St. Stephen's Seminary}*

1924–1927 War Memorial Flagstaff, Pasadena, California (BGG & MMP)

1924–1928 Epworth-Euclid Church, Cleveland, Ohio (BGG, MMP, and Walker & Weeks)

1928   *Governor George Carter's house, Lihiwai, Honolulu, Hawaii** (MMP)*

INDEX

Note: Page numbers in *italic* indicate illustrations.

ILLUSTRATION CREDITS